PICTURING SABINO

THE SOUTHWEST CENTER SERIES

Jeffrey M. Banister, Editor

PICTURING SABINO

A Photographic History of a Southwestern Canyon

DAVID WENTWORTH LAZAROFF

THE UNIVERSITY OF
ARIZONA PRESS

TUCSON

The University of Arizona Press
www.uapress.arizona.edu

We respectfully acknowledge the University of Arizona is on the land and territories of Indigenous peoples. Today, Arizona is home to twenty-two federally recognized tribes, with Tucson being home to the O'odham and the Yaqui. Committed to diversity and inclusion, the University strives to build sustainable relationships with sovereign Native Nations and Indigenous communities through education offerings, partnerships, and community service.

ISBN-13: 978-0-8165-4766-1 (paperback)
ISBN-13: 978-0-8165-4962-7 (ebook)

Cover design by Leigh McDonald
Cover photos: *Women seated on boulders, Sabino Creek*. Item L, album 2, box 14, PC 240, Sykes Family Collection, Arizona Historical Society, Tucson (top); *Shuttlebus crossing stream*. Photograph by the author, May 11, 1991 (bottom)
Designed and typeset by Sara Thaxton in 11/16 Warnock Pro with Arno Pro and Epsom WF

Publication of this book is made possible in part by financial support from the Southwest Center of the University of Arizona.

Library of Congress Cataloging-in-Publication Data
Names: Lazaroff, David Wentworth, 1948– author.
Title: Picturing Sabino : a photographic history of a southwestern canyon / David Wentworth Lazaroff.
Other titles: Southwest Center series.
Description: [Tucson] : The University of Arizona Press, 2023. | Series: The Southwest Center series | Includes bibliographical references, filmography, and index.
Identifiers: LCCN 2022024986 (print) | LCCN 2022024987 (ebook) | ISBN 9780816547661 (paperback) | ISBN 9780816549627 (ebook)
Subjects: LCSH: Natural history—Arizona—Sabino Canyon—Pictorial works. | Human ecology—Arizona—Sabino Canyon—Pictorial works. | Sabino Canyon (Ariz.)—Pictorial works. | LCGFT: Illustrated works.
Classification: LCC QH105.A65 L385 2023 (print) | LCC QH105.A65 (ebook) | DDC 508.791/776—dc23/eng/20220707
LC record available at https://lccn.loc.gov/2022024986
LC ebook record available at https://lccn.loc.gov/2022024987

Printed in the United States of America
♾ This paper meets the requirements of ANSI/NISO Z39.48-1992 (Permanence of Paper).

To Sabino Canyon's photographers, past, present, and future.

Sabino Canyon, Catalina Mountains.
TUCSON, Arizona.

No. 205
PUBL. BY
R. RASMESSEN

Contents

Preface

In the evening of the second of July 1834, an Apache woman was brought to the *comandante* of the garrison at Tucson, which was then a northern outpost of the independent country of Mexico. She was a member of a peaceful band that had settled outside the walls of the presidio, and she had a tale to tell.

Three months earlier, while visiting the Babacómari ranch, about fifty miles to the southeast, she had been kidnapped by renegade members of her own tribe. After weeks in captivity, she stole a horse from her captors, made a brave escape, and began a long and circuitous search for the rest of her band. Traveling at night for safety, she rode westward to the Rio Santa Cruz, then northward along the river until she picked up their trail. She followed that trail eastward to La Ciénega de los Pimas, a marshy area where her band had camped in the past. Failing to find them there, she pursued their trail northwestward until she came to a place where they had collected fruits of the saguaro cactus. Her people weren't there, either. She had then returned to the safety of Tucson.

The woman's name is lost to history. The account of her captivity and escape, transcribed and passed up the chain of command, proved valuable to the Mexican military, which was about to mount an attack on the rebel Apaches and their allies. Today, nearly two centuries later, the report is of special interest to us for the name of the place where the woman's people gathered saguaro fruits: *El Sahuaral del Sabino de la sierra de Santa Catarina*—the Saguaro Forest of the Sabino in the Santa Catalina Mountains.[1]

Were those saguaros at Sabino Canyon? It certainly seems so, but we have only the *Sabino* and not the *cañon*, so perhaps we can't quite be sure.

Thirty-three eventful years later, in 1867, after the Mexican War, the Gadsden Purchase, and the American Civil War, Tucson and the Santa Catalina Mountains belonged to Arizona Territory in the United States of America. On March 5 of that year, Peter R. Brady, sheriff of Pima County, filed a claim to a small ranch he had just purchased. The document described the parcel: "One hundred and sixty acres of unsurveyed public lands . . . situated on the stream known as the arroya of the Cajon Sabino and about thirteen and a half miles North East from the Town of Tucson."[2]

Now we have arrived unambiguously at Sabino Canyon—more precisely, a mile to its south. *Cajon* is a rough synonym of *cañon*, the stream is Sabino Creek, and the rancho Brady claimed (most likely a small farm) had been founded in the previous decade by an American named William H. Kirkland.

These early documents have much to tell us. Among other things, they reveal that the "Sabino" of Sabino Canyon has a long history. It comes down to us from a time when Spanish was the primary European language spoken in what's now southern Arizona, and its origin is anyone's guess. The author's guess, described in an earlier book, is that it refers to the Arizona cypress, a beautiful conifer that may once have been common in the lower reaches of the canyon, but from which it has since vanished, or nearly so, due to a warming climate.[3]

There must have been much earlier names for Sabino Canyon in the languages of Native people, who knew the area centuries before Spaniards set foot in the Southwest. We don't know those older names, but evidence of the people who spoke them, in particular of the ancient farmers we call the Hohokam, is abundant at the canyon in the form of grindstones, fragments of pottery, and overgrown agricultural fields. O'odham people, perhaps descendants of the Hohokam, may still have been harvesting Sabino Canyon's bounty when curious city dwellers began showing up there late in the nineteenth century. An 1883 article in a Tucson newspaper mentions, in the mouth of the canyon, "two mescal heads that had recently been prepared for roasting," nearby pits for the purpose, and "an Indian's grave."[4] Intrigued by those and other reports, Tucsonans soon started arriving in the canyon in increasing numbers. That's when the history in these pages begins, with the "discovery" of Sabino Canyon by city folk. A discovery it was, but they were far from the first.

Back in the spring of 1867, soon after Sheriff Brady bought his ranch, he hired men and oxen to plant crops there. The place received some visitors during the summer, and the tantalizingly brief account of what they saw (and felt) there,

Author photograph

published in a Prescott newspaper, gives us what may be our earliest description of Sabino Creek.

> On the ranch of Mr. Brady, corn is excellent, also melons and other vegetables, including potatoes. This last ranch is at the foot of the mountain and has a beautiful stream of water flowing through it: clear as crystal, and we had almost said, cold as ice.[5]

Sabino Creek is the great constant flowing through Sabino Canyon's history—sometimes rushing vigorously in the foreground, sometimes splashing quietly in the background, but always there—and the story of Sabino Canyon is in large measure a narrative of our evolving relationship to its waters. As we'll see, it's a story that begins with exploitation, in failed plans to dam the stream for irrigation, household water, and electric power. The most ambitious of these schemes would have dried out Sabino Creek entirely, yet it's hard to find any objection by the citizens who were picnicking on its banks. Our relationship was still an infatuation; its longevity wasn't yet assured.

The impulse to dam Sabino Creek revived during the Great Depression, with elaborate plans for recreational lakes and ponds. This was exploitation of a gentler kind; the creek was to be preserved, though thoroughly reshaped and regulated. Our attachment had strengthened, but, like discontented lovers, we were intent on improving the object of our affection. The vision of an aquatic playground became real, in part and for a time. We were still planting trout in Sabino Canyon as late as the 1960s.

But by then attitudes were changing. It was the decade of the Wilderness Preservation Act and a nascent environmental movement. The artificial ponds had all silted in. Sabino Canyon had a new visitor center, with natural history exhibits and a staff offering guided walks. We were growing more enamored of the canyon's natural gifts.

The history in this book ends in 1985, a century after Tucson and Sabino Canyon, once nearly strangers, became acquainted. Today, early in the twenty-first century, our relationship to the canyon and its stream continues to deepen. We're learning to resist efforts to make Sabino Canyon into something it's not and instead to appreciate it for what it is.

What is Sabino Canyon? It's a place of inspiring natural beauty, teeming with life, but it's not a wilderness. As far back in history as we can see, and beginning even earlier than that, people have been there—settled nearby or passing through, picking cactus fruits or grinding mesquite beans, hunting deer or rabbits, resting under the trees, cooling off in the creek, enjoying each other's company, occasionally squabbling, and more lately taking each other's pictures, picnicking, and dreaming of dams. Over the centuries men and women have left their marks on the canyon, and today these marks are to be seen almost everywhere. Sabino Canyon is equally a natural and a historical landscape. Without people, past and present, it would be only half as interesting as it is. We belong there, in the beautiful place with the antique name. At Sabino.

It has been my rewarding task, over many years, to piece together the story of Sabino Canyon and its people. It's my great pleasure now to tell that story to you.

David Wentworth Lazaroff
Tucson

PICTURING SABINO

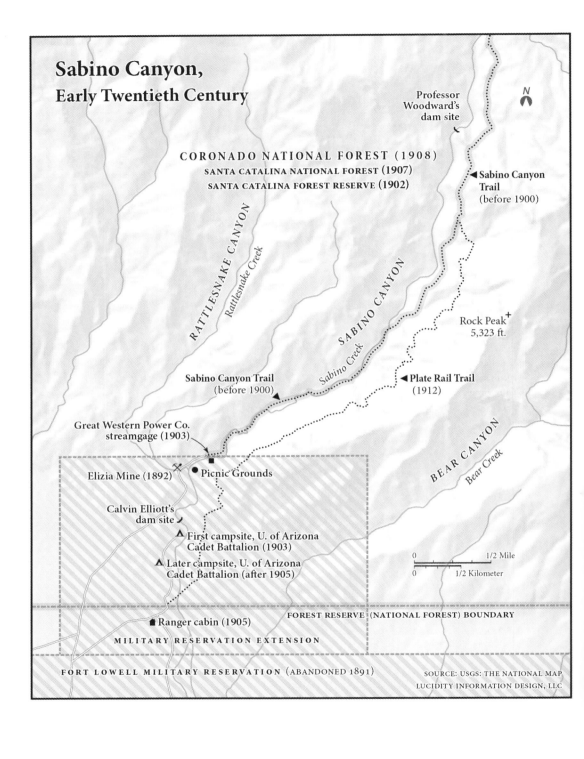

Sabino Canyon,
Early Twentieth Century

Professor
Woodward's
dam site

CORONADO NATIONAL FOREST (1908)
SANTA CATALINA NATIONAL FOREST (1907)
SANTA CATALINA FOREST RESERVE (1902)

◄ Sabino Canyon
Trail
(before 1900)

RATTLESNAKE CANYON

Rattlesnake Creek

SABINO CANYON

Rock Peak⁺
5,323 ft.

Sabino Canyon Trail
(before 1900) ◄

Sabino Creek

◄ Plate Rail Trail
(1912)

BEAR CANYON

Bear Creek

Great Western Power Co.
streamgage (1903)

Elizia Mine (1892)

● Picnic Grounds

Calvin Elliott's
dam site

First campsite, U. of Arizona
Cadet Battalion (1903)

Later campsite, U. of Arizona
Cadet Battalion (after 1905)

0   1/2 Mile
0   1/2 Kilometer

■ Ranger cabin (1905)

FOREST RESERVE (NATIONAL FOREST) BOUNDARY

MILITARY RESERVATION EXTENSION

FORT LOWELL MILITARY RESERVATION (ABANDONED 1891)

SOURCE: USGS: THE NATIONAL MAP
LUCIDITY INFORMATION DESIGN, LLC

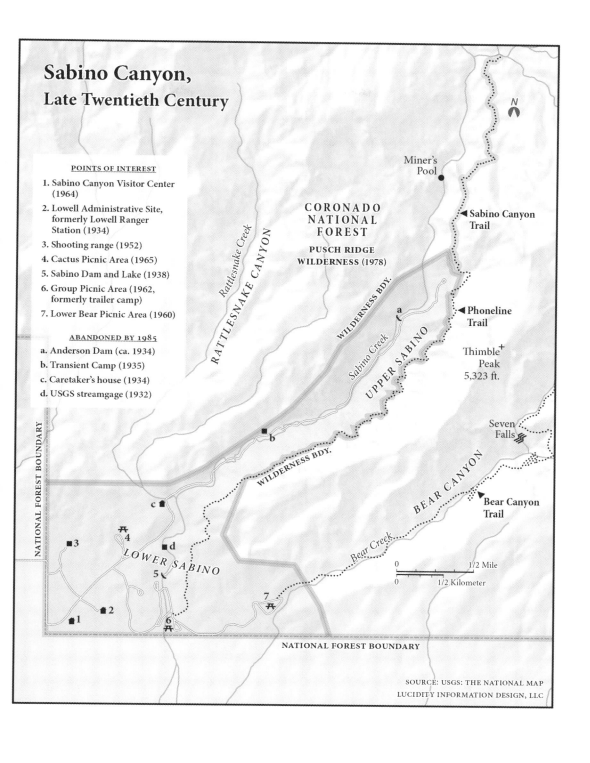

Sabino Canyon,
Late Twentieth Century

POINTS OF INTEREST

1. Sabino Canyon Visitor Center (1964)
2. Lowell Administrative Site, formerly Lowell Ranger Station (1934)
3. Shooting range (1952)
4. Cactus Picnic Area (1965)
5. Sabino Dam and Lake (1938)
6. Group Picnic Area (1962, formerly trailer camp)
7. Lower Bear Picnic Area (1960)

ABANDONED BY 1985

a. Anderson Dam (ca. 1934)
b. Transient Camp (1935)
c. Caretaker's house (1934)
d. USGS streamgage (1932)

Rattlesnake Creek

RATTLESNAKE CANYON

Miner's Pool

CORONADO NATIONAL FOREST

PUSCH RIDGE WILDERNESS (1978)

◀ Sabino Canyon Trail

WILDERNESS BDY.

Sabino Creek

a

UPPER SABINO

◀ Phoneline Trail

Thimble + Peak 5,323 ft.

Seven Falls

■ b

WILDERNESS BDY.

BEAR CANYON

▶ Bear Canyon Trail

c ⌂

☗ 4

■ 3

⌂ d

LOWER SABINO

5

Bear Creek

0 — 1/2 Mile
0 — 1/2 Kilometer

NATIONAL FOREST BOUNDARY

7 ☗

■ 2

■ 1

6 ☗

NATIONAL FOREST BOUNDARY

SOURCE: USGS: THE NATIONAL MAP
LUCIDITY INFORMATION DESIGN, LLC

Prologue

I n the heat of a brilliant midday in the spring of 1880, Carleton E. Watkins, famed photographer of the American West, unpacked his equipment on a hill overlooking the Santa Cruz River, set his massive wooden camera on its tripod, and pointed the lens toward the northeast, across the river. Before him the floodplain, a quilt of green, irrigated fields, stretched away from the foot of the hill. Beyond the fields the adobe town of Tucson lay baking in the sun—most of its citizens, unlike Watkins, no doubt sensibly indoors. And just beyond the town a dark line angled across the scene from left to right, seeming to draw the boundary to nineteenth-century urban civilization.

It was that dark line that had lured Watkins from his home in foggy San Francisco to the uncomfortable warmth of southern Arizona Territory. He had come to document the progress of the Southern Pacific Railroad as it laid track eastward from Yuma, as well as any interesting sights along the way. The first locomotive had reached Tucson only weeks before, to a grand celebration of cannon fire, military band music, and ringing oratory, but by the time Watkins arrived, the tracklayers and the train had moved on toward Texas.[1]

Watkins focused the dim, upside-down image of the scene on the camera's large ground glass. Beyond the railroad tracks, a road snaked across the desert plain and vanished into the distance. Still farther away, perhaps barely discernible on the glass, was the road's most significant destination: Fort Lowell, an army post in the Apache Wars. The soldiers had moved there seven years earlier from a camp near downtown, and the protection the garrison provided, together with the outflow of government cash, had helped foster something of a local boom. Tucson was already a thriving community of seven thousand souls, with shops and hotels, churches and saloons, banks and schools. With the arrival of the railroad, the populace expected still greater things.

Watkins slid a large frame containing a light-sensitized glass plate into the rear of his camera. In the far distance, beyond the army fort, beyond barely seen foothills, lost in the bright haze, was a mountain canyon. Twelve miles away as the raven flies, it had long been outside the limits of casual travel for wary townspeople on the edge of Apacheria. It was as vague in the minds of most Tucsonans as its appearance from the hilltop where the photographer stood, ready to finish his task.

His preparations complete, Carleton Watkins removed the cap from his lens and counted off the seconds of his exposure. In those few moments, he created a portrait of a town poised to become a modern city—and, unwittingly, of the nearly invisible canyon its citizens were about to discover. ■

Smithsonian Institution, National Portrait Gallery

A few years after his expedition to Arizona Territory, Carleton Watkins posed as a gold miner for this self-portrait, taken in his home state of California. His portrait of Tucson is on the following pages.

Bancroft Library, University of California, Berkeley

In April 1880 photographer Carleton Watkins set his camera on Sentinel Peak, better known today as "A Mountain" due to a huge white letter that now stands below its summit. The large building in the middle of the fields is the so-called Convento, a remnant of the Mission San Augustín, founded in the eighteenth century near an O'odham village on the banks of the Santa Cruz. (No trace of the once-impressive building remains today.) But where is the river? By the time of the photograph, it had been reduced to a network of ditches, most for irrigation, but one serving Solomon Warner's water-powered flour mill, at lower left. A decade later floodwaters cut into the fields just beyond the Convento, creating today's steep-banked arroyo.

The thick cottonwood grove at the far edge of the fields near downtown Tucson, left of center, is Levin's Park, which in March had hosted the banquet greeting the Southern Pacific Railroad's arrival. The road to Fort Lowell can be seen beyond the tracks, above the center of the photo, and Sabino Canyon is hidden by haze below the ridgeline of the Santa Catalinas, a little to the left of the road.

Arizona Historical Society

PART I
"Rough and Uncivilized"
1880–1900

The echo of the first locomotive whistle had barely died away before signs of modernity began multiplying in Tucson. A new hospital—St. Mary's, west of town—opened the next month, at the railroad's instigation. The following year, 1881, Tucson got its first telephone exchange, and the year after that, almost all at once, its first gaslights, its first piped water, and its first experiments with municipal electricity. The look of the Old Pueblo began to change. Encouraged by cheaper, rail-imported materials, Tucsonans began to forsake the squarish adobe buildings that had given the city its Mexican character in favor of eastern-style houses with gabled roofs.

Urban folk with time on their hands needed places to spend it, and Tucson provided. Alexander Levin's amusement park, seen in the distance in Carleton Watkins's photograph, offered not only a banquet and music pavilion but also a restaurant, a bowling alley, and a shooting gallery. Across the fields southwest of town (outside the Watkins photo) was the resort called Silver Lake, an artificial pond with bathhouses and its own hotel. Other delights were still farther afield. The last battles of the Apache Wars were being fought very far from the city, and by the early 1880s Tucsonans felt safe in driving their carriages well past Fort Lowell to take the healthful waters at Agua Caliente, more than fifteen miles east of downtown.[1]

Not surprisingly for desert townspeople, water figured in all these amusements. Even Levin's Park featured a running irrigation ditch, or *acequia* (though its brewery and bar suggest other liquids were a stronger draw). Yet these were all tame and civilized places. Tucsonans would soon be tempted by something more challenging. ∎

Within the image:

WATKINS' NEW SERIES
Of Pacific Coast Views, 427 Montgomery Street, S.F.

PARK BREWERY

SALOON TEN PIN ALLEY

Photographic Views of California, Oregon, Nevada, Arizona, Lower Cal., and the Pacific Coast, embracing Yosemite, Big Trees, Geysers, Mount Shasta Mining City, etc., etc. Views made to order in any part of the State or Coast.

Park Brewery, Tucson, Arizona.   4896.

J. Paul Getty Museum

The brewery at Levin's Park, a stereoview taken by Carleton Watkins during his 1880 visit to Tucson.

CHAPTER 1

Discovery

Colonel Eugene Asa Carr, 6th Cavalry, post commander at Fort Lowell, knew he had to take action. Troubling information had appeared in a local newspaper on December 11, 1883, for the second day in a row. He fired off a message to the United States attorney in Tucson, followed immediately by this to his superiors at Whipple Barracks, Prescott, Arizona Territory:

> I have the honor to report that it is stated in the daily papers of Tucson that C. A. Elliott, J. J. Gardiner and J. J. Chatham propose to build a dam across Sabrino [*sic*] Cañon, so called, which is, as I understand it, the principal one of the two Cañons through which flow the streams which unite at Carrillo's Ranch, about the middle of the north side of this Reservation. . . . This dam would most likely interfere materially with the supply of water for this Post.[1]

Colonel Carr seems to have been unfamiliar with the canyon whose name he (or his scribe) misspelled, but he was right about its importance to Fort Lowell. Sabino Creek was a major tributary of the Rillito, a broad, sandy wash that crossed the Fort Lowell Military Reservation east to west, immediately north of the post. Sabino Creek sometimes sank into its stony streambed before joining the Rillito, upstream from Fort Lowell, but even at those times its hidden underflow was essential to filling the fort's wells and *acequias*.

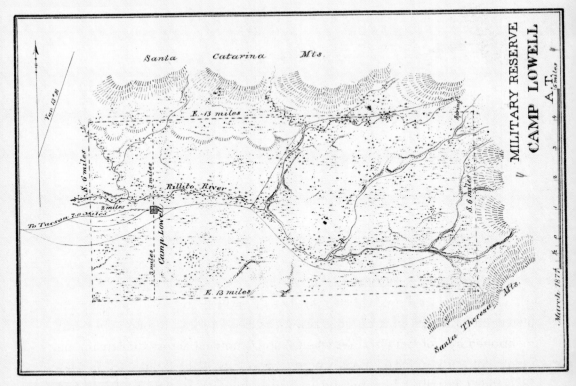

National Archives

This 1877 drawing of the Camp Lowell Military Reserve (more often called a military reservation) may be the earliest printed map to show Sabino Canyon and Sabino Creek, though neither one is named. Sabino Canyon is the opening in the mountains near top center. Sabino Creek emerges from the canyon, meets Bear Creek (also unlabeled) just inside the reservation boundary, and joins the Rillito east of the camp. The army rechristened the post Fort Lowell in 1879.

The crudeness of the map reflects how poorly known the area was in 1877—a situation not much improved by the time of Calvin Elliott's 1883 proposal to construct a dam in Sabino Canyon. The confluence of Sabino and Bear Creeks, for example, is shown more than a mile too far to the east, and some other details bear only a passing resemblance to geographical reality. The "Santa Theresa Mts." are now called the Rincons, but the comically redundant "Rillito River" (little river river) persists on some maps to this day.

alvin Elliott, chief cause of the trouble, was a relative newcomer to Arizona Territory. Once a man of considerable means, he had come to Tucson from Indiana five years earlier after losing his fortune during hard economic times. Elliott had set out in the spring of 1883 to explore the steep-sided canyons along the southern slope of the Santa Catalina Mountains. But unlike many others seeking wealth in the mountains of Arizona, he hadn't been prospecting for precious metals. He had been searching for water. Elliott envisioned fields and orchards in the foothills of the Catalinas—a bit of the green Midwest dropped into the Arizona desert.[2]

Calvin Elliott found even more than he was looking for. Issuing from a deep mountain canyon was a creek so clear and generous in its flow that he could imagine it not only irrigating the nearby desert but also filling bathtubs and drinking glasses in the city, eleven pipeline miles away. The creek wasn't completely unknown. A short distance below the canyon it ran through the ranch mentioned by Colonel Carr. Yet when Elliott stumbled across the stream, he seems not quite to have known where he was. His water claim, filed in May 1883, didn't describe it by name and was vague about its location. But Elliott had figured all this out, amended his claim, and set his plan in motion by the time Colonel Carr read about it in the newspapers.[3]

Despite Carr's concerns, the army didn't immediately interfere with the activities of Mr. Elliott, who proceeded to organize a water company in 1884—though he seems to have done little more than the minimum work needed to keep his claim alive. For more than a year, all was quiet on the Sabino Canyon front. Then, in 1885, the realities of a fickle desert climate caught up with Fort Lowell. In the heat of a parching drought, water in the fort's wells dropped to dangerous levels and the post surgeon pronounced what was left unfit to drink without boiling. Meanwhile, upstream settlers were draining the post's *acequias* so severely that there was little left for the garrison but mud. An army engineer was dispatched to Lowell, and early in 1886 he recommended a drastic remedy: damming Sabino Creek at or near Calvin Elliott's site and building a pipeline to the fort.[4]

And why not? The railroad seemed to make almost anything possible. By then, just a few years after the first locomotive had rumbled into Tucson, water from the Santa Cruz River was flowing six miles to the city through an aqueduct built of California redwood and pipes rolled from St. Louis sheet iron. A conduit from Sabino Canyon to Fort Lowell would be just a mile longer—far less ambitious, in fact, than Calvin Elliott's scheme. The coveted dam site, a narrow spot near the canyon mouth, was just outside the Fort Lowell Military Reservation, but in May of 1886 the War Department neatly fixed that inconvenience by approving a roughly three-square-mile extension to the reservation's northern edge.[5]

Author photograph

Calvin Elliott's choice of a site for his dam was easy: the first conveniently narrow spot above the canyon mouth. A dam one hundred feet tall was to have spanned the lower part of the V-shaped gap seen in this photograph, taken by the author in 2018. The view is from downstream.

Elliott's dam would have backed up a reservoir roughly a mile long. Some of its water would have flowed through a pipe all the way to Tucson, with the rest distributed to fields and orchards in areas that were then uncultivated desert. Elliott's ambitions didn't stop there. For a time he considered building a hotel on the high ground to the left of the gap, and, astonishingly, his Sabino Cañon Water Company proposed to build a sawmill in the forests of the Santa Catalinas and to float logs down a flume through Sabino Canyon. None of these ideas became reality.[6]

By the time Elliott registered his objections with the post commander at Fort Lowell, the army was already having second thoughts, though, and in 1887 it threw out its Sabino Canyon plan altogether in favor of more conservative remedies at the post itself. (It had been wisely pointed out that nature was already delivering Sabino Creek's water to the fort free of charge and purified by filtration through the sediments in the riverbeds.) A new well was dug and a steam-powered pump installed, with two new water tanks for the augmented supply. The pump's engine could also power a saw, and—delightful bonus—an ice-making machine. As for Mr. Elliott, he was appointed Tucson's postmaster that same year, and he dropped his plans as well. Sabino Canyon's first battle over water ended not even in a truce, but when both forces abandoned the field.[7]

At this point we might reasonably conclude that none of these events had any lasting consequence for Sabino Canyon. But that would be a mistake, simply because in 1883, when Calvin Elliott announced his plans, Fort Lowell's commanding officer wasn't the only person reading the Tucson papers. Residents of the city were intrigued. What was this mountain canyon with the flowing stream? A few days after the reports that had caught Colonel Carr's attention, a representative of the *Arizona Weekly Citizen* paid a visit to Sabino Canyon in the company of Messrs. Elliott, Gardiner, and Chatham. His inviting description soon followed.

> On the sides of the canyon grow the omnipresent sahuara, and the amole, yucca, palo verde, mescal and a score of other botanical specimens. The loose sandy soil of the bottom has a growth of willow, ash, sycamore, cottonwood, greasewood and mesquite. . . . This canyon drains the principal portion of the Santa Catalina mountains. It extends way up among the pine forests. Its waters come down from these pineries over its granite boulders and sandy bars as pure and fresh as when it first falls from the clouds.[8]

A month and a half later, in February 1884, a reporter from the *Arizona Weekly Star* interviewed John P. Culver, a civil engineer familiar with Calvin Elliott's proposal. Culver's appraisal was decidedly less effusive.

The Sabino canyon is a rough, uncivilized rent in the Santa Catalina mountains and suddenly debouches out into the low foot-hills some six miles north-easterly of Fort Lowell.[9]

Paradise with a whiff of danger—who could resist? Yet despite continual newspaper updates on Calvin Elliott's progress, and even a Sunday outing to the canyon organized by Elliott himself, it took a while longer for the citizens of Tucson to succumb to the temptations of the newfound oasis northeast of town.[10] By early the next year, the surrender was complete. In March 1885 a brief note appeared in the *Citizen*.

Visitors to Sabino's canyon, in the foot-hills of the Santa Catalinas, report the place to be indescribably lovely, nature having bedecked the canyon in her forest beauties. As a resort for pleasure parties, the canyon is becoming immensely popular.[11]

Sabino Canyon had been discovered. ∎

Instant Legend

Author photograph

In late 1883, when an anonymous reporter toured Sabino Canyon with Calvin Elliott and his collaborators, the place was still nearly unknown to Tucsonans. The canyon seemed like a blank slate, one that the reporter began, playfully, to fill in. His words reveal more about the culture of his place and time than about the unspoiled canyon in the Santa Catalinas.

One large bluff in particular presents a curious spectacle. Its color is almost a bright flannel red. Beneath this skirt descend a number of cones of granite alternately striped white and black and as accurately as the prettiest hose. The whole is a reminder of a sight to be witnessed when a woman is in a predicament on a rainy day in trying to cross a muddy street, and has gathered up her skirts. Only in this scene, sketched by nature's great artist, there appear to be eight or ten pairs of hose behind one big red skirt. As this bluff has no legend one will now be given.

THE LEGEND.
Once upon a time a number of Apache young ladies visited Tucson and saw and longed for some red skirts and striped hose. They besieged their liege lords till the same were bought for them. . . . The new clothes created envy in the breasts of all the other dusky maidens of the pineries of the Sabino forests, and their young men could not kill enough mountain sheep to supply the new demand for hose. The tribe was about to become almost bankrupt, and a council of the chiefs was called. A medicine man, to cut the matter short, bewitched the girls who had the hosiery and metamorphosed them into granite, and the Great Spirit whisked them to the top of this hill, and there they are to this day, all standing behind one big red skirt, with nothing visible but their hose.[12]

Twentieth-century rock climbers later named the same bluff "the Acropolis." It's for the reader to decide whether the formation more resembles a skirt and striped stockings or a hill in Athens.

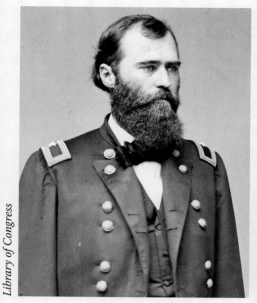

Eugene A. Carr   Calvin A. Elliott

Opponents in the opening maneuvers of the Sabino Canyon water dispute of 1883–1887.

An 1850 West Point graduate, Eugene Asa Carr went west to fight in the Indian Wars, and in 1854 he took an Apache arrow to the arm in a Texas skirmish. He returned east to defend the Union during the Civil War and was wounded several times in the Battle of Pea Ridge, Arkansas. After the Confederate surrender at Appomattox, Carr, by then known admiringly as "The Black-Bearded Cossack," rejoined the Indian Wars. In 1873 he came to Camp Lowell, then situated near downtown Tucson, helped select a new site on the Rillito, and was serving his eleventh and last term in the post's rotating command when he learned of Calvin Elliott's scheme to dam Sabino Creek. Carr retired in 1893 and the next year was awarded the Medal of Honor for his valor at Pea Ridge.

Kentucky-born Calvin Elliott was in his late twenties, living in Missouri, when he heeded the call of the Forty-Niners and headed west to California. After making his fortune there, Elliott returned to the Midwest and ran a successful mercantile business in Indianapolis, only later to be driven nearly into bankruptcy during the financial crisis known as the Panic of 1873. Elliott showed up in Tucson five years later, and in 1883 he announced a plan to dam Sabino Creek for municipal and agricultural use. That project eventually failed, but not before bringing Sabino Canyon, until then little known among Tucsonans, to the city's attention. Elliott served as Tucson's postmaster from 1887 to 1890, ran unsuccessfully for justice of the peace in 1892, and later devoted himself to Arizona's mining industry.

CHAPTER 2

Pioneer Picnickers

It was a long, rough drive to Sabino Canyon in the busy spring of 1885, but Calvin Elliott soon made it smoother by improving the route to his dam site. A note in the *Arizona Daily Citizen* in May seemed to dress up this practical measure as a gesture of civic largesse.

> Mr. C. A. Elliott came in yesterday from Sabino Cañon, and has completed a good wagon road over which picnic parties can drive their teams on a trot clear into the canyon. The water, which is abundant and makes rippling music as it rushes through the rocky cañon, is of splendid quality, and at some future day it will be utilized not only for city purposes, but for motive power and irrigating purposes.[1]

Fortunately for us, when Sabino Canyon's pioneer picnickers parked their wagons at Elliott's dam site, they had their cameras with them. As it happened, the 1880s were years of intense innovation in both cameras and film. Photography, long the province of professionals and well-heeled amateurs, was becoming the pursuit of everyman—and everywoman.

In 1880 Carleton Watkins had needed not just a bulky camera but also a portable darkroom and an assistant to take Tucson's picture. The process required enormous patience and skill. A fragile glass plate was coated with light-sensitive goo inside the darkroom; carried, dripping in its light-tight wooden holder, to the camera for the exposure; then rushed back to the darkroom, still wet, to be developed. Within a decade after Watkins packed up his gear on Sentinel Peak, any Tom, Diego, or Hattie with a few dollars to spare could buy a handheld Kodak and film to put in it. At Sabino Canyon, as everywhere else, these advances revolutionized personal photography.

This faded card-mounted photograph from the watershed year 1885 is one of the earliest dated images of Sabino Canyon. Like most such photos, it features a large collection of well-dressed urbanites, and it's plain to see these visits were as much social events as outdoor explorations. Tucson's citizens must have felt safer in numbers when venturing into a wild and unfamiliar place so far from town.

It's likely that many (perhaps all) of the people in this picture have come to Sabino Canyon for the first time, and they've assembled for a photograph to commemorate the occasion. A trickle of water across the ledge divides the carefully arranged group, except for one man who's straddling the flow. As with almost any old photograph, the details are fascinating, and this one deserves a closer look.

Arizona Historical Society

This is a detail from a second print of the same photograph. More than time and fashion separate us from these early visitors to Sabino Canyon. Notice the rifle held by the young woman at left. Guns show up in many early photos taken in the canyon, and surprisingly often in the hands of women, but we'll wait for more examples before considering why. The two young men at right front may be expressing no more than friendship—it's impossible to say. Such displays of male affection would become uncomfortable in later decades. Hats are evidently de rigueur in 1880s Sabino Canyon (and sensibly so), but the headgear on the man at upper right is downright peculiar. He seems to be the joker of the group, one hand holding a bottle, the other thrust into his jacket, parodying a Napoleonic pose often struck in formal portraits of the time.

Only a few of these adventurous people can be identified with confidence, and they're all seated in front. In the group at right, it's Marie Alexander wearing the bonnet. In the group at left, the woman looking toward the camera is Jennie Crepin, daughter of a French-born doctor practicing in Tucson. Not far to the left of Jennie, with a parasol across his lap, is twenty-eight-year-old Willis P. Haynes. Might there be a budding romance here? The two married six years later.

From the very beginning, people of all ages came to Sabino Canyon. This undated picture from the 1880s is among the earliest to show children. The three kids with their feet in the water bring life to the mostly stiff-looking group, as do the two languidly reclining adults at center.

Curly-haired Jennie Crepin, whom we saw in the previous photograph, seems to be here again, this time in a striped dress, standing in the right foreground. Willis Haynes may be seated at left (it's hard to tell), but it's also possible he's operating the camera. Haynes achieved recognition as a talented photographer by the late 1880s, and his prints were shown as far away as Paris.[2]

Like the previous photo, this one may have been printed from a glass plate negative—not a cumbersome wet plate like the ones Carleton Watkins so skillfully prepared, but one of the precoated dry plates that had recently become available. Exposures were still lengthy by modern standards, so the camera needed to be set on a tripod to keep it still, and anybody or anything that moved—like the impatient child at far left and the hat (or parasol?) in Jennie's hand—would be recorded as a blur.

We might gain the impression from the previous two photos that only Anglos visited Sabino Canyon in the early years, but this image seems to show a number of Hispanic faces, and the names of three of the subjects—Ben Soza, Juan Elias, and Gertrude Angulo, marked by *X*s on the card—confirm this is so. Tucson had been gradually losing its Mexican character even before the coming of the railroad, but it was still very much a multicultural community, as it is today. The photographer is unknown.

This is clearly a very well-disciplined and cooperative group. They're carefully arranged, many hats have been politely removed, and almost no one has moved a muscle during the exposure. We see mostly young people, and the few adults, except for the ostentatiously posed man at center, are arranged near the sides. A school picnic? A church youth outing? What do you think?

W hy does almost everyone in these photographs look so serious? Didn't nineteenth-century folks know how to have fun?

Many have wondered about the somber expressions seen in old photos, and most agree the explanation lies partly in the long exposures required. It's hard to hold any smile for more than a few seconds, let alone a natural-looking one. Yet a close look at the faces in these early images reveals some very pleasant expressions, and a few of the young people in the last one are genuinely smiling. By the time of that photograph—the 1890s, judging by the clothing—exposures were short enough for anyone to grin, yet most of the group still chose not to. Why?

The answer may lie in the culture of portraiture. Before the invention of photography, having one's picture painted was a prolonged and expensive undertaking, and most subjects put on a serious expression to suit the occasion. The tedium of posing lessened greatly with the first photographic studio portraits, but exposures were still uncomfortably long and prices were still high. By then the solemnity of formal portraits had become the model for anyone being photographed anywhere. This was how people in photographs were *supposed* to look, even on happy picnic outings.

In the earliest Sabino Canyon photographs, we don't see the fun, or even the picnics. They happen outside the frame. We see only the ritual moments when the participants have taken their places before the camera, the photographer has given his signal—not "say cheese," but "hold still," or something like it—and almost everyone has frozen, wearing the appropriate expression. Even the person in the funny hat; in fact, that's part of the joke.

All that changed when film became sensitive enough for the camera to escape the tripod and be held in the hands, ready to capture the candid moment. A refreshingly new kind of photograph was born: the snapshot. ∎

Arizona Historical Society

Despite the deterioration of the image, the moment caught in this 1897 shot seems as fresh as the day it was snapped. The bluish print (a cyanotype) was pasted in an album by a lively and intelligent young woman named Clara Fish. We'll meet Clara herself in a moment.

The 1890s were still the Victorian era, but these young citizens of Arizona Territory were not the queen's subjects. Even so, this may appear to be an unseemly degree of public touching among well-bred youth of that epoch. The explanation lies in the next photograph.

Arizona Historical Society

There's Clara at center, caught in midbite. To her left is Mary McEwen, whom you'll recognize from the previous photograph. According to Clara's carefully labeled album, Mary has come from San Francisco to Tucson for her health. Mary's maiden aunt, Jean Parker, has accompanied her and is seated at right. She's serving as chaperone for this group of youthful picnickers. Behind Miss Parker, leaning against a stone, is the key to the previous photo: Mary's crutches.

"Perfect contentment" is Clara's title for this snapshot. By 1897 Sabino Canyon has become a familiar place, and visitors no longer seek the comfort of large groups. Informality reigns at this sunny picnic, fresh fruit is on the menu, a rifle stands at the ready (for what?), and a carriage awaits in the background to take everyone home.

Arizona Historical Society

Clara sips from the creek while Mary looks after her hat.

Twenty-year-old Clara Cramond Fish, who in 1891 had been the first student to enroll at the brand-new University of Arizona, would graduate a few months after these photographs were taken. Sabino Canyon outings seem to have been a tradition in Clara's family; her socially prominent parents, Edward Nye Fish and Maria Wakefield Fish, were among the canyon's pioneer picnickers in the spring of 1885. Her childhood home, once at the edge of the fields in downtown Tucson, is today an annex of the Tucson Museum of Art. Clara became a teacher shortly after graduation, married Frederick Roberts in 1905, and remained devoted to public education throughout her life.

In the early years, most of Sabino Canyon's visitors were content to spend their time socializing in the mouth of the canyon, at or near Calvin Elliott's dam site, and few were interested in exploring the little-known territory farther upstream. There were occasional exceptions, though, like this hardy group of men who made their way two miles beyond the end of the road in 1890. Their identities are unknown, but we do know the exact day when they took their places among the boulders for this photograph: June 10, a very hot time of year to be rock-hopping in Sabino Canyon.

It's often said that the many huge stones in Sabino Creek tumbled from the canyon walls during a powerful earthquake centered in northern Mexico, three years before this photo was taken. There were indeed rockfalls in the Santa Catalinas during the famous earthquake of 1887, but there's scant evidence of any in Sabino Canyon. Many of the boulders on the canyon floor seem to have been delivered there by prehistoric landslides and debris flows.

University of Arizona Libraries, Special Collections

The posed group portrait of course lived on into the era of the snapshot. All the young subjects in this beautiful photograph can be named: Minnie and Fred Watts (upper left), Hattie Ferrin (seated below them), Lulu Hilzinger (standing, center), Paul Noble (bottom center), and Willie Drake (at right). The original print is marked 1898, but it may actually date from the 1894–95 academic year, when all pictured here were freshmen at the University of Arizona. Miss Ferrin later served several years on the faculty as an English and Latin instructor.

It's tempting to suppose that Mr. Drake helped set up the picture before walking into it. (Is that something camera-related in his hands?) As for who snapped the shutter, there was at least one faculty member present: Miss Gertrude Hughes, Instructor of Elocution and Physical Culture, and perhaps she did the honors. We'll hear her name again (chapter 6).[3]

Notice the similar career paths of several of the women in these photographs. Teaching was one of relatively few professions readily available to educated American women in the late nineteenth century.

Arizona Historical Society

A photograph of family or friends in Sabino Canyon catches only a moment, but sometimes a thing as subtle as a gesture or a look hints at interesting lives led outside the canyon walls. If the wary expressions here suggest to you that this pair aren't mother and child, your instinct is correct. In fact, these are aunt and niece—Pauline Wood (known to most as Lena) and her sister's daughter, Beppie Leslie. It's about 1892, the photographer may be Beppie's mother, Sallie, and we're witnessing a lasting relationship in the making.

Lena married a prominent surveyor several years after this photograph was taken. Beppie, meanwhile, grew into a beautiful young woman, married a navy man, John Harding Culin, in 1913, and the couple moved away from Arizona. Tragically, while on duty in Haiti in 1925, Lieutenant Commander Culin died of malaria. Lena and her husband welcomed Beppie into their home in Tucson, but a few years later he died, too. The two widows, Lena and Beppie, her trusted companion, lived together in the same home nine more years until Lena's death in 1937. Beppie Leslie Culin resided there alone another five decades. She was buried in 1988 next to her husband in Arlington National Cemetery.

Lena's surveyor husband, George Roskruge, had his own very interesting connections to Sabino Canyon, as we'll see in chapters 4 and 5.

Arizona Historical Society

Young visitors like these in 1895, carefree and unafraid in a beautiful canyon miles from town, were only a generation removed from Arizona's dangerous pioneer past. The first and third women from the left in this photograph are Mercedes Anna Shibell and Georgia Hazel Scott, whose lives were linked by a violent episode their mothers had endured thirty-five years earlier.

In the spring of 1860, Larcena Pennington Page, a married woman of twenty-three, and a ten-year-old girl named Mercedes Sais Quiroz were kidnapped by Apaches in another mountain canyon near Tucson—Madera Canyon, in the Santa Ritas, south of town. As the Indians forced their captives rapidly northward on foot, Larcena became too exhausted to keep up. The Apaches stripped her to her underwear, stole her shoes, stabbed her repeatedly, pounded her with rocks, and left her for dead. They then pressed onward with Mercedes. Two weeks later, starving, sunburned, caked with blood, and nearly unrecognizable, Larcena stumbled into a lumber camp near where her ordeal had begun. Mercedes was later recovered at an Apache camp north of the Santa Catalinas.[4]

Larcena survived. After the death of her first husband, John Page, she married William Scott, and their daughter, Georgie, was born in 1873. Mercedes Quiroz married Charles Shibell, and their daughter, named Mercedes after her mother, was born in 1875. (Twenty years later she was one of the University of Arizona's first three graduates.)

The others holding hands in the photo are brothers Will and George Kitt, at far left and far right; Otis Hale, between Mercedes and Georgie; and Anna Taylor. The feisty young woman with her hands on her hips is Millie Brown. Next time we see her, she'll threaten us with a pistol.

CHAPTER 3

Bonanza

In the spring of 1892, seven years into Sabino Canyon's newfound popularity, a well-known visitor noticed some interesting rocks. Excitement ensued.

Originally from New York, Charles Patterson Sykes had arrived in Arizona Territory in the late 1870s, following a string of newspaper and mining ventures in his home state and in the West. He had embarked at once on a scheme of breathtaking ambition, focused on an unprepossessing settlement called Calabasas, about fifty miles south of Tucson, on the banks of the Santa Cruz River. Sykes envisioned the little community transformed into the territory's prime portal to Mexico, thriving on profits from mines, farms, and cattle, and linked to parts north and south by a railroad running along the Santa Cruz—a line that as yet existed only in his fertile imagination. By 1878 he had enlisted the help of San Francisco and Boston financiers, laid out a new town site, begun work on a fancy new hotel, and was promoting his plans across the country and even abroad.[1]

Hotel Santa Rita,
CALABASAS, A. T.
C. P. SYKES, Prop.   WM. R. LANE, Manager.

Arizona Historical Society

The Hotel Santa Rita, opened in Calabasas by C. P. Sykes in 1882, was a vision of eastern refinement set in the wilds of Arizona Territory—a two-story building with broad verandas, hot and cold running water, and, in the lobby, an ornate case displaying two dozen stuffed birds. For some guests, at least, the attraction of the dining room's sumptuous fare was exceeded only by that of the Boston girls hired to serve it. This delicately illustrated notecard conveys the luxuriousness of the establishment.

Among the many notables who signed the massive, leather-bound register around the time of the hotel's opening was Sabino Otero, a well-to-do rancher from the nearby town of Tubac. A decade later Otero received a homestead grant at the mouth of a canyon in the Baboquivari Mountains, about thirty miles west of his hometown.[2] That canyon eventually came to be called Sabino Canyon, and, inevitably, the two canyons with the same name became confused in folk history. The erroneous story that the better-known canyon in the Santa Catalina Mountains was named for Sabino Otero has proven utterly resistant to debunking, and the author suspects it will be told until both the Santa Catalinas and the Baboquivaris have eroded entirely away and washed into the Sea of Cortez.

Things began to go sour for Sykes in 1882, when the Santa Fe Railroad opened a line through Calabasas from the east, then snubbed the town and established its own international gateway on the border at Nogales. Unfazed, Sykes held a gala celebration at his newly opened hotel, then over the next decade stubbornly sought financing for his own railroad between Calabasas and Tucson. By May 1892 the entire enterprise was very much in doubt, but the persistent promoter was making a pitch to still another potential investor—Mr. W. J. Broadwell, a banker visiting from New York.[3]

Toward the end of the month, Sykes paid a visit to Sabino Canyon. While most visitors were looking for no more than a few pleasant hours in a beautiful place, Sykes, as always, was looking for opportunity, and to this end he was "accompanied by a photographer . . . for the express purpose of taking some views."[4] To his evident surprise, he found a much greater opportunity in plain sight on the ground. He took a rock to a Tucson assayer, who confirmed that it was rich with gold. Over the next week, Sykes returned with Broadwell and local miners to collect more samples and to stake claims for several gold mines near the confluence of Sabino and Rattlesnake Creeks. It wasn't long before the word was out.

> Tucson is about to experience one of the biggest mining booms ever yet known in the territory. Some very rich discoveries of gold have been made in the Sabino Canyon during the past week. Heretofore no one has even so much as dreamed of such a thing as gold being in the mountains in the vicinity of Sabino Canyon. Men who have spent years in the mining business and who have reached that point where they are looked upon as experts in all matters pertaining to mining have often gone to the canyon on picnic parties, have gazed at the mountain sides, have drank [sic] from the sparkling stream wending its way down the canyon and have come home no wiser than when they left it.[5]

A few weeks later, Sykes left by train for the East Coast to seek capital for his latest undertaking. It took more than three years to make a start, but in November 1895 the new Sabino Gold Mining Company was officially organized in New York City. Two years later the company held legal claim to ten gold mines in and near Sabino Canyon. Then it vanished.[6]

What happened? We may never know. Perhaps there simply wasn't enough precious metal to make the company profitable. Just possibly, there was no gold at all. Like many business ventures in the late nineteenth century (and even in the twenty-first), this one was launched in public but sank in private.[7]

Colonel Sykes died in New York not long afterward, in 1901. His widow lived on for a decade in the beautifully furnished hotel her husband had built in Calabasas. The settlement fell into rapid decline, then disappeared entirely. Today it's no more than a ghost of a ghost town, haunting the modern community of Rio Rico. At Sabino Canyon, not one of the gold company's mines was ever developed. Only shallow prospects remain, many too overgrown to be noticed. ■

Author photograph

The Rough and Ready Mine, claimed in 1892 by C. P. Sykes and his associates, is typical of the prospects eventually taken over by the Sabino Gold Mining Company. Those identified by the author are all short horizontal tunnels, rather than vertical shafts. With one exception, described on the following pages, they are off the beaten path and seldom seen by today's visitors to Sabino Canyon.

All in the Family

Indefatigable, skilled in the arts of persuasion, possessed of boundless confidence, and a master of hype long before it was a word, Colonel Charles P. Sykes was the very model of a late-nineteenth-century entrepreneur. Despite being prone to extravagant claims and impossibly elaborate schemes, Sykes was widely admired for his vision and "pushahead." By the time he found gold in Sabino Canyon, he had become known in the territory as "Colonel" Sykes—an indication of respect rather than military rank.

During the busy two weeks following his gold discovery in Sabino Canyon, Sykes and his associates staked claims to nine mines. To some of these he gave traditional names like "Bonanza" and "Rough and Ready." Others he named after individuals, most notably "Broadwell" for the New York financier he drew into the project. But one, the "Lizzie Mine," stands out for bearing a woman's name. It seems to have been an affectionate gesture to his wife, Mary Elizabeth Knight Sykes.

Both: Arizona Historical Society

Colonel and Mrs. Charles P. Sykes

(*continued*)

(continued)

Colonel Sykes later renewed the Lizzie claim, upgraded its name to the more elegant "Elizia," and defined its location relative to a local landmark. Like most of the canyon's natural features at the time, this one was still unnamed, so he took it upon himself to name it after a second individual he evidently held in high regard.

> The claim is situated and located in the Sabino Cañon Mining District in Pima County, in the Territory of Arizona about 2½ miles in a southeasterly direction from a prominent and Conspicuous Chimney Shaped Butte by the name Sykes Observatory.[8]

The gentleman so honored was of course the colonel himself, and the name is the earliest known for what we now call Thimble Peak. It never came into general use.

Elizia Mine   Sykes Observatory

Author photograph

CHAPTER 4

The Man from Cornwall

George James Roskruge, whose future wife we met in chapter 2, began his life thousands of miles from Sabino Canyon, in Cornwall, England. In 1872, shortly after his twenty-seventh birthday, he showed up in Arizona Territory, where he found work as a packer and cook for a surveyor's crew. It was a fortunate misemployment. Although the food he prepared was indigestible (by his own account), he discovered a natural talent for surveying.[1] In 1874 his skills caught the attention of the territory's surveyor general, who hired him in his office in Tucson, the city that would remain Roskruge's home for the rest of his life. Over the years he earned a living as a private surveyor and in many official capacities, including as city surveyor, county surveyor, U.S. Land and Mineral surveyor, and ultimately, by appointment of the president of the United States, as Arizona's surveyor general himself.

Roskruge's long career connected with Sabino Canyon on several interesting occasions. In 1883 and 1884, shortly before the first wave of curious picnickers arrived, he was at work with Calvin Elliott's partner John Gardiner, surveying Elliott's dam site and drawing up plans for the project. Although Elliott eventually lost interest in Sabino Canyon (as did his military rival, Fort Lowell), his dam site lingered in the minds of Tucsonans for years afterward as a possible source of city water, and Roskruge returned to the canyon just before the turn of the century for another look. The circumstances of this later survey are unknown to the author, but it left us valuable early photographs of Sabino Canyon, several of which are reproduced in this chapter.[2]

Tucson's surveyor extraordinaire, George J. Roskruge, flanked by two members of his crew at Calvin Elliott's dam site on an unrecorded date during the late 1890s.

Compare the two trees behind Roskruge with the trees behind Clara Fish and her friend, when Clara is sipping from the creek in chapter 2. Details like these are often helpful in determining time and place for historical photographs of Sabino Canyon.

Roskruge took a deep interest in public education, and he served on both the Board of Regents of the University of Arizona and the Board of Directors of the Tucson School District. Unfortunately, the latter role landed him in a kerfuffle in the spring of 1906, when five members of the district's all-female teaching staff were accused of scandalous public behavior: they had been observed at a picnic in Sabino Canyon, smoking cigarettes while drinking beer and wine. After investigating, two of the three school board members decided the event was too insignificant to warrant anything more than a reprimand. Roskruge, however, saw it differently. He insisted that four of the teachers be suspended or resign. Outvoted, he was the one to resign—from the board, several days later.[3]

By this time accounts of the episode were being printed in newspapers as far away as Flagstaff and Albuquerque. According to one version of the story, a happy teacher, enjoying the aftereffects of way too much alcohol, had fallen off her horse on her way back to Tucson. As it turned out, the young lady's tumble had been quite innocent.

It was true that a young lady had fallen from her horse but that calamity had occurred in the course of the performance of an act of mercy. As she was riding homeward she noticed a burr sticking to the knee of her horse and she leaned forward to brush it off. Though her motives were all right and her offense was entirely unintentional she violated the law of gravitation and the statute relating to equilibrium and was punished for it.[4]

George Roskruge was a man of great personal pride and integrity. Despite his forbidding appearance in photographs, an occasionally gruff manner, and perhaps some slightly antiquated social views, he was at the end of his life a beloved figure in his adopted city. Known to all as "Uncle George," he died in 1928 at the age of eighty-three. Flags in Tucson flew at half-mast, and at his Masonic funeral, the coffin was draped with both the Stars and Stripes and the Union Jack.[5] ■

Arizona Historical Society; background, author photograph

Canyon Panorama

During his survey of Calvin Elliott's dam site in about 1900, George Roskruge made a series of photographs showing the small basin to be filled by the reservoir. Six photos are known, but the gap suggests there may have been one more. Roskruge's images are here superimposed on a panorama taken by the author in 2011 from the exact location where Roskruge set his camera. The dam site is just outside the left edge of the panorama.

Old photographs can illuminate more than history. In 1962 and again in 1995, ecologists revisited the same spot and repeated several of Roskruge's photographs. Since his survey, the appearance of the canyon floor has changed dramatically as mature oak trees have fallen, mesquites have invaded once-open areas, and floods have scoured away streamside vegetation.[6]

The road crossing the background, today the well-traveled route into what we call Upper Sabino, appears on a map Roskruge drew in 1893. We'll have a look at that remarkable document in the next chapter.

Author Photograph

In 2011 a small cairn and a chiseled X marked the ledge where Roskruge had set his tripod.

CHAPTER 5

Getting There, Late Nineteenth Century

Sabino Canyon is becoming quite a popular place for picnics, the only objection being its distance. One has to begin the trip at an early hour in order to reach town again in the evening.[1]

S o reported the *Arizona Weekly Citizen* in the spring of 1885, as eager Tucsonans were venturing for the first time to the beckoning retreat northeast of town. As the years went by, distance proved to be no obstacle. Families and friends sometimes hitched up their horses at dawn so they could enjoy a day under the cottonwoods and still arrive home by dusk.

Fortunately for bleary-eyed travelers, the first part of the journey—a six-mile drive across the monotonous, creosote-bush-dotted plain east of town—was so easy the horses could almost do it themselves. Eventually a stripe of green and a patch of red, white, and blue appeared in the distance—welcome signs that Fort Lowell wasn't much farther ahead. This small military outpost, with its double row of leafy cottonwoods along officer's row and its flagstaff on the parade ground, was the halfway point on the journey to Sabino Canyon, and, in the early years, a pleasant place to rest and perhaps chat with soldiers and their families before pressing on.

So far the route was familiar, almost routine. Townspeople had been driving to Fort Lowell for years to enjoy dances and band concerts hosted by the soldiers. Beyond the fort things grew more interesting.

East of Fort Lowell would-be picnickers turned north toward the Rillito—and the most memorable moment in the journey. Even in the late nineteenth century, long reaches of the "little river" were normally dry, but here a sheet of water flowed over the riverbed for much of the year. Some drivers and passengers climbed down from their carriages to reduce the weight and keep the narrow wheels from sinking too deeply into the wet sand. Wading, they led their horses gingerly across to the northern bank.[2]

Before this crossing, Sabino Canyon's most prominent landmark, today's Thimble Peak, had been inconspicuous against the more distant background of the Santa Catalina Mountains. Now it rose above the skyline, where it would stay boldly in view most of the rest of the way to the canyon. The road followed a dry wash—a natural desert highway—northward into a sandy-floored valley bordered by cactus-studded hills. Mile by mile the rugged escarpment of the Santa Catalinas loomed closer. Then the valley opened up, the road climbed onto a mesquite-covered plateau, and it turned eastward toward its destination.

At long last, two or three hours after leaving the city, the travelers dropped into the mouth of Sabino Canyon. With the rush of the creek in their ears, they followed the canyon upstream until the walls closed in and the way grew too narrow to continue. There, at Calvin Elliott's dam site, thirteen bumpy miles from Tucson, the horses were unhitched and watered and everyone settled in for a fine day at Sabino Canyon's unofficial first picnic ground.[3] ■

Arizona Historical Society

This photograph of travelers at Fort Lowell reminds us that many early visitors to Sabino Canyon arrived on horseback rather than in wagons or carriages. There are familiar folks here. Third and forth from the left, on horseback, are Willis Haynes and Jennie Crepin, whom we met in chapter 2. Jennie is riding side-saddle, as are the other female equestrians. Behind the travelers are the army residences and cottonwoods along officers' row. The photographer is unknown.

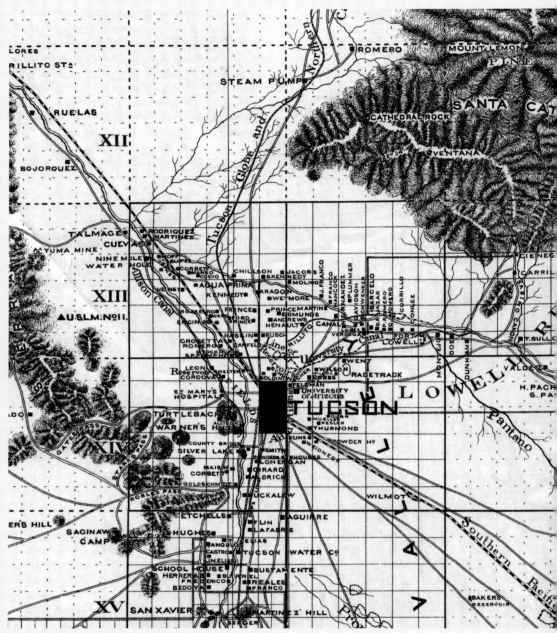

Arizona State Library, Archives and Public Records

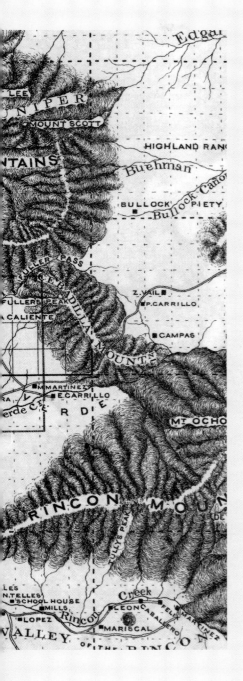

Surveyor George Roskruge's "Official Map of Pima County," published in 1893, is remarkable not only for its size—fully five feet across—but also for the beauty of its execution. This is only a piece of that extraordinary document. The small squares are a mile across.

Many details relate to the story so far, among them Sentinel Peak, here called "Warner's Hill," where Carleton Watkins set his camera in 1880; the fields along the Santa Cruz; the city of Tucson; the Southern Pacific track; the young University of Arizona; Fort Lowell and its Reservation (though not the 1886 Sabino Canyon extension); and Sabino Creek, labeled "SABINO CANON"— the first known appearance of the canyon's name on any generally available map.[4]

Eight years after Sabino Canyon's discovery by picnickers, people were still taking the same route to get there, usually on horseback or in carriages or wagons. Most broke up the journey with a stop at Fort Lowell, though by 1893 only empty buildings awaited there; the post had been abandoned by the army two years earlier. East of the fort, travelers turned north just past the Doe ranch and crossed the Rillito (curiously unlabeled here). Farther north they bypassed a road branching eastward toward the Carrillo ranch and bore right at the next fork, near the military reservation boundary. They then turned north again at the Cienegita ranch and drove another half mile to the road's end, at Calvin Elliott's dam site.

The Sabino Canyon area is enlarged on the next page.

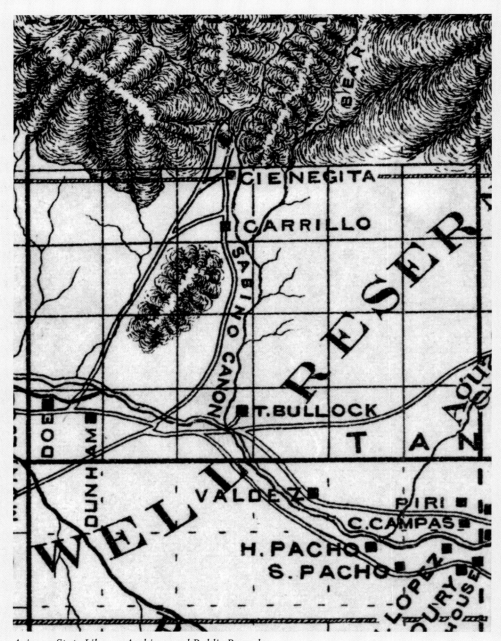

Arizona State Library, Archives and Public Records

This detail from Roskruge's 1893 "Official Map of Pima County" shows Sabino Canyon and its surroundings. The Carrillo ranch, near the confluence of Sabino and Bear Creeks, is the one founded by William Kirkland and later purchased by Peter Brady (preface). By the time it was mentioned by Fort Lowell's commander in his message concerning Calvin Elliott's plans (chapter 1), it had been acquired by Leopoldo Carrillo, a wealthy Tucson entrepreneur. Carrillo planned a resort hotel on his property—a genteel alternative to the "rough, uncivilized" canyon—but he died without building it, several years before this map was drawn.[5]

Farther north, there are two roads into Sabino Canyon. The longer road, on the left, is the one we saw in the previous chapter, in George Roskruge's photographic panorama. It may have been constructed to provide access to mines claimed by Colonel C. P. Sykes and his associates (chapter 3), or to another mine in the same area. The shorter road, on the right, north of the Cienegita ranch, ends at Elliott's dam site. The dam site is unlabeled, but look carefully. Has George Roskruge drawn the tear-shaped reservoir the dam would have created? After expending so much effort to make it real, Roskruge might be forgiven a bit of wishful cartography. He wouldn't have been the last to publish a map with a phantom lake in Sabino Canyon.

Mar 17th 1900

University of Arizona Libraries, Special Collections

Every sort of wagon and carriage was to be seen plying the road to Sabino Canyon, but surely among the most picturesque was this mud wagon stage that carried University of Arizona students to a picnic in the year 1900. Students jammed the interior seats and piled onto the roof, where they held on tightly as the creaking vehicle, of a design already verging on the antique, pitched and rocked through the desert. Behind the wagon we glimpse the roof of a more ordinary carriage; most likely it's transportation for faculty members supervising the outing.

It's evening in this snapshot, and the picnickers are just about to depart from Sabino Canyon. We might well suppose the next stop is the university, but that may not be the case. Many years after her graduation, Clara Fish Roberts recalled a similar occasion, when the returning students were met by a small orchestra at Fort Lowell. There, by the light of candles nailed to the crumbling adobe walls, they danced among the ruins until midnight.[6]

PART II
Engineers at the Oasis
1901–1928

City folk making their way to Sabino Canyon at the dawn of the twentieth century drove through a desert in the grip of a deepening drought. There had been signs of trouble as early as 1885, when soldiers at Fort Lowell were boiling their scarce well water just as the canyon's first picnickers were passing through. Since then the climate had lurched unpredictably between damp and desiccating. During the summer of 1890, violent floods sliced a deep arroyo through the fields along the Santa Cruz River, dropping the water table and leaving *acequias* high and dry. When drought struck again the next year, some farmers on the floodplain turned entirely to wells and pumps to irrigate their fields.

Nor had the city itself been spared. By the early 1890s, the springs feeding the pipeline into the city were drying up too, and pumps and wells had been installed to supplement the flow. Tucson had become a thirsty town. Water was needed to sprinkle the dusty streets and to nourish the trees planted alongside them, and citizens complained when they couldn't keep their fashionable lawns and gardens green or when their kitchen taps ran dry. In 1899 the region plunged into a drought that wouldn't be relieved for six years.[1]

Meanwhile, an energy shortage had been deepening in tandem with the water crisis. As at Fort Lowell, many of the pumps that farmers and city dwellers relied upon to tap into underground water were powered by steam engines, and many of those engines were fueled by wood fires. Similar engines ran the machinery of local industries, and during the cooler months wood was in constant demand to heat homes, stores, hotels, and public buildings. It didn't take long for most woodlands near the city to be depleted and for enterprising (and sometimes dishonest) woodcutters to look farther afield. Fuelwood theft from the Fort Lowell Military Reservation had become an irritant to the army, and when the post was abandoned in 1891, even the beautiful cottonwoods that had shaded officers' row were felled, sawed up, and burned. By the next year, most of the trees within ten miles of the city had been cut down and some woodcutters were resorting to digging out the stumps and roots.[2] ∎

Falls on Santa Cruz River 107. 150

Flooding on the Santa Cruz in 1889, a prelude to the greater flood of the following year. In the background is Sentinel Peak, from which Carleton Watkins took his view of Tucson in 1880.

CHAPTER 6

The Professor's Idea

Long before the picnickers arrived, there was a crude trail up Sabino Canyon. It began on the canyon floor, where it crossed and recrossed the creek more than a dozen times. When the way grew too narrow and boulder choked, the trail climbed out of the canyon bottom and continued along the steep eastern canyon wall. Eventually it passed through a broad, oak-filled basin, then followed the steep ridges of the Santa Catalina Mountains upward into the pine forests. Native Americans may have been the first to walk this trail, or parts of it, soldiers from Fort Lowell may have improved it, and by the early 1880s a few hardy civilians were following it to seek their fortunes in minerals or timber. Called the Sabino Canyon Trail, or sometimes the Apache Trail, it was the most traveled route into the Santa Catalina Mountains from the south.

In the year 1896, Sherman Melville Woodward joined the University of Arizona faculty as professor of physics and mechanics. A Harvard graduate in his midtwenties, he soon married fellow faculty member Gertrude Hughes, of a prominent Tucson pioneer family, and took to exploring his fascinating new surroundings with colleagues and friends. Woodward was very likely traveling the old trail when, around the turn of the century, he came upon a riveting natural formation. About four miles up Sabino Canyon, at the lower end of the inner basin of the Santa Catalinas, was a narrow gorge with steep stone walls over three hundred feet high. It was a scene of beauty and one to quicken the pulse of any hydraulic engineer—a spectacular natural dam site, a potential source of both water and hydroelectric power, less than twenty miles from a city both thirsty and energy starved.

Author photograph

The dam site found by Professor Sherman M. Woodward, several miles upstream from Calvin Elliott's site, seemed almost to have been designed by nature for the purpose. The steep V shape of the solid rock walls was immediately impressive, and the gorge also narrowed downstream so that a dam would wedge solidly into the gap under the pressure of a reservoir. The sheer seductive perfection of the site would drive a succession of engineers and speculators to pursue the dream of a great dam in Sabino Canyon relentlessly for many years. All these schemes would eventually fail, and when the author photographed the site in 2017, it was still very much as Woodward had seen it, more than a century earlier.

Woodward acted quickly. In the spring of 1901 he filed a claim on the waters of Sabino Creek, talked up his idea with Tucson men of means, and organized a survey for a dam and reservoir.[1] On June 7, the day after commencement, a team of nine (five men, two boys, and two mules) started out from the university. Accompanying Woodward was a fellow professor, G. E. P. Smith, responsible for the surveying, with two student assistants, Phil Reilly and Walter Wakefield. Professor F. Yale Adams and his nine-year-old son, Charley, joined them. Adams had offered to serve as cook if the two could tag along for the camping trip. A young local named Juan minded the pack animals.

The group soon reached the basin and set up camp. The entire reservoir area was rugged, but it was the precipitous dam site itself that truly challenged the surveyors, who removed their shoes to climb barefoot up the smooth rock walls and lowered each other down the sides of the gorge on ropes. After several days of this difficult and sometimes dangerous work, the men were seized by the urge to explore (and doubtless to cool off), so they agreed to shelve the job temporarily in favor of a hike up the trail to the lofty, forested peaks of the Santa Catalinas. Evening had fallen by the time they reached a small, vacant cabin among the pines. Years later, Professor Smith described what happened next.

> No one was in the cabin and we bedded down for the night, three in the bunks and three on the floor. We were just about asleep when the night was pierced by the most horrible, long, drawn-out shriek, which literally made our hair stand up on end. After a period of dead silence, someone whispered, "Do you think that was a locomotive?"[2]

It was an understandable reaction from anyone connected with the University of Arizona, situated as it was within earshot of the Southern Pacific tracks. Smith's guess had the advantage of plausibility: "It probably was a mountain lion or leopard calling to his mate."[3]

The next day the team ascended through the green, spring-fed headwaters of Sabino Creek into the aspen grove at the summit of Mount Lemmon, the highest peak in the Santa Catalina Mountains. Then, after a second, less eventful night in the cabin, they returned to the reservoir site, where they completed the survey in less than another week. The expedition seems to have been satisfactory for all—except for one of the pack animals, which, according to Smith, had an unhappy experience on the last day.

> Juan was trying to get the two mules up the steep slope onto the trail. One mule lost its footing and was poised to fall over backwards, but Juan was holding on by the head strap. He finally let go, and the mule rolled down the mountain slope, end over end, struck a dead tree which broke and continued rolling. We all rushed over to the foot of the slope and found the mule on its back in a crevice between two rocks. We loosened the pack; suddenly the mule gave a big stretch and came up on its feet, stretched again and seemed to be all there.[4]

With care and coaxing, the animal made it back to Tucson, bruised but still braying.

The next step toward building a dam was measuring the creek's flow to demonstrate the project's feasibility to potential investors. That phase began in June 1903, when Woodward hired David Cochran, a local contractor, to help him build a streamgage in Sabino Canyon. The place they chose was as far upstream as was then convenient to haul lumber and cement—near the end of the upper road into the canyon. During the years of the streamgage's operation, it was the only manmade structure of any consequence in Sabino Canyon.

In September 1904 Sherman Woodward accepted a professorship at the University of Iowa and resigned from the University of Arizona. The faculty threw him a farewell banquet, students and alumni hosted a reception and dance, and the next day many turned out again to say goodbye to him, to Gertrude, and to their two children at the Southern Pacific depot. Their train steamed eastward and out of sight, but what the professor had set in motion in Sabino Canyon would roll on for decades.[5] ■

Professor Woodward's streamgage was a magnet for visitors with cameras. This group posed there in about 1907.

In the box at the top of the streamgage's wooden superstructure was a pair of French clockwork mechanisms called nilometers, each of which slowly moved a paper chart, wrapped around a drum, under a pen linked by a wire to a float. Sabino Creek's great range of flow, from trickle to torrent, made two devices necessary—one for low water, the other for high. The water level at the streamgage was controlled by a precisely shaped dam, or weir, extending across the creek.

Technicians visited weekly to change the charts, and they doubled as repairmen. Leaves and sticks sometimes jammed the floats, and at least once a packrat had to be evicted from the instrument box. In 1905, when record-breaking rains at last broke the turn-of-the century drought, the creek overtopped the superstructure, filled the instrument box with mud, and rusted out the clock springs, putting the streamgage temporarily out of service. It was soon repaired, and it would stay in operation until 1912.[6]

A Young University

All but about a half dozen faculty members at the University of Arizona gathered for this group portrait on May 7, 1901. A decade after the institution had admitted its first students, it was still a small school, and Sabino Canyon was a familiar place to faculty and students alike.

(*continued*)

(*continued*)

Seated in front are Mary Elizabeth Plimpton (English), George Edson Philip Smith (physics and engineering), Millard Mayhew Parker (university president), David Hull Holmes (manual training), and Mary Bernard Aguirre (history and Spanish). At rear are William Woolford Skinner (chemist, Agricultural Experiment Station), Frank Yale Adams (history and pedagogy, commandant of cadets), Louise Henriette Foucar (botany, mathematics, and languages), Sherman Melville Woodward (mathematics and mechanics; meteorologist, Agricultural Experiment Station), Emma Monk Guild (subcollegiate instructor), Frank Nelson Guild (mineralogy and chemistry), Howard Judson Hall (English, librarian), Robert Humphrey Forbes (chemistry; director, Agricultural Experiment Station), and Nora Towner (stenography and typing, president's secretary).[7]

Exactly one month after this photograph was taken, several of the dapper male academics seen here departed for a survey of the promising new dam and reservoir site that Professor Woodward had found in Sabino Canyon. Woodward led the expedition, Smith was chief surveyor, and Adams—who would become university president later the same year—was the cook.

CHAPTER 7

Men in Green

I n September of 1901, a few months after Professor Sherman Woodward and associates surveyed his Sabino Canyon reservoir site, a gun-wielding anarchist assassinated President William McKinley, catapulting his energetic and ambitious vice president, Theodore Roosevelt, into the nation's highest office. McKinley and his predecessors had been setting aside western forest reserves for a decade, and Roosevelt took up the cause with characteristic gusto.

The following spring, Royal Shaw Kellogg, an agent of the Bureau of Forestry, Department of Agriculture, paid a visit to the Santa Catalina Mountains to support their being designated a new forest reserve, administered by the Department of the Interior. Over six days he and University of Arizona botanist John James Thornber walked up the Sabino Canyon Trail to Mount Lemmon and back. A local guide led the way, and two barely adequate burros carried provisions at a pace so painfully slow it might have been unbearable if Kellogg and Thornber hadn't wanted to stop so often to collect specimens and take notes.

USDA Forest Service, Southwestern Region

On April 12, the last day of his explorations in the Santa Catalinas, Kellogg snapped this picture on the way back down the trail. While his title for the photo, "Giant Cactus in lower Sabiño Canyon," shows its botanical purpose, it might just as well have been an illustration of his impression of the nearly finished hike, which he guessed to have been sixty miles long—"but estimates are difficult to make in the mountains, and fatigue is not in proportion to the number of miles traveled, but to the rocks met en route, and there was no scarcity of them any-where."[1] Other than that, his description of the mountain range was glowing, reinforcing a report filed the previous year by the reserve's chief proponent, Interior agent Samuel J. Holsinger.

few months after Kellogg's reconnaissance, Roosevelt created the Santa Catalina Forest Reserve by presidential proclamation. For the city folk who were flocking to Sabino Canyon, the big event was little more than an announcement buried in the local newspaper, two weeks after the fact.[2] In the early years forest rangers were scarce as roadrunner teeth, and among their chief preoccupations were resentful cattlemen, loggers, and fuelwood cutters, not contented Sunday picnickers. The rapid bureaucratic evolution over the next half dozen years was mostly invisible to anyone visiting Sabino Canyon: the transfer of the forest reserves from the United States Department of the Interior (USDI) to the Department of Agriculture (USDA) in 1905, the renaming of the reserves as national forests in 1907, and the merging of the Santa Catalina National Forest with the Santa Rita and the Dragoon to create Coronado National Forest in 1908. By then the USDA's Bureau of Forestry had been renamed the Forest Service under Roosevelt's friend, Gifford Pinchot, and the agency was starting to take on its modern shape.[3]

In the midst of all these changes, Thomas F. Meagher (pronounced "mar") spent three busy years as supervisor of the Santa Catalina Forest Reserve. Meagher had followed an unlikely path to southern Arizona. Born in Indian Territory in 1878, oldest son of an Irish immigrant and a Native American woman, Meagher was a member of the Muscogee (Creek) Nation in what would later become the state of Oklahoma. He was a few weeks short of finishing high school when recruiters for volunteers in the Spanish-American War appeared in his hometown in the spring of 1898. He joined up, missed graduation, and was shipped off to Cuba as a trumpeter in Roosevelt's Rough Riders. Within days of reaching the island, he was wounded by a gunshot to his left forearm. A war correspondent who happened to be nearby handed him a five-dollar bill, "because you are a plucky youngster."[4] He was twenty years old.

After the war, suffering from tuberculosis in the aftermath of yellow fever contracted during his service, Meagher headed to Arizona for his health. He arrived in Prescott in 1900 to a scene of smoke and destruction: a massive fire had swept through downtown the previous day. He helped with the rebuilding, served briefly in the Arizona Rangers, and near the end of the year accepted an appointment as a forest ranger in New Mexico. In 1904, after only a few years' service, he was promoted to supervisor of both the Santa Catalina Forest Reserve and the Santa Rita Forest Reserve, to its south.

No more than a handful of rangers assisted the new supervisor in his work, and they were often on the move between the two reserves. In July 1905 Meagher wrote to Pinchot in Washington that he had done something to make that travel easier.

> For the convenience of the men in passing from one district to another, I built a small frame shack in Sabino Canyon, on the south edge of the Santa Catalina Reserve, which cost $50.50 for the material. This house is situated on a well established trail and will come in handy for the shelter of the forest officers during the rainy season.[5]

Meagher's shack, nailed together two years after Professor Sherman Woodward's streamgage, was the first building constructed by the Forest Service at Sabino Canyon. Located on high ground just west of the canyon mouth, the "ranger cabin" would become a familiar landmark for travelers into the Santa Catalinas.[6]

Around this time, a movement was growing in Tucson to create a summer resort in the mountaintop forests of the Santa Catalinas. Before this beguiling notion could become reality, though, there would need to be a better way to get there than the primitive trails then in use. Tom Meagher became a spirited advocate of a wagon road into the mountains, not only to help city dwellers retreat uphill during the hotter months, but also to reduce the price of pine lumber and to ease the fuelwood crisis gripping the city. A road was not to be, but in the spring of 1906, Meagher put several rangers to work refurbishing the old Sabino Canyon Trail. When word reached town, private citizens contributed $500 toward the effort in less than twelve hours. The cash paid the wages of local laborers, and with their help the trail was ready for travelers by the Fourth of July.

The first stop on the trail was at the confluence of Sabino and Rattlesnake Creeks, by then one of the most popular places in Sabino Canyon. Even before the work was done, some grateful Tucsonans named the spot Meagher's Lodge in the supervisor's honor. It was a generous gesture, but the name didn't stick.[7]

Thomas Meagher left his job as supervisor early the next year. During his short time in southern Arizona, he had built something more valuable than a shack and a trail, and the *Arizona Daily Star* had taken notice: "Supervisor Meagher has been assiduous in his duties touching these reserves. He has popularized the forest reserve system with our people who are coming to appreciate the value to the community at large of the same. He has brought the people in harmony with the purposes of the government which has always been in the interest of the same."[8]

By the time of Meagher's departure, interesting things were starting to happen in connection with Professor Woodward's dam site, as we'll see, but those heady developments were well beyond the authority of local officials. Those were matters for higher-ups in Albuquerque and Washington. ■

Thomas F. Meagher

During his several years as supervisor of the Santa Catalina and Santa Rita Forest Reserves, at a time when rangers were often regarded with hostility by westerners convinced of their right to unfettered use of public lands, Thomas Francis Meagher Jr. won the gratitude and respect of Tucsonans for his efforts to ease travel into the Santa Catalinas.

Unfortunately, Meagher seems to have had an uncomfortable relationship with others in his own agency. Some may have resented his rapid rise to supervisor, suspecting it was due to his Roosevelt connection. It probably didn't help that Meagher was an outsider in Arizona and of part-Indian ancestry. In February 1907, after one too many disagreements with his coworkers, he abruptly resigned.

Following a brief time as a fur trapper in the Northwest, he settled in 1908 in Tulsa, not far from the place of his birth. Oklahoma had recently become a state, and oil discoveries were bringing new wealth to its citizens. Meagher worked as an engineer in the industry while in his spare time avidly studying the customs and past of the region's Native American tribes—many of which, including his own, had been forcibly moved into Indian Country during the previous century. When oil prices plummeted during the Great Depression, Meagher's reputation as a historian won him a position in the Indian-Pioneer History Project, a Works Progress Administration program gathering local oral histories.

The photograph shows Meagher in his blue wool U.S. Army uniform, around the time of his service in the Spanish-American War. It was a defining moment in his life. He died in 1945, and his tombstone in Tulsa reflects his pride in the great adventure of his youth.

THOMAS F. MEAGHER

OKLAHOMA

TRUMPETER 1 U.S. VOL. CAV.

ROOSEVELT ROUGH RIDER TROOP L

CHAPTER 8

Power and Water

By the time Professor Sherman Woodward stepped onto the train to Ohio in 1904, his idea was firmly planted in the consciousness of Tucsonans, thanks in no small part to the *Arizona Daily Star*, whose reports and editorials—like this one from 1902—had kept it continually in the public eye.

> There is one of the most inviting reservoir sites in the territory located not over ten miles distant, which with an outlay of less than $300,000 can be made to produce over five hundred horse power during the entire year, day and night. . . . There should be a concerted movement on the part of our business interest to crystallize this suggestion into a veritable fact. Let us join hands and encourage the construction of this power plant reservoir that Tucson may be the beneficiary of the forces of the rain and snow fall of the Santa Catalinas.[1]

It may not have been mere coincidence that the newspaper's publisher was former Territorial Governor Louis C. Hughes, the professor's father-in-law and a financial backer of his plans.[2]

In the spring of 1906, a newly organized and grandly named venture, the Great Western Power Company, took up the challenge. William Phipps Blake, respected professor emeritus of geology at the University of Arizona, accepted the ceremonial role of president of the corporation, but its prime movers were its two younger officers—Vice President William B. Alexander, a former engineering student of Professor Woodward's, then serving as Pima County surveyor, and Secretary William H. Daily, a local mining investor. The company issued the bulk of its capital stock to Alexander and Daily, and a lesser portion to Woodward. It then purchased the professor's streamgage, Sabino Creek water rights, and survey notes, and boldly went on to claim rights to Bear Creek, in the adjacent canyon to the east.[3]

For more than two and a half years, Alexander and Daily sought backers, ran surveys, drew up plans, and negotiated for a permit from the still-evolving Forest Service bureaucracy. On January 19, 1909, the precious document was signed. The Great Western Power Company had a mere three years to fulfill a stunningly ambitious plan: two large dams high in two rugged mountain canyons, two hydroelectric power plants, and miles of electric lines and water conduits.[4]

The clock was running, but progress was frustratingly slow. A year passed while the company dithered over the design of the Sabino Canyon dam and struggled to gain financial support. Then Vice President Alexander took a risky step—perhaps a desperate one. In April 1910, after acquiring Secretary Daily's stock, he sold a controlling interest in the company to a consortium of capitalists headquartered in Chicago.[5] With the eastern backers installed as officers, the corporation took on its first paid engineer, Mr. George C. Hinckley, and by the end of May, laborers were hauling tools and supplies up the Sabino Canyon Trail to Woodward's dam site. There they began laboriously digging a tunnel through which the creek could be diverted while the dam was built.

Author photograph

When William B. Alexander ran surveys to prepare for the planned developments in Sabino Canyon, he and his assistant left markers along the way. These chiseled artifacts are rarely noticed today. This one, at the sixteenth station on a survey line along the canyon wall, is more conspicuous than most.

After years of seemingly endless discussions, suddenly it seemed to Tucsonans that the dam might become concrete reality. A presentation by the Great Western Power Company so impressed the mayor, the city council, and the Tucson Chamber of Commerce that planned improvements to the city's water system were put on hold. There was eager talk in town of a resort hotel above Woodward's dam site, with cabins and tents set on the shore of the reservoir-to-be.[6] Farmers along the Rillito voiced worries about the loss of underflow caused by the diversion of water from Sabino Creek, but this sour note—an echo of Fort Lowell's objection to Calvin Elliott's plans a quarter century earlier—was soon drowned out by the chorus of enthusiasm. "The Sabino Canyon proposition means millions to this city and should not be talked to death or driven under cover by selfish interests," admonished the *Star*.[7]

Late in 1910, about the time the Rillito farmers were raising their concerns, the Great Western Power Company got wind of competition. Others were planning to dam Tanque Verde Creek—like Sabino Creek, a major tributary of the Rillito—for irrigation and hydroelectric power. Alexander and Hinckley squelched that idea by throwing together a sham proposal of their own for the Tanque Verde, then filing first for a federal permit. Itching for revenge, their rivals then tried to jump the Great Western's Sabino Creek water claim by filing for rights upstream from the dam site. It was an ineffectual ploy. The Great Western Power Company survived this exercise in cutthroat capitalism, but more serious trouble was brewing within.[8]

Even before the Tanque Verde Creek episode, Alexander had begun to feel cheated by the investors who had taken control of his company. They had refused to pay several thousand dollars he believed were his due for engineering services in the corporation's early years. After all, it was he who had conducted the surveys, made the calculations, and drawn up all the maps and plans—a huge amount of work, and none of it compensated. By the fall of 1911, he was ready to make his move.

Working behind the scenes, Alexander recruited a brakeman and a conductor from the Southern Pacific Railroad to front for him as officers of a new corporation, which he named the Federal Power and Water Company. On November 6, 1911, engineer Hinckley presided over the Great Western Power Company's pro forma annual stockholder meeting. That same day, unbeknownst either to Hinckley or to the eastern backers, Alexander held a Great Western stockholder "meeting" of his own. Only he attended. Claiming that the transfer of stock to the easterners had never been completed, and that he alone represented the true stockholders, he brazenly declared that the Great Western Power Company was abandoning its entire project. Then he voted—unanimously—to sell all of Great Western's rights and property to his own newly created company for $35,000 in promissory notes.

From that moment, the entire enterprise sank into a morass of recriminations, shady maneuvers, and double-dealings that only a lawyer could love. Daily, already at legal odds with Alexander over previous dealings, swore out a warrant against Alexander. Hinckley and the Great Western Power Company sued. Alexander departed eastward, out of Arizona.[9]

Coronado National Forest

In early December 1911, about a month after the dueling stockholder meetings held by the Great Western Power Company's engineer and its former vice
president, Forest Service engineer Theodore W. Norcross led a small group of
inspectors on a tour of the company's work in Sabino Canyon. Despite the nearly
three years Great Western had held its permit, the single accomplishment of any
consequence at the dam site was the diversion tunnel, which was still under
excavation. Norcross found only two men at work on the tunnel, using hand
tools. His photo leaves out the laborers, but we catch a glimpse of their tools and
provisions—including, to the right of the entrance, a bulging sack of Peerless
High Patent Flour, milled in Tucson. Ironically, the Peerless Flour slogan, "Give it
a test—it will do the rest," didn't apply to the Great Western Power Company.[10]
Norcross recommended an extension to Great Western's permit, but the corporation was already nearing collapse.

Today the tunnel's entrance looks much as it did in 1911, and a careful explorer with a good flashlight can follow the cave to its dark terminus, roughly
125 feet into the bedrock.

For a while it seemed Great Western might emerge unscathed. In January 1912, when the company's three-year completion deadline passed, the Forest Service granted it one more year, and in May its laborers finished a new, more direct trail up Sabino Canyon to the dam site, to speed construction. But the legal warfare was sapping the confidence of the eastern financiers, and by July all work had ceased. A new contender appeared on the scene: the New State Development Company, headed by a group of Tucson speculators. The corporate vultures were circling.

When the Great Western Power Company's one-year extension expired in January 1913, the Forest Service offered the corporation one last chance—and a firm ultimatum. If by May 1 of that year Great Western couldn't present proof of its capability to proceed, its permit would be permanently revoked. Sensing the end was near, key players began hedging their bets. Engineer Hinckley, by then dropped from Great Western's payroll, claimed water rights in his own name, secretly sold them to the New State Development Company, then turned around and made a last plea to the City of Tucson for support of Great Western. William Daily, too, appealed to the city on Great Western's behalf, but enlisted his brother, John W. Daily, to file for water rights. William B. Alexander mailed an impassioned letter to Secretary of State William Jennings Bryan, hoping to capitalize on an acquaintance with the famous man's son. The handwritten plea had no effect on the course of events.[11]

As the Great Western Power Company's do-or-die May 1 deadline drew near, three rivals were waiting for the axe to drop: the New State Development Company, with Hinckley in its camp; the Daily brothers; and the Federal Power and Water Company, with its creator, Alexander, relocated in Massachusetts. There was about to be a fourth.

On the last day of April 1913, hours before the Great Western Power Company's permit was set to expire, two men secretly made their way from Tucson to Sabino Canyon and up the new trail to the dam site. One was the city engineer, J. Mos Ruthrauff. The other was a city councilman named David Cochran. It was he who had helped build Professor Woodward's streamgage in 1903, and he had been watching for a decade as events unfolded. The sun set, a moonless night fell over the canyon, and the conspirators waited. Then, just after midnight, they posted a water-rights claim for the City of Tucson.[12]

By the time the secretary of agriculture canceled the Great Western Power Company's permit, Mayor Ira E. Huffman had telegraphed the Forest Service, declaring the city's interest in developing Sabino Creek for municipal water. Meanwhile the three private competitors were racing to complete their applications and gain federal priority. Relentlessly pressed from multiple directions, Forest Service officials took their time considering. In August 1913 the secretary of agriculture decided in favor of the city. The other applicants were outraged—and didn't hesitate to make their feelings known—but the roadblock was only temporary. In December, advised that the Sabino Canyon project was far greater than any small city could possibly undertake, and assured by the Forest Service that Tucson would always have the legal right to buy out any private developer, the mayor withdrew the city's claim.[13]

In March 1914 the Forest Service reopened Sabino Canyon to private applications, and so began a long endgame that played out against the background of the First World War. Each applicant got its chance in turn, according to filing priority. The Federal Power and Water Company dropped out in 1915, and the New State Development Company followed suit the next year. This left only John Daily, still working on behalf of his persistent brother, William. Finally, on November 1, 1917, the Daily permit expired.[14]

More than sixteen contentious years after Sherman Woodward had led the survey of his Sabino Canyon dam site, the professor's idea had at last run its course. Or so it seemed. ■

The breadth of the Great Western Power Company's unfulfilled ambitions is made clear by this map, drawn in 1908 by the company's de facto engineer at the time, William B. Alexander. If the company had succeeded, there would have been not one but two artificial lakes in the southern Santa Catalina Mountains.

A reservoir in Bear Canyon had been proposed by a failed corporation in 1899, even before Professor Woodward had conceived of his dam in Sabino Canyon.[15] Under Great Western's plan, water from this Sycamore Flats Reservoir was to have passed through a tunnel to a hydroelectric plant on the shore of the Woodward Basin Reservoir in Sabino Canyon. From that reservoir, water would have flowed down a sinuous pipeline to a second power plant in the canyon mouth. Another conduit (not shown) would then have carried the water to Tucson.

Eventually the name "Woodward Basin" faded with the memory of the professor himself, and the area came to be called Sabino Basin. The great Sabino Canyon dam was never built, but in the late 1930s a small dam was installed at the Bear Canyon site, to provide water to a camp for federal prisoners building a scenic new road into the Santa Catalina Mountains (chapter 22). The pond that dam created has long since silted in.

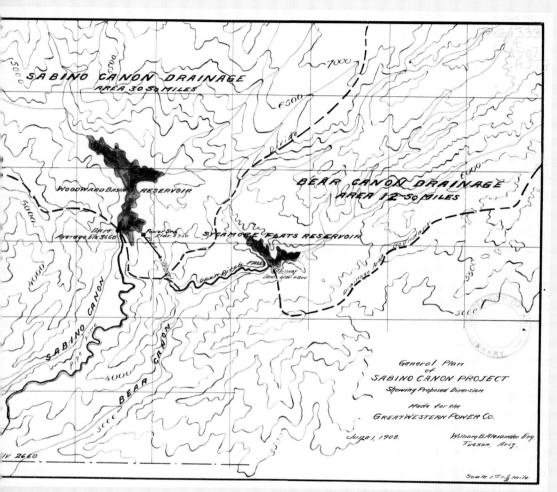

SABINO CAÑON DRAINAGE
AREA 30 SQ MILES

BEAR CAÑON DRAINAGE
AREA 12 SQ MILES

Woodward Basin RESERVOIR

SYCAMORE FLATS RESERVOIR

Dam
Average Elk 3660

Power Sta.
Elev 3750

Open Ditch FALLS

Spillway
Dam Elev 4300

SABINO CAÑON

BEAR CAÑON

Pipe Line

Divide

Drainage Area Boundary

General Plan
of
SABINO CANON PROJECT
Showing Proposed Diversion

Made for the

GREAT WESTERN POWER CO.

June 1, 1908.

William B Alexander Eng.
Tucson, Ariz.

Scale 1" = ½ mile

93

Arizona Historical Society

William Burnham Alexander and friends during their student days at the University of Arizona, May 1902. Alexander is the imposing figure at right in the dark suit. At far left is his engineering classmate, Frank Kelton, and between them, left to right, are Frances Cheyney, Arthur Hess, and Emma Culver.

Alexander transferred from the University of Vermont in 1901 and studied engineering with Professors S. M. Woodward and G. E. P. Smith. He and his fellow Vermonter, Kelton, became trusted student assistants to the faculty and performed together in the school's military band. After graduating in 1904, Alexander served for a time as Pima County surveyor, then became exclusively a private civil engineer.

Alexander's life changed dramatically in 1906 when he helped to found the Great Western Power Company, for which he acted over several years as secretary and unpaid engineer. His obsession with the doomed vision of twin reservoirs in Sabino Canyon and Bear Canyon led him to alienate his colleagues, push the boundaries of the law, and come to be regarded by some—rightly or wrongly—as a scoundrel. He never forgot the promise and heartbreak of his Sabino Canyon venture, and decades later described it as "one of the outstanding efforts of my life."[16]

Postmortem for a Dam

In the end it wasn't skullduggery that killed Professor Woodward's dam; it was economics. The Great Western Power Company was foremost a scheme to produce electricity, as its name implies, but by the time its permit was issued, fossil fuels arriving by railroad could conveniently power electric generators right in the city. It was hard to justify the enormous expense of building a hydroelectric dam miles up a canyon, far from town.

As for municipal water, always a secondary consideration, the end had been foreshadowed decades earlier at Fort Lowell. For Tucson in the early twentieth century, just as for Fort Lowell in the late nineteenth, wells and pumps were simply cheaper than mountain dams and reservoirs. What's more, the water buried beneath Tucsonans' feet seemed limitless and much more dependable than what might have collected in the reservoirs.[17] It wouldn't be until 1992, when Tucson's groundwater had been seriously depleted, that the city would receive surface water from elsewhere, and then it would be from a watercourse far greater and more distant than Sabino Creek—the Colorado River, via the Central Arizona Project canal.

While the Great Western Power Company was struggling to begin its dam in Sabino Canyon, a thousand miles to the north, another dam was rising. It, too, would supply both electricity and water. But unlike the ill-fated dam in Sabino Canyon, it was a federal project under the National Reclamation Act of 1902.

When the Shoshone Dam near Cody, Wyoming, was completed in 1910, it was the highest dam in the world. It was 325 feet tall. By 1912 the planned height of the Great Western Power Company's Sabino Canyon dam was 360 feet. It would have been an engineering wonder for its time. We may question the fiscal sense of the men who aspired to build it, but there is no doubting their audacity.[18]

CHAPTER 9

≡ 🌰 ≡

Military Occupation

During the first decade of the twentieth century, while battles over Professor Sherman Woodward's dam site were being waged in corporate meetings, government offices, newspaper editorials, courtrooms, and heated correspondence, Sabino Canyon was repeatedly invaded by military forces. Not once did Forest Service officers offer resistance, nor did civilians ever take up arms to defend the picnic grounds. Nevertheless, the occupiers always withdrew within days.

The invading force was the cadet battalion of the University of Arizona. In the university's early years, military training was standard for all healthy male students through their sophomore year. Men were required to own West Point–style gray uniforms, and many chose to wear them to all their classes, lending a distinctly military atmosphere to the campus. Parade drills and target shooting were routine features of university life.

Beginning in the fall of 1903, the battalion mobilized once each academic year for a practice encampment, almost always in Sabino Canyon.[1] After assembling at the university, the troops set out for the canyon on foot, while their gear and supplies were hauled out in wagons. The adventures began even before they arrived.

Naturally during the march the main body became considerably separated from the wagon train and its guard and when the latter arrived in camp they reported that while going through the foothills they were attacked by a band of hostile Indians. Cadets Hazzard, Hardy, Wheeler, and Grosetta, on the guard accompanying the train, made a valorous defence [*sic*] and with well aimed volleys dispersed the marauding Apaches.[2]

That was the *Arizona Daily Star* amusing its readers during the first encampment. In 1903 the cadets were about as likely to encounter hostile Apaches as musket-bearing redcoats.

Once in camp, the cadets kept to a regular schedule from reveille through taps. Still, despite the discipline, there was fun to be had. The cadets swam in the creek during breaks from training, they sang around campfires in the evening, and during the night, more experienced campers led gullible first-timers in "snipe hunts," tracking down imaginary wildlife. Because the camp was so close to Tucson, friends often came out to visit, and when wagons returned to town for supplies, mothers sent out treats for their boys to enjoy—not always with beneficial effects on their digestion. The speed of the march home was a matter of pride, and in 1908 the cadets broke the record by reaching campus only two hours and fifty minutes after leaving Sabino Canyon. Another newspaper account, this one from 1907, summed up the whole experience.

> The youthful soldiers had a great time at the Canyon. There were many stirring incidents especially in the night time when the sentries had to walk their beats with only the silent rocks as companions. It is stated that the rocks show numerous evidences of having received sentries' bullets but this report is not verified. At all events none of the enemy in the form of coyotes, wildcats, mountain lions or bears stormed the camp.[3]

The Sabino Canyon encampments were memorable events in the lives of the men of the University of Arizona, and we're fortunate to have their own snapshots to show us what went on.[4] ■

At 8:00 am on November 24, 1903, a battalion of thirty-nine cadets, led by Captain Mason M. Maxon, U.S. Army veteran of the Indian Wars, professor of military science and tactics, marched out of the University of Arizona campus, headed for Sabino Canyon. They arrived in the early afternoon and staked their tents in a neat row along the road in the canyon mouth. There the cadets camped for five days over the Thanksgiving break, during which they arranged targets in the rocks for rifle practice, advanced their military training, and honed their outdoor skills. Sometime during the encampment, a photographer (probably one of the cadets) climbed a bluff across the creek from the camp and snapped this photo.

The end of the road, seen at right, and Elliott's dam site just beyond it, outside the frame, had been Sabino Canyon's most popular picnic ground in the previous century, but by this time most visitors were parking their carriages farther up the canyon, so the battalion probably had this area mostly to itself. Headquarters were at the second tent from the left, and that's where the next photograph was taken.

The collapsed pup tent behind the cadets at right suggests the battalion is break-ing camp on the last morning—as does the impressive array of wildlife that has been sacrificed in the service of military education. Captain Maxon stands at left. His son, Kimball, is at his side, and the gentle way the boy is cradling the desert tortoise suggests it's still very much alive and not destined for the soup pot.

The obvious youth of most of the cadets seen here may seem surprising, but there had been no public high school in Tucson since 1896, and the university was helping to fill the gap by offering college preparatory instruction. During the 1903–1904 academic year, subcollegiate students like Kimball Maxon outnum-bered college students by more than two to one.

The battalion marched out of Sabino Canyon on November 29, perhaps car-rying with it a forlorn turtle, and camped one more night amid the ruins of Fort Lowell before returning to the university to rest its sore feet.

A few years later, the cadet battalion has grown in number and the encampment has moved a quarter mile down the road to where the canyon floor is broad enough to serve as a parade ground. According to one account, it's a Sunday, and admiring families have come from town to watch the cadre perform its military drills. Beyond the cadets, who are standing smartly in formation with their sabers and rifles, are some of the two-man tents where they sleep, and behind these tents a carriage packed with onlookers has stopped on the old road to the Elliott dam site.

The cadet who so skillfully composed this photograph was sophomore Albert R. Buehman, captain of Company A. Al's father, German immigrant Henry Buehman, ran a portrait studio in town, and Al would later take over the business. Prints of this image seem to have been offered to the cadets as souvenirs. Multiple copies have survived, unhelpfully marked with multiple dates, but other evidence shows this encampment was in April 1907.

It's daybreak and these bleary-eyed cadets have just been rousted from their tents. They're lined up, disheveled, trying not to look into the rising sun, and the one closest to the camera hasn't quite finished putting on his pants.

The morning is in April 1910, and if the cadets seem older on average than the ones in 1903, it's because a public high school has reopened in Tucson, and the University of Arizona's preparatory classes are on their way out. During the 1909–1910 academic year, college students outnumbered prep students at the University of Arizona for the first time.

The 1910 encampment would be one of the last in Sabino Canyon. It's sobering to consider that some of the young men in this photograph may later have been conscripted for combat in the Great War. A few nights in a tent in Sabino Canyon would have seemed a quaint and comforting memory to a soldier in a trench in France.

Author photograph

The cadets left little behind to remind us of their campouts in Sabino Canyon—with one intriguing exception. High on a bluff in Lower Sabino is a fading set of white, painted figures, pockmarked with bullet holes. These seem to be the targets the cadets used in 1903 (and possibly in later encampments as well) to sharpen their shooting skills. Over the decades weather has taken a severe toll on these artifacts, and by 2020, when the author took this photograph, several of the figures were nearly gone. Eventually only the bullet scars will remain—last, cryptic evidence of the youthful invaders who occupied Sabino Canyon more than a century ago.[5]

CHAPTER 10

One Visit

On a fine Sunday morning at the tail end of February 1904, four people with a camera set off from Tucson for Sabino Canyon in a fringe-top surrey. Two of them were Gaius and Lydia Upham, a young couple who had moved to Tucson from Wisconsin about two years earlier. The identities of the others are unknown to the author, though one may have been Lydia's unmarried younger sister, Olga Reiner. Gaius, who had found work with the Southern Pacific Railroad, was a skilled amateur photographer. He used a camera as most people did then and do now—to photograph his family, his friends, his workplace, the scenery, and anything else that struck his fancy.

This day was something special. Gaius seems to have set out to tell the story of a single outdoor adventure almost from beginning to end. The photographs he and his companions took on that late winter day give us a lighthearted visual narrative of a visit to Sabino Canyon shortly after the turn of the century.[1]

By the time of the outing, most visitors to Sabino Canyon had abandoned their old haunts at Calvin Elliot's dam site and were spending their time about a half mile farther upstream, at the end of the upper road into the canyon— the road seen in George Roskruge's photo panorama, taken a few years earlier (chapter 4). This beautiful area, at and near the confluence of Sabino and Rattlesnake Creeks, became known as the Picnic Grounds, a straightforward designation that long survived the 1906 proposal to rename the place after Supervisor Meagher (chapter 7). It would remain the recreational heart of Sabino Canyon throughout the first few decades of the twentieth century. ■

After crossing the plain northwest of Tucson, the travelers paused at Fort Lowell for their first picture. Thirteen years earlier the soldiers had departed, and nearly every scrap of wood and metal had been auctioned off and carted away. By 1904 the unprotected adobe buildings—stripped of roofs, floors, windows, and doors—had fallen into picturesque decay, and the abandoned post had become a destination for curiosity seekers.

Here Lydia holds the reins while Gaius has stepped out of the surrey with the camera near what may once have been a fine house on officers' row. The late winter morning is still cool enough for scarves and jackets.

Arizona Historical Society

The day is warming, jackets have been shed, and the friends have crossed the Rillito and stopped for a drink about two miles west of Sabino Canyon. In 1904 few saguaros stood among the creosote bushes between the city and Fort Lowell, but the giant cacti added welcome interest to the scenery in the foothills north of the river. The imposing plants may have been especially fascinating to Gaius and Lydia, who were still relative newcomers to Tucson.

The magnificent canteen is the other center of attention, but what's the object slung over Lydia's shoulder? (We'll see it again.)

Arizona Historical Society

A short time later, the surrey is approaching the upper entrance to Sabino Canyon on the one-carriage-wide road to the Picnic Grounds. The vegetation in the foreground is much sparser than today. In 1904 Sabino Canyon was still deep in the turn-of-the century drought, which wouldn't be relieved until the following year.

Arizona Historical Society

In Sabino Canyon at last, the group has parked in the Picnic Grounds and walked just beyond the end of the road to Professor Sherman Woodward's streamgage—eight months after its installation, already one of the most popular spots in the canyon. The streamgage's weir crosses the center of the picture, just upstream from Lydia, and the instrument box is to the left of her raised elbow, mostly hidden by a tree. On the distant horizon is the stony dome that Colonel C. P. Sykes named after himself, but by this time it has become known as Rock Peak.

Notice how low the water level is for February—a sign of the persistent drought.

Arizona Historical Society

Arizona Historical Society

A little farther along, the intrepid four have climbed atop a boulder, high above the canyon floor, and Lydia snaps a photograph of her husband brandishing a pistol. A breeze has come up, and the woman in the photo is holding on to her hat. By now the bulky canteen has been left behind in favor of a cup, held by the man at left. In 1904 few people thought twice about drinking from Sabino Creek, whose water many expected would eventually flow from taps in Tucson homes.

Landscape photographs of the time often featured figures posed on precarious perches for dramatic effect, and the photographer may have had such popular images in mind when arranging this composition. Gaius and Lydia appear to be taking their lives in their hands at the edge of the slanting rock, but this is no more than a clever illusion: the trees at lower right show the two are only a short distance above the canyon floor. While Gaius points theatrically into the distance, Lydia is less preoccupied with posing than with maintaining her modesty in the breeze.

The object slung by a strap from Gaius's shoulder is the same one Lydia was carrying when she drank from the huge canteen on the way to the canyon: the leather case for his folding camera.

Arizona Historical Society

Arizona Historical Society

The two friends of the Uphams share a cup of Sabino Creek water. How does it taste? In 1884 engineer John Culver, after pronouncing the canyon "a rough, uncivilized rent" in the mountains, went on to describe the creek's water as "not nearly as good as the water now supplied to Tucson by the Water Company. The Sabino Canyon water, when I examined it, was somewhat bitter, and had a yellowish discoloration," qualities he correctly attributed to plant material over which it had flowed.[2]

It's easy to confirm the water's color today, but in the age of giardia and bacterial contamination, its taste is best left to the imagination.

By late afternoon the four are recrossing the dry bed of the Rillito, nearing the halfway point on their drive back to Tucson. If there has been a picnic—and there must have been one—it hasn't been judged worthy of a snapshot. The air is cooling, a breeze is fluttering the fringe on the surrey, and jackets are on again as the passengers patiently wait for Gaius to take one last picture. Perhaps a trifle weary after their day of fun and photography, the travelers still have time to reach home before sunset.

CHAPTER 11

=== 🍃 ===

Gunplay

We glimpse Sabino Canyon's past in a photograph, but we hear it only in the mind's ear. It's tempting to imagine the early days to have been quiet ones, when the laughter of friends blended with the murmur of the creek, the rustle of a breeze through sycamore leaves, and the sweet counterpoint of birdsong. No doubt on some days the canyon did offer up such idyllic soundscapes. But on other days its walls echoed the crack of gunfire.

Why did so many people bring guns to Sabino Canyon? Imagined Apaches may be part of the answer, at least in the beginning. By the mid-1880s the Tucson area was quite safe for travelers, yet the memory of the old threat was still fresh. In 1885, when picnickers were first venturing into Sabino Canyon in numbers, the Indian Wars were still very much in the news. That spring, Geronimo and his followers escaped the San Carlos Indian Reservation for the last time, and his epochal surrender wouldn't come for more than a year. All this was happening a long way from Sabino Canyon, but the newspaper reports were enough to make Tucsonans uneasy.

If Apaches didn't worry the picnickers, wildlife might. Those early visitors to Sabino Canyon were mostly city dwellers, after all, and not all of them would have been entirely comfortable in an untamed landscape where mountain lions and black bears might conceivably lurk. Having a firearm at hand made the "rough, uncivilized" canyon feel just a bit safer.

But if anything it was the wildlife that needed protection. People packed up their picnics in town before they set off, but they sometimes supplemented the fare with small game shot along the way—quail, dove, and rabbits. And, of course, some people continued to hunt once they arrived in the canyon, though there are surprisingly few photographs to confirm it. The image of the cadets showing off their harvest of game (chapter 9) is quite unusual, and of course reflects special circumstances.

Yet even all these motives together can't explain the sheer number of photographs of people with guns in Sabino Canyon, especially after the turn of the century. When Gaius Upham raised his pistol in 1904, he wasn't protecting his companions or enhancing the lunchtime menu. He was fooling around. A visit to Sabino Canyon had become an opportunity for urban folk to play at being wild westerners in the fading afterglow of the pioneer era. ■

Four firearms are clearly in view here on the banks of Sabino Creek, but there are five if the boy in the jacket, across the stream, has shouldered a rifle, and six if his friend is waving a blurry pistol, both of which seem likely. The three men in the photograph appear to be showing off their rifles for the camera, while the woman at left has laid hers carelessly across her lap.

Henry Buehman, founder of his family's studio in Tucson, may have been the photographer. This extravagant display of firepower was at Calvin Elliott's dam site, just as one would expect for an early outing to Sabino Canyon, perhaps in the 1880s.

A photograph from Clara Fish's remarkable album shows a group enjoying a Sabino Canyon outing in the spring of 1899. It's among the earliest photos to show visitors in the area that would come to be known as the Picnic Grounds.

You may recognize Clara in the top row, at right, next to her friend Millie Brown. We met them separately in chapter 2. Just below them are Elbridge Graves, at left, and a married couple, Elizabeth and Stuart Bayless. Stuart's mother, Margaret Bayless, at right, is acting as chaperone. Sadie Etchells (who will later marry Mr. Graves) is the one with the pistol on her hip, and we might take it to be a casual part of this western woman's outfit if it weren't for certain other photos taken the same day.

Both: Arizona Historical Society

It's Millie's turn to enjoy the novelty of strapping on a holster and handling a gun. Evidently the pistol is being passed around for everyone's amusement.

Clara's title for the second picture, "a snap-shot," captures the lightheartedness of the moment with clever wordplay. "Snapshot" originally meant a hurried gunshot without careful aim, but by Clara's time it had already taken on a second meaning: a quick photo taken with a handheld camera.

Arizona Historical Society

Anyone handling a firearm was a subject of photographic interest, but a woman with a gun seems to have been irresistible to male photographers. Gaius Upham was probably the man with the camera on this occasion, in the Picnic Grounds, about 1907.

In the first decade of the twentieth century, when crowding still lay in Sabino Canyon's future, horsing around with guns was relatively harmless—though we don't know how the horses themselves reacted when the trigger was pulled.

Although the photographic evidence is sparse, there was indeed hunting in Sabino Canyon in the early years, and not all of it was for food. Here, a group of friends from the University of Arizona are spreading the wings of an unfortunate owl.

Thanks to official university picnics at Calvin Elliott's dam site, and later to the annual cadet campouts nearby, the lower reaches of Sabino Canyon were familiar territory to the men and women of the University of Arizona during the early years of the twentieth century. Some students made return visits on their own, bringing their guns (and cameras) with them. This photo was taken at Elliott's site in 1902.

Both: Arizona Historical Society

We can only hope it wasn't loaded.

Photos like these were still being taken at Sabino Canyon into the second decade of the twentieth century, but by then Arizona's gunslinging past was becoming a more and more distant memory, and the increasing number of picnickers was making it less and less safe to fire a gun. Recreational shooting may already have been on the wane in 1919, when the Arizona legislature established a game preserve in the Santa Catalina Mountains, and it became unlawful to carry a firearm in Sabino Canyon without a permit. "Bring your cameras but not your guns," admonished the Forest Service.[1] After that, pistols and rifles went the way of parasols and carriages at Sabino Canyon, and vanished from snapshots.

CHAPTER 12

On the Trail

Perhaps a few Tucsonans were relaxing in their favorite canyon on the unremarked day, sometime during the first decade of the twentieth century, when the town's population slipped past the ten-thousand mark. The warm and dry desert climate was helping to entice newcomers to the city, but there was no denying that while winters were a treat, summers were trying. Every year, when the hotter months arrived, residents with time and train fare exited westward to enjoy the ocean breezes along the California coast. The problem was, they took their wallets with them.

As yet another sizzling summer loomed in 1911, the Tucson Chamber of Commerce began a campaign to induce the sweltering populace to spend its dollars closer to home. Why pack one's bags for San Diego when there was cool air to breathe right next door, in the green forests of the Santa Catalina Mountains? Even before the turn of the century, small numbers of adventurous Tucsonans had been riding the Sabino Canyon Trail to spend their summers amid the pines, but now the old trail, which had been upgraded with such fanfare only five years earlier (chapter 7), was judged to be the chief impediment.

In May of 1911, the chamber of commerce approached the Forest Service with an offer of $500 toward opening a new trail into the mountains if the agency would match the funds. To choose the best route, a "committee of two" was appointed: Coronado National Forest's supervisor, Robert L. Selkirk, and Emerson O. Stratton, a well-known rancher and miner. By fortunate coincidence, at that very moment the Great Western Power Company was beginning work on a wagon road from near old Fort Lowell to its Sabino Canyon dam site, for the efficient transport of men, equipment, and materials. The company's engineer, George Hinckley, lent his assistance to the trail committee and a decision was quickly made. The new trail would follow Great Western's route up Sabino Canyon as far as the dam site, from there skirt the eastern shore of the projected reservoir, then head upward into the pines a few miles east of the older trail.[1]

In early June workers set up camp in Sabino Canyon and began laying out the stretch of trail from the canyon mouth to the dam site. A few days later, Stratton led another team of men up the Sabino Canyon Trail, established a second camp above the dam site, and began blazing the new trail from there to the top. As work proceeded simultaneously on both sections, Chamber of Commerce Secretary H. Virgil Failor was busy in the city soliciting private contributions, and with funds and labor from Pima County, the Forest Service, and the Great Western Power Company, the new trail seemed well on the way to being ready for vacationers by mid-July. This, it soon became apparent, was wishful thinking.[2]

Coronado National Forest

The new trail was still under construction in December, when Forest Service engineer Theodore Norcross made his inspection tour of the Great Western Power Company's work (chapter 8). The route ran along the eastern canyon wall, paralleling the planned pipeline from the dam to the canyon mouth. At the time of the inspection, the trail's leading end was still advancing slowly through steep and rugged terrain, just over halfway up the canyon to the dam site.

Great Western's idea was first to build a trail to the dam site, then later to widen it into a wagon road. Norcross visited and photographed the trail's lowest section, which was already being widened. At the same time, the Forest Service was stringing a telephone line along the route. Near the canyon mouth, cacti served as no-cost telephone poles. Look carefully: just beyond the horses a board with a wooden peg is attached to a saguaro. Farther up the canyon, where saguaros were fewer and farther between, wooden poles and upright metal pipes would be installed instead.[3]

Author photograph

Some of the old wooden telephone poles still stand—including this one, with an insulator peg still attached, photographed by the author in 2012, a century after the trail opened. Other wooden poles have long since fallen over or burned in wildfires, and some of the remaining ones may be replacements, but the metal poles have fared better over the years. Surviving poles, and even lengths of the wire itself, can still be spotted with a little effort. The line ran mostly upslope of the trail (seen here in the background with a lone hiker, below Thimble Peak), but one of the old iron poles is in plain sight, set in a boulder right next to the trail, where it serves today only to mystify passing hikers.

On May 26, 1912, a year after proposing a new trail into the Santa Catalinas, the Tucson Chamber of Commerce proudly announced the route's opening with a full-page notice in the Tucson papers, complete with a map. It was just in time for the summer season.[4]

The U.S. RANGER CABIN, a black dot just west of Sabino Creek, near the foot of the NEW TRAIL TO MT LEMON, is the shack that Supervisor Tom Meagher had built seven years earlier. A mile upstream from the cabin is the popular PICNIC GROUND, and beyond there the old Sabino Canyon Trail is a barely visible dashed line crossing and recrossing the creek. The old trail joins the new one south of the BASIN, which was meant to be filled by the Great Western Power Company's reservoir. Above the basin, the old trail (today called the Box Camp Trail) climbs toward SOLDIER CAMP, while the new one (today's Palisade Trail) runs farther eastward, to BURNED CABIN. The new telephone line (not shown) connected the ranger cabin in Sabino Canyon to one at Soldier Camp.

WEBER'S, northwest of Soldier Camp, was a cabin resort that would soon become part of a town called Summerhaven. MT LEMON is a common misspelling of the name of the summit of the Santa Catalinas. That peak was christened by E. O. Stratton in honor of botanist Sara Plummer Lemmon, whom he guided there with her husband and scientific partner, John Gill Lemmon, when the Lemmons were enjoying a plant-collecting honeymoon in 1881.

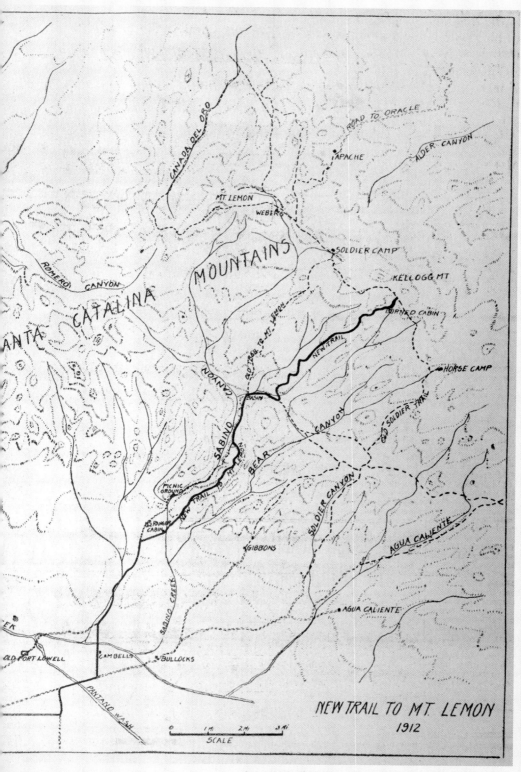

Arizona Daily Star, *courtesy Arizona Historical Society*

J ust as the Tucson Chamber of Commerce had predicted, the new trail instantly replaced the older and more primitive Sabino Canyon Trail as Tucson's favored route into the shady forests of the Santa Catalina Mountains. Everyone's first ride up the trail was an experience to remember, yet one of the most vivid accounts of such a journey was written not by a local, but by a tourist from Missouri.

In midsummer 1913 Oswald and Elsie Weigelt, a married couple from St. Louis, came to Tucson to visit Elsie's sister and brother, Marie and Otto Haeber, who had moved there a year or two earlier. The Weigelts took eagerly to local customs. At the Haebers' rented home near downtown, they slept outdoors under mosquito nets, Tucson style, and for their first Sunday outing, they cavorted with their hosts among the boulders in Sabino Creek. That cheerful excursion seems to have whetted their appetites for more.

Elsie Weigelt; her husband, Oswald Weigelt; and her brother, Otto Haeber, photographed by Elsie's older sister, Marie Haeber, during their visit to Sabino Canyon on the tenth of August 1913. Oswald, Elsie, and Marie had immigrated from Germany as children (and may have spoken with German accents), but Otto, the youngest, had been born in the United States. He was working as a clerk for the Southern Pacific Railroad. A few weeks after this photo was taken, the four left on a pack trip into the Santa Catalina Mountains. Oswald, who was in the glass and mirror business in St. Louis, later wrote an account of their adventure.

On an afternoon in early September, the Weigelts and the Haebers set out again for Sabino Canyon. This time the high Santa Catalinas were their goal, and to help them get there they had hired the Haebers' irascible landlady, Miss Amelia Franco, among whose qualifications was that her sister was married to James F. Westfall, the Forest Service ranger stationed at Soldier Camp. Oswald, who later chronicled the expedition, described what they found that evening near the mouth of Sabino Canyon.

> At about 5 O.cl. we arrived at Lowell Station. Lowell Station belongs to the U.S. Forest Reserve, and consists of a makeup of rough boards and canvas, called the Cabin, in which the mountain ranger stays during the winter months. The mountain stream terminates here only a short distance from the cabin, and peculiar enough, disappears altogether, flowing into some underground river.[5]

Tom Meagher's ramshackle building had by then acquired an official name, which almost certainly reflected its nearness to old Fort Lowell. In fact, the land where the cabin stood had once been part of the Fort Lowell Military Reservation—appended to it in 1886, when the army had briefly considered piping Sabino Creek water to headquarters (chapter 1). Of course, the reservation was already long abandoned when Supervisor Meagher wielded his hammer in Sabino Canyon in 1905. But let's return to the Weigelts and the Haebers on that September evening in 1913.

After supper the women laid their bedding on the ground, and the men spread theirs on a broad wooden step outside the door of the cabin. For a while Oswald and Otto were kept awake by thoughts of dangerous wildlife.

> At last we began to doze away a little when suddenly I discovered some noise under the platform. I poked Otto into the ribs and called his attention to the fact that I thought a Rattle Snake was roaming under us, he denied the fact, as snakes don't exist there, his view in the matter was Skunk, well we turned over on our stomachs and looked and listened. I discovered something dark looking in the distance, picked up a club I had laying along side of me and just got ready to throw, when Otto yelled: don't throw for God sake that's our lantern! well the whole bunch burst their sides laughing.

The lantern survived the night—as did Amelia's riding boots, saved by her shout before Otto could fill them with buckshot in the dark.

After breakfast the travelers forded Sabino Creek and started up the trail that had opened the year before. They had five horses, but two were loaded with supplies, so the women rode and the men walked. Amelia took the lead, driving one of the pack horses ahead of her. The others, feeling "a little shaky" on the narrow trail along the steep canyon wall, soon fell behind. Amelia stopped to wait for them at the entrance to the basin, gave them a thorough scolding when they caught up, and then directed them down a steep pathway toward the canyon floor. According to Oswald, the descent was like "sliding down the side of a house."

To everyone's dismay, once they reached bottom, it became clear that they had taken a wrong turn. Otto was appointed to climb back up and reconnoiter, and after a while the others spotted him on a rock far above, "apparently the size of a frog." He had found the trail. The party then struggled back up the slope—a heroic effort for humans and horses alike. Oswald reached the top crawling on all fours, "the next thing to being ready for embalming," and was persuaded not to return to Tucson only after Elsie and Marie massaged his temples with whisky and administered a medicinal dose by mouth.

The steep trail that had caused the trouble was the path that laborers paid by the Great Western Power Company had followed to reach the diversion tunnel at the dam site (chapter 8). By 1913, when Amelia led the Weigelts and the Haebers astray, all work had stopped and Great Western's permit had been revoked, but the trail was still fresh enough to cause confusion. (It can still be found today, and it has been made even worse by erosion during more than a century of rainstorms.)

The tale of the intrepid travelers has a happy ending. After further scoldings from Amelia, they camped and recuperated in the basin, and early the next morning resumed their uphill climb. The women went ahead with the horses and were first to reach Soldier Camp. By the time Oswald and Otto showed up several hours later, Elsie had been reduced to tears, fearing that her husband had lost his way in the woods, never to be seen again. Happily reunited, they boiled up a restorative pot of beans, but were too ravenous to leave them long enough on the fire. "It was fairly good," Oswald later wrote. "I mean the bacon and gravy, for the beans we almost had to use a nutcracker." All had a fine story to tell, and Elsie even sported a souvenir row of tooth marks on her hip, courtesy of one of the pack horses.

The mountaineers and their hosts near Soldier Camp in September 1913. The affectionate couple at center are Elsie and Oswald Weigelt, looking rested after their two-day journey up the trail. Elsie's sister, Marie, is standing at left. More at home in the woods are the two spirited tree climbers: ranger Jim Westfall and his formidable wife, Leta. They gave the Weigelts and the Haebers a grand tour of the mountaintop during their stay. The stern-looking woman with the rifle is Leta's sister, Amelia Franco, who led the Weigelts and the Haebers up the trail and repeatedly chewed them out for encouragement. Elsie's brother, Otto, snapped the picture.

The Weigelts and the Haebers packed provisions for a two-week trip, but those who stayed the summer needed supplies all season long. When the new trail had opened, the Tucson Chamber of Commerce had encouraged local businessmen to establish a commercial packing service, and within a week a pair of enterprising University of Arizona freshmen had declared their intention to do just that.[6]

Over the next few years, the numbers of city folk migrating uphill for the summer grew. Around 1914 the packing service was taken over by John W. Knagge, a furnace man from Indiana who had homesteaded with his family about a mile from the ruins of Fort Lowell. Running the pack trains was mainly the job of his capable sons, Ed and Tom, with younger Dick and Francis pitching in as they could. After taking orders over the telephone line from Soldier Camp, they hauled supplies by wagon or automobile from the city to Sabino Canyon, where the pack animals—mostly burros—were held in a corral near the Lowell Ranger Station cabin. From there the boys drove the animals up the trail to the family's camp near Burned Cabin.

A half dozen pack animals was about the limit, Tom later recalled. The burros, oblivious of the profit motive, were inclined to stop and snack along the trail, "and if we had too many we couldn't throw rocks and keep them moving."[7] Despite the interruptions, the uphill trip often took only a day, and the next morning the boys made their deliveries to vacationers at Soldier Camp and Summerhaven. The burros then got a rest while the Knagges took a fresher set back down to Sabino Canyon for the next load.

The Knagges became masters of the burro-packing art, and they skillfully loaded their animals with everything imaginable—food, household supplies, lumber, and, in season, Christmas trees. They were especially proud of packing a massive woodburning stove up the mountain, but for that they sensibly took a shorter route, beginning at some mines on the north side of the Santa Catalinas. Those mines could already be reached by road, and with the cooperation of their owners, William H. Daily and Emerson O. Stratton (both of whose names you may recognize), by 1921 that road was improved and extended to Summerhaven and Soldier Camp. After that the honking of automobile horns replaced the braying of burros when supplies were delivered on the mountain.

Courtesy Terry DeWald

Not many photographs have survived to show us the burro-packing business run by the Knagge family in the Santa Catalinas. The stoical animals in this photo, taken on an unknown date, appear to be waiting at the family's camp in the ponderosa pine forest near Burned (or Burnt) Cabin, loaded with lumber for delivery to Soldier Camp and Summerhaven.

The figure near the center may be Edwin Knagge, John W. Knagge's oldest child, who had chief responsibility for running the operation. The work helped turn Ed into a highly regarded outdoorsman. He later fought fires in the Santa Catalinas, assisted on a solar eclipse expedition to Mexico, served in the Chiricahua Mountains as a foreman for the Civilian Conservation Corps, and spent several decades doing road construction for Pima County.[8]

Travelers into the Santa Catalinas were hard to please. In 1916, just four years after the new trail opened, a survey was completed to replace it with an automobile road up Sabino Canyon. Fiscal realities seem to have relegated that plan to the shelf, and the opening of the road up the north side helped to keep it there.

But dissatisfaction soon set in again. The drive from Tucson around the northern end of the Catalinas was much too long, it seemed, and the last seven miles, twisting up the forested slope toward Summerhaven, were so narrow that traffic could move in only one direction at a time. The old call to "keep the money at home" was heard in the city again, but the estimated cost of a southern road had quadrupled since 1916, and bond elections for a road up Sabino Canyon failed in 1928 and again in 1930.

The vision of a southern road into the Catalinas, dating back at least to Supervisor Meagher's time, was too compelling to be dimmed by a mere quarter century of disappointment. A fresh survey for a southern route was run in 1931, and with surprising results. The long-touted Sabino Canyon route was dismissed as too winding and steep for a modern roadway, and engineers selected another, starting up the slope several miles to the east. This time federal funding was forthcoming, with federal prison labor as well, and construction of today's Catalina Highway began in 1933.[9]

Yet road builders still weren't quite finished with Sabino Canyon. The next year would see the ground broken for a new road beyond the old Picnic Grounds. Its destination wouldn't be Soldier Camp or Summerhaven, and it would change the canyon profoundly—but that's a story for another chapter. ■

Two young riders on the 1912 trail, about a mile below the Great Western Power Company's dam site. The long-ago scene is in deep shadow, so the photo is underexposed, but it's easy to see why the ride might give pause to newcomers like the Weigelts and the Haebers. In the foreground the narrow trail is notched into the bedrock, and it continues, barely visible, across the steep slope in the distance.

Sometime during its heyday in the second decade of the twentieth century, the vertiginous pathway up Sabino Canyon to the dam site came to be called the Plate Rail Trail. The name was homespun poetry—a reference to narrow shelves built high on the walls of rooms for displaying crockery—and it was always good for a chuckle. But as architectural fashion changed in later years, plate rails disappeared from both homes and vocabularies, and the trail's colorful name faded away with them. It's a shame. Today the route is known, prosaically, as the Phoneline Trail.

CHAPTER 13

Postcard Perfect

The early decades of the twentieth century were wonderful times to visit Sabino Canyon. The route from town was by then familiar, well traveled, and, except during the very worst of weather, quite safe. When visitors arrived, they stepped into a leafy oasis that must have seemed a perfect refuge from the busy desert city. Every stream-polished ledge and shady sycamore within a half mile of the Picnic Grounds had become a place to while away the hours with family and friends. As the old photographs show, people were seldom dressed to wander much farther than that.

Even with the ever-growing numbers of visitors, and despite multiple schemes to exploit the creek for power and water, the canyon was still much as the first picnickers had found it—and just as beguiling in the imagination. A note in the Sunday paper captured the anticipation of a springtime outing in 1912.

Girl in younger set says: "Well, it will soon be time for picnics, chaperones and sandwiches. Spring is coming also the day of the Thermos basket! Sabino Canyon will once more come into its own."[1]

Yet we must be cautious about viewing the past through the warm filter of nostalgia. As we'll see in a later chapter, the precept "Take only pictures, leave only footprints" hadn't yet entered the culture of the American outdoors, and some of those early picnickers were leaving behind more than the imprints of their shoes. Fortunately, though, the urge to spend film was already in full force, and we have a fine legacy of photographs to show us the pleasures of being in Sabino Canyon in the early years of the new century.

If we could follow a family of picnickers home from Sabino Canyon around the turn of the century, we'd be likely to find a stack of stereoscopic cards in the parlor and a simple viewer nearby. In those days commercial stereo photography played a role that today is mostly filled by electronic media: it was a convenient and vivid window into worlds outside one's everyday experience. It was also part of the bread and butter of some professional photographers. When Carleton Watkins paid his visit to Tucson in 1880, he didn't only lug a camera up Sentinel Peak. He also took stereo photos of downtown—western exotica for his customers around the country. We saw one of his popular stereoviews in the introduction to part 1.

For amateurs, though, stereo photography remained an unusual specialty. This rare Sabino Canyon stereograph, taken on the first of May 1903, shows the Moffitt clan and friends among the rocks near Calvin Elliott's dam site. The individuals are difficult to identify with certainty, but Byron Moffitt and his older brother, Albert, appear to be standing at upper left and upper right, respectively. Both were Southern Pacific locomotive engineers.

Not even the most splendidly dressed could resist nature's temptations in Sabino Canyon. In this tiny cyanotype, reproduced here near actual size, Myrtle Drachman and her friends are the elegant ladies testing the waters at the Elliott dam site. Both the date and the photographer are unknown.

Myrtle's father, Samuel Drachman, was a well-known and civic-minded businessman who had the misfortune to be serving on the board of the Tucson School District with George Roskruge at the time of the notorious Sabino Canyon teacher scandal of 1906 (chapter 4). Myrtle became a teacher in that district too, but a year too late to have been among the reprobates.

The occasion captured in this wonderful image is anyone's guess, but perhaps Miss Drachman's companions are fellow members of the University of Arizona's fun-loving Gamma Phi Sigma sorority, which included Beppie Leslie (chapter 2) and Mary Virginia Jones, whom we'll meet later in this chapter.

SABINO CANYON, TUCSON, ARIZ.

Nov. 9 '06. Do you remember this? Sister.

Author's collection

By the first decade of the new century, Sabino Canyon had become popular enough to make its debut in picture postcards. Just as now, many cards were kept as souvenirs, and those actually posted were often delivered to people in faraway places—in this case to a Louisiana woman in November 1906. At that time, postal regulations permitted nothing other than an address to be written on the back of a postcard, so space was often left on the front for a message. This card's recipient had evidently visited the canyon herself. The message reads, "Do you remember this?"

The setting is just upstream from Elliott's dam site, and the photographer may be Henry Buehman, founder of Tucson's prestigious Buehman Studio. In a more detailed print of the same photograph, held in the archives of the Arizona Historical Society, the man standing at left bears a very striking resemblance to the portrait of Colonel C. P. Sykes in chapter 3.[2] Recall that Sykes brought a photographer with him the day he claimed to have discovered gold in Sabino Canyon. Might this photo have been taken on that interesting occasion?

Sabino Canyon, Catalina Mountains. TUCSON, Arizona.

Author's collection

In 1907 Congress passed a law allowing a message to be written on the reverse of a postcard. The new divided-back style encouraged publishers to devote the entire front to a photograph. A brief golden age of fine postcards ensued, ending less than a decade later, when the printing industry was disrupted by the First World War.

Sometime before 1911 Rudolph Rasmessen produced a beautiful set of Sabino Canyon postcards to sell in his curio store in downtown Tucson. The cards proved so popular that they were reissued multiple times right into the 1920s—though with diminished quality in the later years. This card shows carriages parked in the Picnic Grounds at the confluence of Sabino Creek and Rattlesnake Creek. The image is one of the best surviving views of the area that by then had thoroughly supplanted Calvin Elliott's dam site as the favored place to spend a day in Sabino Canyon.

Arizona Historical Society

Unlike picnic areas in national forests today, those in turn-of-the-century Sabino Canyon were almost completely free of manmade improvements. No one seems to have minded. Stone circles served as fireplaces, and picnickers spread their cloths on the ground in time-honored fashion.

This particular meal is being enjoyed on the first weekend of spring 1911, on the tree-lined bank of Sabino Creek, a short distance up the canyon from the Rattlesnake Creek confluence. The woman at right has placed her dark, feathered hat on the ground and has been caught chewing, much like young Clara Fish on an earlier occasion. We've already been introduced: this is Lydia Upham, seven years after her visit in 1904 (chapter 10). With her this time are her daughters, Helen, at left, and younger Muriel, mostly hidden behind her mother. (The second woman and child haven't been identified.) Gaius is here, too, taking the picture and represented by his rifle (leaning against the tree at left) and, once again, the case for his camera (just right of that tree).

If the people in many of the old photographs seem to be wearing their Sunday best, it's no accident. An outing to Sabino Canyon after church was a very popular pastime. In this photo, taken on a Sunday in about 1910, three generations of the Failor family have wandered nearly a half mile upstream from the Picnic Grounds. Civil War veteran Samuel Failor sits on the boulder at center with his wife, Lucy, behind him. At right is their son, Virgil, with his wife, Olive. The youngest pictured are Virgil and Olive's children—Marian, sitting with her grandfather; son Gillmor, standing nearby; and Edith, getting a helping hand from one of the two women at left (who may also be family members).

There's an unmistakable note of melancholy about the image. In the several decades surrounding the turn of the century, tuberculosis sufferers were drawn to Tucson by its dry climate. Virgil, Olive, and their two daughters immigrated from the Midwest in 1905 after Virgil was diagnosed. Despite continuing poor health, he served ably as secretary of the Tucson Chamber of Commerce, and he took special interest in the creation of the new trail that opened in 1912. Unfortunately, he died the following year. Olive continued rearing their three children herself, and had a long career in the legal profession.

Author's collection

Author's collection

As one might expect, one of the Rasmessen postcards depicts what was then the best-known landmark in all of Sabino Canyon: the Great Western Power Company's streamgage, located at the upper end of the Picnic Grounds (and built, coincidentally, with the help of Rasmessen's father-in-law, David Cochran). The instrument cabinet is just left of center, and the weir extends across the stream toward the right. Rock Peak is in the distant background. The wooden superstructure was destroyed by a powerful flood in the summer of 1912, but the weir, slowly deteriorating in place, remained a curiosity at least into the 1920s.

The inviting ledge at left was the setting for many early-twentieth-century gatherings, but Rasmessen left people out of his Sabino Canyon compositions—with one notable exception, as we're about to see.

The tiny figure sitting next to the Sabino Canyon trail (near bottom center) is Rudolph Rasmessen himself. Can you spot him? He's impossible to miss in another of his postcards, opposite this book's table of contents.

Rasmessen ventured about two miles up the canyon from the Picnic Grounds, into territory seldom seen by casual day-trippers, to take his place in this scene, snapped by an anonymous assistant. The venerable pathway would soon fall into disrepair after the creation of the new trail (the Plate Rail) by the Great Western Power Company.

Mr. Rasmessen would later serve on the University of Arizona's Board of Regents during the wartime years, then four years as mayor of Tucson during the 1920s, and two more as chairman of the Pima County Board of Supervisors. Originally from Sweden, he had arrived in Tucson from Chicago in 1898, weighing about 115 pounds after a long bout of typhoid fever, and expecting to stay only a few weeks to recover his health.

Arizona Historical Society

Arizona Historical Society

Social strictures were loosening in Arizona, and the dour chaperones who had once enforced decorum in Sabino Canyon were disappearing from photographs. This exuberant group posed for the camera in the Picnic Grounds, and the photo was pasted in an album by Mary Virginia Jones, a young woman from Alabama. Mary Virginia herself may well have been the photographer. (You may have noticed her fiddling with her camera on the dedication page of this book.) The large boulder with the climbers is the same one seen at far left in Rudolph Rasmessen's postcard photograph of the streamgage.

The new freedoms for young people brought certain activities out of the shadows of the mesquites and openly into the sun in view of camera lenses. This particular freedom wouldn't last much longer, though. Arizona became a dry state in 1915, fully five years before the country as a whole, and it remained so until the repeal of national Prohibition in 1933.

A comparison of this photograph with the previous one shows they were both taken during the same high-spirited outing. Mary Virginia's older brother, Sam Jones, is front and center, raising his bottle highest and with the greatest enthusiasm. It's significant that only the men of the group are featured in this image. At this time—about 1910—a collection of young women hoisting bottles of Schlitz might still have raised eyebrows.[3]

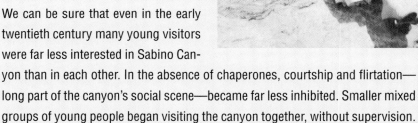

Both: Arizona Historical Society

We can be sure that even in the early twentieth century many young visitors were far less interested in Sabino Canyon than in each other. In the absence of chaperones, courtship and flirtation—long part of the canyon's social scene—became far less inhibited. Smaller mixed groups of young people began visiting the canyon together, without supervision. They passed their cameras around, and affectionate horseplay became commonplace in photographs.

The photo at left, another from the Jones album, shows a pair of Mary Virginia's friends staging an almost kiss next to the creek. The time hadn't yet arrived for the real thing to appear routinely in snapshots. At right, in a print from an album kept by a young woman named Margaret Eldred, a couple are enjoying themselves a short distance upstream from the Picnic Grounds.

M omentous political events brought change to Arizona in the second decade of the twentieth century. In 1912 Arizona became a state—the last of the lower forty-eight. A few months later, the all-male electorate approved an amendment to the state constitution granting Arizona women the right to vote. It was a remarkable moment. Women's suffrage wouldn't be written into the federal constitution for another eight years.

Stressful times arrived later in the decade, with the entry of the United States into the First World War. Mary Virginia Jones had married Albert Montgomery, a handsome civil engineer, not long after the photos in her album were taken. The young couple had lived together in a railroad car for a time, while Albert worked for the Southern Pacific Railroad. Albert volunteered during the war and was shipped off to Europe, where he was involved in heavy fighting. Debilitated by his battle experiences, he developed the symptoms of tuberculosis soon after the Armistice, and he died in 1924. ■

Arizona Historical Society

During the war, the creek flowed through the Picnic Grounds just as it always had, with only the occasional appearance of a man in uniform to serve as a reminder of the terrible events unfolding a continent and an ocean away. The man in this photograph, identified only as Frank, is wearing the overseas cap of the American Expeditionary Force. (The woman at right may be Geraldine Sampson, who pasted the photo in her album.)

"I'd walk a mile for one" is the title inked on the album page, echoing the re-cently minted and relentlessly repeated advertising slogan "I'd walk a mile for a Camel," as well as lyrics from a popular song of the day, "I'd walk a million miles for one of your smiles, my Mammy!"[4] In the freewheeling 1920s, some might have judged that the standards of propriety at Sabino Canyon had become *too* relaxed. Even today this 1922 photograph of three women in the Picnic Grounds carries a faint whiff of the disreputable, though the scene is certainly quite inno-cent. Margaret Tait is the one lighting Viola Steinfeld's cigarette, while Pat Casey puffs away between them. The words on the rock were true, if the spelling was unconventional. "Admition" to Sabino Canyon was still free to everyone, and it would stay that way for another forty-three years.

University of Arizona Libraries, Special Collections

Much had changed since Myrtle Drachman and her friends moistened the hems of their dresses in Sabino Creek. Despite highlighting the bare knees and some fashionably rolled stockings, these bathing suits were quite modest for the 1920s, when more revealing one-piece suits were already coming into vogue.

The exact site where these arboreal bathing beauties posed is uncertain, but another photo taken on the same 1922 outing suggests it may have been near Calvin Elliott's dam site, where there were some fine swimming holes, less in the public eye than anywhere in the more popular Picnic Grounds.

Arizona Historical Society

Seeing the world in monochrome can be deceptive, but this snapshot, taken in the Picnic Grounds in the early 1920s, can't help but remind us of Henry Ford's infamous words: "Any customer can have a car painted any colour that he wants so long as it is black."[5]

The 1920s saw the beginnings of crowding in Sabino Canyon. Early in the decade, fifty to a hundred cars were showing up on weekdays, and far more jammed the canyon on Sundays. The numbers were increasing year by year, but the size of the canyon—that is, of the small part of it most people knew and loved—was not. Change was waiting impatiently at the threshold, but it would take a national crisis to open the door.

CHAPTER 14

=≡ ◆ ≡=

Getting There, Early Twentieth Century

During the early years of the twentieth century, the journey to Sabino Canyon was still part of the adventure—miles of sometimes rough dirt roads through open desert, with little more than the ruins of Fort Lowell and an occasional ranch building as signs of past or present human habitation. It was possible to cross the distance on foot, of course, like the hardy cadets from the University of Arizona, but most sensible people did otherwise.

Professor G. E. P. Smith, Sherman Woodward's friend and colleague at the University of Arizona (chapter 6), became all too familiar with the route's minor hazards. In the late spring of 1903, after classes had ended, Woodward was camped in Sabino Canyon with his contractor, David Cochran, installing the canyon's first streamgage. Smith and Frank Guild, another faculty member, decided to pay them a visit.

> At the end of a very hot June day, Professor Guild and I mounted our bicycles and rode out to the canyon. The road was not graded, but had wheel tracks in grooves—and we rode in or tried to ride in the grooves. This was difficult and at one point I was thrown from the bicycle and unfortunately landed on a bed of cholla. Professor Guild and I worked for a long time in the gathering darkness pulling the spines out of my skin and my clothing.[1]

For a while it was Smith's job to visit the streamgage regularly to change the paper on the recording drums. Usually he drove himself to the canyon in a horse-drawn buggy, but on one day in the rain-drenched year 1905, he sensibly hired

Cochran to take him there. The two set off in a light wagon pulled by a pair of small mules. Cochran was the proud owner of an expensive new shotgun, and during the monotonous early part of the drive, he amused himself by discharging it in the direction of roadside rabbits.

The tedium ended at the Rillito. It was running bank to bank. The time had come for Cochran and his mules to show what they were made of.

> Without hesitating he drove in and, as soon as the small mules got into the water, they began to flounder for the quicksand was deep. We could not turn back. Mr. Cochran lashed his mules and yelled at them and they did their best. But if they pulled one leg out of the deep sand, they would sink their other legs into the quicksand. He used his whip till it was broken, and he threw it away. Then he took his hundred dollar gun and struck the mules over the back with the gun, bending it so badly that he had to send it back to the factory. . . . He was standing up and shouting. I leaned away to give him room, expecting that the next minute I would be floundering in the water also. But the little mules never gave up and eventually they got us out![2]

Few trips to Sabino Canyon were quite so harrowing, but the condition of the roads often left much to be desired. In 1906, in response to a citizen petition, the county took responsibility for the route, but by the next year it had again deteriorated so badly that some picnickers were returning to town with lame horses and damaged carriages. In 1908 things were looking up again, and tire tracks were to be seen next to the imprints of horseshoes. By then Sabino Canyon had become *the* place to be on a weekend in March.

> Sunday by a sort of common consent all the outing seekers headed for Sabine canyon [sic]. Autoing parties out there were numerous and every livery team in the city was sold for the day to pleasure seekers who went up there. The roads were never in better condition and the more than 300 people who went up had a day of days.[3]

Two years later, in 1910, it was still possible for predawn travelers to become disoriented in the maze of roads at the eastern edge of the city, but once the sun came up, no one could possibly get lost. According the *Arizona Daily Star*, it seemed that an unknown "philanthropist," or perhaps more than one, had placed helpful guides every twenty to thirty feet all the way to Sabino Canyon.

The expense was not great, the donor or donors getting "full" value for the cash expended. The marks are durable, because if broken their remains can be seen afar off in the sunlight. Hereafter travelers . . . need have only one motto and remember only one thing to keep from getting off the road. The motto is "Follow the empty beer bottles."[4]

Just a quarter century had passed since the pioneer picnickers had found their way to the canyon. A thoughtful traveler, contemplating the sparkling scenery, might have foreseen a time when there would be too many vehicles and too much beer in Sabino Canyon, but that day was still decades away. ■

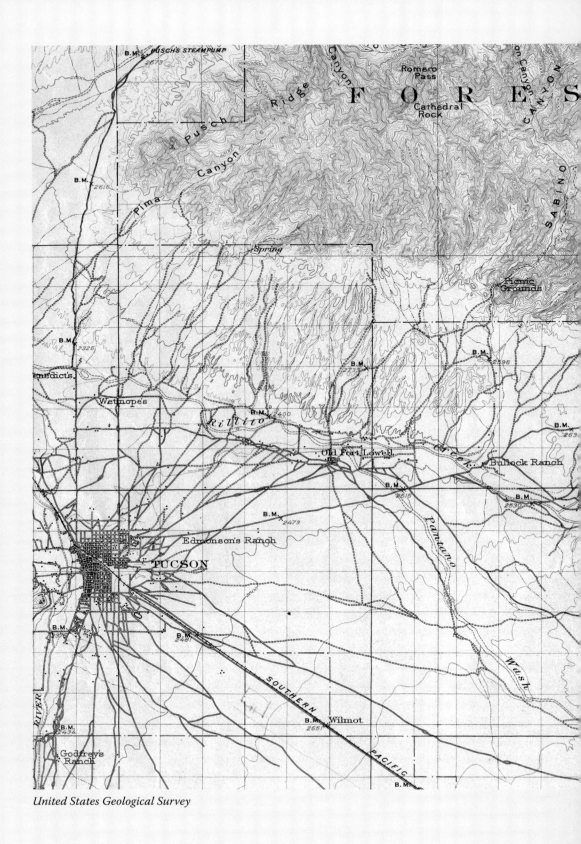

United States Geological Survey

The United States Geological Survey's Tucson Quadrangle, published in 1905, provides an invaluable overview of the Tucson Basin and the Santa Catalina Mountains in the first decade of the twentieth century. Only a dozen years had passed since the appearance of George Roskruge's "Official Map of Pima County" (chapter 5), yet the advances in detail and precision are striking. As on that earlier map, the small squares are a mile across.

Tucson's surroundings had become much more accessible, as the proliferation of roads attests. By 1905 Sabino-bound travelers could take their choice among several primitive roads through the creosote bush desert to the ruins of "Old Fort Lowell." As in the previous century, many made their way eastward another two miles before turning north to cross the Rillito. That was where Cochran, Smith, and the mules braved the current in the year this map was published. But by then another crossing had opened directly north of the abandoned fort. That was the one taken by the cadets when they marched to the canyon for the encampment in 1903, as well as by the Uphams and their friends on their well-photographed outing the following year (chapters 9 and 10).[5]

The old military reservation has vanished from the map, as one might expect. The Southern Pacific tracks are still shown, running through the center of the city. By this time the railroad had become much more than a link to distant places. It was an important employer in Tucson, providing livelihoods for several of the people we've met.

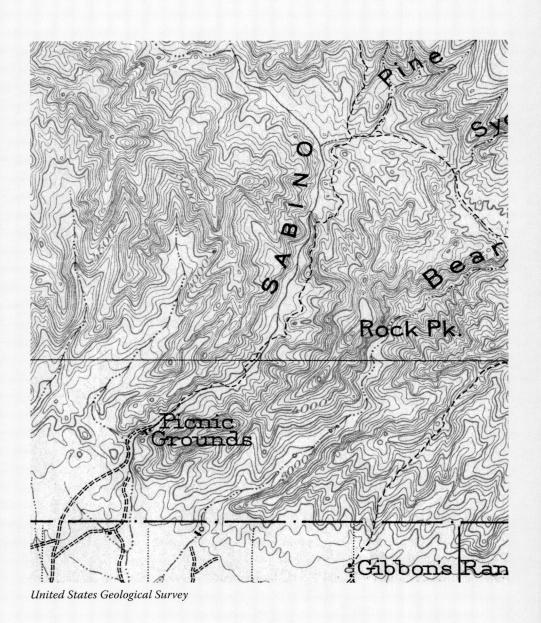

United States Geological Survey

This enlarged detail of the Sabino Canyon area shows many of the features we've come across so far. Rock Peak is prominently featured, as are the Picnic Grounds—the only such place mapped in the Santa Catalinas, and by 1905 the canyon's best-loved destination. Some other important items are drawn but not labeled. The small marks at the stream, just to the left of the *G* of "Picnic Grounds," indicate Professor Woodward's streamgage, installed two years earlier. The dotted line running up the canyon from there is the Sabino Canyon Trail, soon to be refurbished under Supervisor Meagher. It passes the professor's unmarked dam site, about two miles farther up, near the "I" of the word "SABINO." (No sign of the Plate Rail Trail, though; it's seven years in the future.)

The two roads seen in George Roskruge's earlier map are still the only carriage-worthy routes into the canyon. The lower (eastern) road passes Supervisor Meagher's shack—shown as a tiny rectangle just south of the boundary of the Santa Catalina Forest Reserve—before heading northward toward Calvin Elliott's dam site. Notice that the upper (western) road extends farther into the canyon than on Roskruge's map—right into the Picnic Grounds. That change helps to explain the area's new popularity early in the twentieth century.[6]

Rillito Crossing

The first automobile arrived in Tucson to great excitement around the turn of the century, and it wasn't long before horseless carriages were braving the Rillito on their way to Sabino Canyon. This Curved Dash Oldsmobile may have been among the earliest. In that very popular model, America's first mass-produced motorcar, the single-cylinder engine was mounted crosswise under the seat, where it made a noise like a contented lawnmower—when it was running. Here it has stalled in midcrossing. The driver has let go of the tiller (steering wheels weren't yet standard) and is applying elbow grease to the side-mounted crank.

The elderly operator of this recalcitrant vehicle is almost certainly John J. Gardiner, one of Calvin Elliott's partners in his ill-fated Sabino Canyon enterprise two decades earlier. An engineer, he was just the sort we might expect to try out one of the newfangled automobiles, and he had the skills to keep it in repair.

Arizona Historical Society

Despite the advent of the motorcar, most visitors arrived at Sabino Canyon under natural horsepower even into the second decade of the twentieth century.
We may imagine the long carriage drive to have been uncomfortable, but these
refined and time-tested vehicles were reliable and blessedly quiet, and their
well-designed springs smoothed out the bumps in the road. The combination
of long-legged animals and tall wheels made these the ultimate high-clearance
vehicles, and they shifted smoothly into "low gear" whenever conditions required
it—which was often. They lent themselves perfectly to leisurely outings in an era
less hurried than our own.

These twin surreys, rented from a Tucson livery stable, are parked at the
end of the road in the Picnic Grounds. It's about 1910. The afternoon shadows
are lengthening, and the members of this extended family are about to head for
home. Do you recognize them? They're the Failors, whom we encountered earlier
in the day, gathered among the boulders in Sabino Creek (previous chapter).

Sometime during the second decade of the twentieth century, a traveler stopped on a hill about a mile southwest of the mouth of Sabino Canyon and snapped a picture of the view. This photograph, long preserved in a family album, gives us a rare glimpse of the well-traveled road itself.

Gone are the deep ruts that caused Professor Smith's mishap with the chollas in 1903 (though a prickly pear seems poised to ambush bicyclists at the rough spot just ahead). The Great Western Power Company has improved the road and picnickers are the incidental beneficiaries. The narrow tracks of wagon or carriage wheels are easily seen, and there may be faint tire prints as well.

Look closely. Just ahead, the road drops over the side of the hill and disappears among the dark mesquites on the plain west of Sabino Creek. In the distance, right of center, a threadlike white stripe climbs a ridge. It's the same road. Great Western has widened the lower part of its new trail (today's Phoneline Trail) in its failed effort to extend the road all the way to Professor Woodward's dam site (chapter 12).

By 1920 the transition from carriage to automobile is essentially complete. It's November of that year, and this Overland touring car has left the Picnic Grounds and pulled to the roadside just west of the upper entrance into the canyon. The driver (and unseen photographer) is Glenton Sykes, an engineering student at the University of Arizona.[7] With him are, left to right, the McCluskey sisters, Hazel, Anna, and Hilda. Anna, in the light-colored frock, is Glenton's future wife, and it's hard to say whether this is a more admiring portrait of his sweetheart or of the automobile.

The cars of the 1920s, impressive as they were, were no match for the older, horse-drawn technology on narrow, primitive roads. By the middle of the decade, the Rillito had been bridged and the rough track north of the river had been straightened, widened, and graded, creating today's Sabino Canyon Road. The drive to the canyon from town had shortened to about an hour. No longer an adventure, it could be undertaken on a whim. The pace of life was quickening in Sabino Canyon, as everywhere else.

PART III
The Great Expansion
1929–1939

A busy scene in Tucson's flourishing downtown, 1926.

If the twenties didn't quite roar in Tucson, Arizona, at least they purred. The town was growing, money was begging to be made, and the words of a popular song sounded like they might have been written just for the Old Pueblo:

Never saw the sun shining so bright
Never saw things going so right[1]

No one seemed to notice in September 1926 when Mr. Joseph Wittman of Morristown, New Jersey, filed application with the Federal Power Commission (FPC) to build a hydroelectric dam at Professor Woodward's site. Nor did anyone seem to notice the following January when Wittman expanded his application to take in Bear Canyon as well. History was starting to repeat itself in the Santa Catalinas, but so far it was just background noise in the hubbub of Tucson's Jazz Age.

Delay set in immediately for Wittman, much as it had for his predecessors earlier in the century. Like almost every other water power project in the Colorado River Basin since 1921, Wittman's was put on hold while states depending on the river haggled over water rights. (On maps, at least, Sabino Creek flows to the Colorado through the Rillito, the Santa Cruz, and the Gila—though the notion of a drop of Sabino's amber-tinted water passing under a bridge at Yuma may seem farfetched.)

In March 1929 the Gila River and its tributaries were dropped from the Colorado River moratorium. Wittman's dormant application sprang to life, the *Tucson Daily Citizen* printed a legal notice, and the city began to pay attention. The mayor and council, preoccupied as always with water needs, registered objections, and the chamber of commerce concurred. Tucson might eventually need Sabino Creek's water for itself, they claimed.[2]

By this time William B. Alexander, residing in Wittman's state of New Jersey, had gotten wind of developments and, through a government friend, requested his old Federal Power and Water Company application papers from the Forest Service, hoping to get in on the action. The voice from the past could hardly have been welcome to

Forest Service officials, but nothing would come of Alexander's revived interest.[3]

In late October, with local objections still unresolved, Joseph Wittman's engineer met Forest Service officials for a field investigation of his Sabino Canyon project. As they worked, curious news was coming out of New York.[4]

The last day of the investigation was October 29, 1929. It was Black Tuesday: the day the stock market crashed. ■

CHAPTER 15

◆

Alphabet Soup

I t took time for the turmoil on Wall Street to spread across the country, but by the end of 1930, Arizona banks were collapsing, once-comfortable Tucsonans were out of work, and vagrants were showing up on the city's doorsteps, begging for handouts. The drought-driven Dust Bowl soon took hold in the Midwest, uprooting families and pushing them westward, desperate for work. Tucson's charities struggled to provide for the stricken among its own citizens as well as for those passing through, but local generosity was not enough, and not much help was coming from the federal government. Times were tough in Tucson, as almost everywhere else, when Franklin Delano Roosevelt took the inaugural oath in March 1933.

The blizzard of legislation blowing out of Washington during the prolific "Hundred Days" that launched the Roosevelt administration brought hope to suffering communities. It also initiated a mind-numbing succession of new federal programs, most of which came to be best known by their initials. It's not surprising that many decades later we find these "alphabet agencies" confusing; even at the time it was hard to keep them straight.[1]

For the Forest Service, Roosevelt's New Deal brought a sudden surfeit of free labor. It would prove to be a daunting opportunity. Coronado National Forest's supervisor, Fred Winn, saw it coming, and in mid-1933 he gave fair warning to his troops.

Not in the life time of the oldest Forest officer in point of service, has the Forest Service had such an opportunity to get much needed public work performed at a very moderate cost. The Forest officer who is not alive to this opportunity and especially the District ranger . . . is dead from the ears down and will probably be tetotally and officially dead all the way up and down if he is not wise enough to grasp this chance when it is offered to him and see that his district is improved while the going is good.[2]

At Sabino Canyon, the 1930s would be a decade of utter transformation, from a quaint, barely developed picnic spot into an immensely popular recreation area with all the expected amenities of its time. Images of a new kind would flood the historical record: agency photographs documenting federal construction projects.

As it happened, though, one of Sabino Canyon's first construction projects during the Great Depression came even before FDR was elected. In 1932, perhaps spurred by the renewed interest in Professor Sherman Woodward's old dam site, the United States Geological Survey (USGS) built a new streamgage, replacing the professor's original installation, which by then had been defunct for two decades.

The USGS streamgage was only a few months old when its picture was taken in October 1932. The concrete structure in the creek controlled the water level much as the weir had done for Woodward's gage. The tall pipe (a stilling well) admitted water at the bottom, and a float inside it was linked to a recording mechanism in the box at the top, which technicians reached by means of a short catwalk.

The USGS also stretched a cable across the canyon with a small suspended car—here seen parked at an angle near the left end of the catwalk. The cable car allowed a technician to hang a measuring instrument into the current anywhere across the creek.

May '34   *May '34*

Both: Arizona Historical Society

Once again a streamgage was the most significant manmade structure in Sabino Canyon, yet the new device seems not to have attracted nearly as much attention as Woodward's installation had in earlier years. While the professor's streamgage had been installed right in the popular Picnic Grounds, the USGS chose to build farther downstream, at Calvin Elliott's old dam site—a spot that by the early 1930s was much less favored by visitors.

But if the gage itself was of limited interest, the cable was another matter. The suspended car was wisely kept on a locked chain to prevent joyriding, but that didn't stop testosterone-charged youths from climbing out over the canyon floor hand over hand—like Mr. May, here, from the nearby Southern Arizona School for Boys. We can hope he lived to graduate with his friends in the class of 1934. The gage would survive another forty years after that.[3]

On March 21, 1933, less than two weeks into the Hundred Days, Roosevelt proposed a Civilian Conservation Corps (CCC) in an address to Congress. The catchy name, with its even catchier initials, was embraced by almost everyone from the start, though it wouldn't become official until 1937. Until then, in government paperwork at least, the name was the eminently forgettable Emergency Conservation Works—ECW in alphabet-agency parlance.

In the beginning, CCC enrollees were mostly young, unmarried men, aged eighteen to twenty-five, whose families were on the relief rolls. (The requirements changed over the years, and there were special programs for war veterans and Native Americans.) CCC boys lived together in camps run by the army, worked mostly on outdoor projects, and were required to send much of their pay home to their families. The benefits to parks and forests were matched by those to the enrollees themselves—income, good food (and plenty of it), discipline, training, self-respect, camaraderie, and the satisfaction of doing useful work with their hands. Years later, many would remember their days with the "Three Cs" as high points in their lives.

For the members of CCC Company 838, who in November 1933 traveled from Wyoming to the Tanque Verde Camp, east of Tucson, first impressions were particularly memorable.

> The personnel of Camp F-42-A from the Medicine Bow Forest, left there when it was 7 below zero. They arrived at Tanque Verde when it was above 90 in the shade; from 9000 feet elevation to about 2700 feet; from a lodge-pole pine area to a giant cactus area in which everything which grows has a sticker on it and a duck carries a canteen to insure sufficient water. They wanted a change and they got it.[4]

The Wyoming CCC boys soon came to appreciate the mild winter climate of the southern Arizona desert, and by early March 1934 some of them were starting work on a new ranger station at Sabino Canyon.

Construction of the new ranger station had just gotten underway when these men were photographed "making dobes" for the new buildings. In traditional fashion they mixed mud of the right consistency in a pit (center background), then shoveled it into a three-compartment wooden form laid on the ground. After a few minutes they lifted the form, leaving a neat row of three adobe bricks to dry in the desert sun. The rows of bricks can be seen drying in the background at left. The men in the foreground may be mixing the mortar that will bind the bricks together.

If anyone here seems older than twenty-five, it may be because the CCC sometimes hired older men with valuable skills to provide guidance and supervision. These special personnel were called local experienced men, or LEMs. Forest Service employees also helped to supervise work on national forest lands.

Coronado National Forest

During the spring of 1934, the building that was to become the district ranger's residence was taking shape. The high quality of the work is clear in this photograph. While adobe bricks composed most of the walls, smaller fired bricks were substituted in certain areas for greater precision and strength—such as here, for the front porch.

There seem to have been several Black men in Company 838, and it's just possible one of them appears in this photograph. Regrettably, racial segregation later became the norm in the CCC, and Mexican-American enrollees often experienced discrimination in the Southwest.

Coronado National Forest

Toward the end of May 1934, CCC Company 838 headed back to Wyoming, and in July Company 1838, composed mostly of presumably more heat-hardened Arizona boys, moved into the Tanque Verde Camp. They finished the new Lowell Ranger Station later that summer, and District Ranger Gilbert Sykes and his wife held a housewarming in the fall.

In 1936 Richard H. Lewis photographed the completed ranger residence and its surrounding landscaping against the imposing backdrop of the Santa Catalinas. The flagpole stood in front of a smaller office building, just outside the photo to the left, and behind the residence was a combination garage and barn. Compared to Thomas Meagher's simple shack—perhaps only a memory by the 1930s—these modest structures were almost a palace. Lowell Ranger Station was listed on the National Register of Historic Places in 1993, and all three buildings are still in use today.[5]

Young unmarried men, deserving though they were, were far from the only people in serious need of help in 1933. In May, about a month and a half after approving the CCC, Congress authorized another agency to aid a much broader segment of the unemployed. The new Federal Emergency Relief Administration (FERA) was empowered to make grants to the states for relief programs tailored to local needs. The Emergency Relief Administration of Arizona (AERA) received the funds for the state and passed them on to county welfare boards. People often found it easiest to call the whole multitiered bureaucracy simply "the ERA."

Over several busy years, the ERA provided direct relief payments as well as work relief. It created mostly construction jobs, but it also hired teachers for adult education, employed women to manufacture household goods for the needy, and even ran programs in research and the arts. However, as the first winter approached, it became clear that something else was needed—and quickly. In November 1933 the Civil Works Administration (CWA) was established within FERA so that the federal government could temporarily bypass state intermediaries and pay workers directly through the colder months. Across the country, communities and government agencies scrambled to come up with short-term construction projects for the CWA.

For the Forest Service personnel responsible for Sabino Canyon, the choice was easy. The CWA was a windfall, and the obvious place to put it to use was in the almost-too-well-loved Picnic Grounds at Rattlesnake Canyon. There was no time to waste; the program would last only about four months. CWA laborers went to work in the canyon almost immediately, well before formal plans were drawn up.[6]

It was the dawn of the Age of Furniture at Sabino Canyon. Tables, fireplaces, and restrooms built in the Picnic Grounds by CWA laborers during the winter of 1933–34 were among the very first New Deal constructions in the canyon itself, preceding even the completion of the new Lowell Ranger Station by the CCC.

Many of the original tables installed by the CWA, including this one, are still in use today. Each is unique and was created on-site. Workers gathered stream-rounded stones to make the pillars, then poured green-dyed concrete into wooden forms to cast the tops and benches in place. As a final step, they usually stamped two symbols into opposite corners of the wet tabletops: a Forest Service shield and an arrow pointing north.

Veteran Forest Service employee F. Lee Kirby took this shot during the summer of 1934. Twenty years earlier, while on duty in the Galiuro Mountains, northeast of Tucson, Kirby had taken a shot of a very different kind, killing a belligerent miner in self-defense. Much had changed in the life of a forest ranger since the early days.

National Archives

Another photo by Kirby, probably taken the same day, shows one of several restrooms built by the CWA, and it prompts a question: Was there anything similar in Sabino Canyon before the 1930s? Among the many earlier photographs examined by the author, only a few show something resembling a restroom, and we can't be absolutely sure that's what it was. This may suggest that pre-Depression sanitation in the canyon left much to be desired, but documentary evidence indicates the little buildings were there and we just don't see them.[7] After all, who takes pictures of outhouses?

The answer, of course, is the people who build them, and beginning during the Great Depression, federal employees have been remarkably prolific in recording their accomplishments along this line at Sabino Canyon. It has been the author's dubious privilege to catalog more than two dozen historical portraits of outhouses, some with copies in multiple archives. You may thank him for publishing just one.

Coronado National Forest

USDA Forest Service, Southwestern Region

Both the newly furnished recreation spot and the people enjoying it would need protection, and it fell to the men of the CWA to provide a home for a resident caretaker. The workers built this sturdy cabin of locally quarried stone, rather than of adobe and fired brick as at Lowell Ranger Station. It stood on a rise near Rattlesnake Creek, from which it commanded a fine view of the new developments.

Over the decades the stone cabin would be home to several hard-working caretakers, one of whom, with his family, we'll get to know in chapter 23. This snapshot was taken within a year or two of the cabin's completion. Neither the photographer nor the woman near the Ford pickup have been identified.

The CWA's laborers extended the old Picnic Grounds road about a thousand feet farther up the canyon, where it terminated in a broad new turnaround, not far past where Professor Woodward's stream gage had once stood. Beyond the road's end, winding along the canyon floor, was the venerable Sabino Canyon Trail—improved in the days of Supervisor Meagher, then neglected after the Plate Rail Trail, high on the canyon wall, had supplanted it as the prime route into the Santa Catalinas. CWA men thoroughly rehabilitated several miles of the Sabino Canyon Trail to serve as a scenic pathway for the canyon's visitors—complete with stepping stones at creek crossings, as shown in this rare Forest Service photograph from May 1934.[8]

The CWA's time ran out at the end of March 1934, before all the improvements planned by Coronado National Forest could be finished. Over the following winter, CCC boys from Company 1838, by then attached to a camp in the Santa Rita Mountains, took over. Bivouacked in a "fly camp" in Sabino Canyon, they added camper registry booths, stairways, more restrooms, and a fine stone footbridge across Rattlesnake Creek.[9]

A good number of the early installations in the Picnic Grounds have survived into the twenty-first century, but the restored Sabino Canyon Trail was remarkably short-lived. By the time the CCC boys started work in the Picnic Grounds, laborers from another agency had begun an ambitious new construction project on the canyon floor, one that would bury the trail and nearly erase it from memory. Sabino Canyon would soon change at a speed and scale unmatched before or since. ∎

CHAPTER 16

Reservoir Renaissance

What happened next—and what nearly happened, but not quite—was a series of events driven by the dedication and preternatural persistence of the Tucson Chamber of Commerce and an influential ally in the United States Congress. It was a prolonged and determined effort, overcoming daunting obstacles and repeated setbacks. Though in the end it fell short of its goals, it transformed the landscape of Sabino Canyon.

The Tucson Chamber, founded in 1896, had by the time of the Great Depression become a force to be reckoned with in local affairs. Anything and everything of consequence to the city's economic health and growth was of interest to the organization—including significant goings-on at Sabino Canyon. The chamber had joined controversies surrounding power and water projects, pushed the creation of the Plate Rail Trail, and unsuccessfully backed a road up the canyon to take its place. It had advocated improvements to the Picnic Grounds years before the New Deal had made them a reality. With the chamber's encouragement, the county road to Sabino Canyon had been improved during the 1920s, and the steep approach to the Picnic Grounds—long a challenge to vehicles of all sorts—had been straightened and smoothed.[1]

That last project had come in the first troubled months after the 1929 stock market crash, during Herbert Hoover's presidency. By December of the next year, the economic crisis was tightening its grip on the nation. Congress provided emergency funding for relief work, and Coronado National Forest received a hefty share for a temporary road-improvement program. A close collaboration organized projects in Pima County: the chamber of commerce hired the men, the national forest paid their wages, and the county provided the equipment. One of the places chosen for attention, naturally enough, was Sabino Canyon.[2]

A newly formed reemployment committee handled the hiring at the chamber of commerce offices. Its chair was a capable and charismatic woman named Isabella Greenway. A familiar figure in the city and a rising star in the Democratic Party, she was an intimate friend of Eleanor Roosevelt and a valued supporter of Eleanor's husband, Franklin, who was then governor of New York. As expected, Greenway did her committee work well. In March 1931, near the end of the program, twenty-one workers camped at Sabino Canyon expressed their gratitude with an act of generosity.

> Realizing that other people are in want, each man agreed to give one day's wages to relief work. The money was pooled last Saturday, and given to the committee, which purchased groceries at wholesale from Baffert and Leon. Families at an auto camp, and the family of a patient in the U. S. hospital were among those aided.[3]

The employment of these men, all of whom had lost their jobs in the deepening Depression, was the first federal relief program at Sabino Canyon—two years before Franklin Delano Roosevelt's inauguration as president. We know virtually nothing about what was done in the canyon in the early months of 1931. It was a short-lived program, limited in scope, and its accomplishments were undoubtedly limited as well. Far more significant, as it would turn out, was the relationship forged between the Tucson Chamber of Commerce and Isabella Greenway.

Meanwhile, in a campaign to conserve floodwaters in the Tucson area, the chamber had arranged a survey for a dam at Calvin Elliott's old site, but nothing had come of it. The excitement of Roosevelt's Hundred Days, with their promise of federal funds, reenergized the effort. In late spring 1933, the chamber's president, John J. O'Dowd, appointed a Sabino Canyon Dam Committee to push the project forward. Then, in a bold leap, the committee picked up its plans and dropped them several miles upstream—at Professor Woodward's dam site.[4]

Electric power and water supply had been the primary incentives driving all the failed proposals for a dam at Woodward's site earlier in the century, but the Tucson Chamber of Commerce thoroughly reimagined the professor's idea to suit the times. Power and water were erased from the picture, and recreation, never before more than an afterthought, was put front and center.

While the CCC was laying adobe bricks at Lowell Ranger Station and the CWA was cementing together tables in the Picnic Grounds, a much grander plan was taking shape at the chamber of commerce. As in the days of the Great Western Power Company, an access road to the dam site would need to come first. The Forest Service, wary of the scheme being pressed upon it, insisted that any road should follow Great Western's route—the Phoneline Trail, along the canyon wall—but the men of the chamber of commerce would have none of it. They wanted the road to start up the canyon floor from the Picnic Grounds. It would cross the creek multiple times over small dams, each of which would create its own recreational pond. These, along with new roadside picnic areas, would be features of a spectacular recreational complex, anchored by a magnificent 250-foot dam at Woodward's site. A mountain lake, high above the desert, would be both a cooling getaway for Tucsonans and a draw for tourists from around the country. Of more immediate importance, the creation of all this would provide sorely needed relief to Tucson's unemployed.

It seemed a compelling vision to the chamber of commerce, but the community was frustratingly slow to embrace it. After months of little progress, attorney William R. Misbaugh, a particularly industrious member of the Sabino Canyon Dam Committee, reached out to an influential friend of the chamber: Isabella Greenway, who earlier that year had been sworn in as a member of the United States House of Representatives from the state of Arizona. Writing in June 1934, Misbaugh mentioned both the Elliott and the Woodward sites, but he made it very clear where the committee's preference lay. Water conservation, the chamber's original motive for dam building, was relegated to a distant second place, and a dash of interstate rivalry spiced the appeal.

> Would it not be possible for you to induce the Forest Department for a dam either in lower Sabino or one four miles up the canyon where there is an ideal dam site and a large basin surrounded by many trees and greenery, which is at an altitude somewhat higher than Tucson and would make an ideal recreational area for thousands of people in this vicinity[?] We could have fishing, boating, swimming and camping and as you know we do not have any too much water in this country anyway and it seems a shame to me to have this run-off water finally get to the Colorado River and have California take it.[5]

Greenway quickly took up the cause. The Forest Service declined the project, pleading lack of funds, but the congresswoman's support helped convince others to climb aboard the chamber of commerce bandwagon. The advance was swift. By October 1934 the ERA had committed labor for the access road and cement for the first creek crossing. Pima County had signed on as the project's local sponsor and was standing by with a truck, a tractor, and enough blasting powder to get started. Everyone was ready to go, and all that was still needed was a permit from the Forest Service. But there was a problem, and it was a serious one: Joseph Wittman's 1926 application for a dam at Professor Woodward's site.[6]

That application was in legal limbo. After the field investigation that had ended on Black Tuesday, 1929, the Forest Service engineer had reported that a Sabino Canyon–Bear Canyon hydropower project would be even more impractical than it had been at the turn of the century. The state of Arizona had denied water rights, and the Federal Power Commission had threatened to reject Wittman's power site application without them. Yet the FPC had never followed through, so Wittman's application was still active—at least on paper. He had done no work at all in Sabino Canyon for years.[7]

Faced with this obstacle, the Tucson Chamber of Commerce and its allies mustered all their political clout. The chamber, Representative Greenway, both of Arizona's senators, the City of Tucson, and Pima County all focused pressure on the FPC. It worked. On Wednesday, October 24, 1934, the FPC formally denied Wittman's application. The news sped across the country by telegram, the Forest Service granted its permit, and on Friday construction of the road to the dam site began.[8]

Meet the men who began the new road up Sabino Canyon. Folk history often credits this road to the Civilian Conservation Corps, but these are not CCC boys. These are local men in need—residents of Tucson and its environs who have been thrown out of work by the nation's economic crisis. They've been offered paid employment by the ERA's Work Relief Program and they're being trucked in daily to labor in the canyon.

The photograph seems to have been taken during the first days of work in late October 1934. The laborers are just beyond the Picnic Grounds, as enlarged the previous winter under the CWA. The pointed rock at upper left is where Gaius and Lydia Upham posed on a breezy day thirty years earlier (chapter 10).

The men have stopped work for just a moment to turn toward the photographer. The hardships of the Great Depression are written on their faces.

Arizona State Library, Archives and Public Records

The four men sporting ties and facing the camera appear to be officials conducting an inspection. They're standing where the first of nine small stone dams will be built across the creek, each one carrying the road along its top. The tall figure near the center of the group is Albert H. Condron, secretary of the Tucson Chamber of Commerce. His energy and commitment will help to keep the chamber's project alive through multiple challenges over the next several years.[9] Notice the large boulders behind Condron. Two friends of the Uphams shared a cup of Sabino Creek water while sitting on those rocks in 1904.

This is the first of several photographs, most likely taken by an ERA photographer, documenting the creation of the first crossing. As construction is about to begin, the canyon is deep in a postmonsoon drought, the stream is barely flowing, and laborers are already roughing out the roadbed beyond the crossing.

Boulders have been shattered to make way for the dam, leaving fragments strewn across the streambed, and a sturdy wooden trestle has been installed. A truck-mounted crane, on loan from the state highway department, has been driven onto the trestle to lift the heaviest stones into place, while to the trestle's right the core of the masonry dam is being assembled.

A close examination of this and other photos showing the ERA's laborers at work reveals quite a few dark-complexioned faces. Hiring discrimination on the basis of race was forbidden in the ERA. The contribution of persons of color to the legacy of the Great Depression at Sabino Canyon has rarely been recognized or appreciated.

Arizona State Library, Archives and Public Records

Arizona State Library, Archives and Public Records

It's late November or December 1934. The winter rains have arrived, the convenience of low water has ended, and construction is continuing even as the creek flows. This time the view is back down the canyon. At left we see the scaffolding that has been built to support the workers, as well as the curved forms that are guiding them as they shape the dam's masonry walls. A few of the stone "dragon's teeth" that will line the roadway (next photograph) have been set in place at the far end of the dam, and a small cement mixer is spinning in the background.

The first crossing was finished on the fifth of January 1935. The next day, Sabino Creek put the freshly completed structure to the test with a sudden spike in streamflow. The dam passed without difficulty, and it has survived far more severe floods in the decades since.

Judging by the still-leafless trees, this photograph was taken soon after the dam was completed. Compare it to the earlier photograph of the inspection, which was taken from nearly the same spot. Over just a few years, the natural appearance of the canyon floor would be profoundly changed by recreational developments.

"Lake in Catalinas Assured" read the headline in the November 1934 issue of the Tucson Chamber of Commerce's monthly magazine, as work was beginning on the road to the dam site. Tucsonans were already applying for lakeside cabin permits and making plans to stock the water with fish.[10] Week by week, fun-seekers followed the construction up the canyon, and certain activities in the new swimming holes at the crossings inspired an indignant letter to the editor of the morning paper.

> In the past it was not uncommon to see couples taking advantage of the seclusion of the canyon, and much drinking was also the common order of the day—now, when decent people wish to take their families for an outing in the mountains they have nude bathers added to the "attractions" of this, the only recreational area available to the average people of Tucson, who nevertheless do not like to see things like this everywhere they turn![11]

The steady progress in the canyon belied difficulties behind the scenes. Even before the workers had broken ground, Representative Greenway's secretary, Howard Caffrey, had expressed misgivings in a note to his boss. "It is quite an extensive undertaking—much beyond the scope of Relief Labor as I gather it," he had written. "In fact, if they are counting on the FERA for cement, materials, etc., I'm sure they are going to stub their toes."[12]

Caffrey's concerns were proving well founded. The ERA provided surveys, plans, labor, supervision, and what few supplies it could, but it had no cash for anything else. The county and the state were helping out by lending heavy equipment, but they had no money to offer either. To the great annoyance of the chamber of commerce, the Forest Service was contributing nothing at all. It was left to the local community to scrounge for materials, which were continually in short supply. According to Bill Misbaugh, of the chamber's Sabino Canyon Dam Committee, it was "just like pulling teeth from day to day in order to accomplish anything."[13]

Beginning with the third crossing, the roadside "dragon's teeth" were replaced by concrete curbs. A more significant change was invisible to the eye. While the first two crossings had been made of solid masonry, all the rest would be built with masonry sidewalls and a rubble core—a redesign lending itself to faster completion.

Today most people call all these crossings "bridges," but when they were created they were usually (and more accurately) called "check dams" or simply "dams." Each one backed up a small pond on its upstream side, as seen here. Spillways passed water under the road during moderate streamflow, while the dip in the middle of the dam directed the water across the top during floods.[14]

One more crossing would be constructed by the men of the ERA before Roosevelt stirred the alphabet soup and another agency took over.

By late March 1935, three crossings and a half mile of roadway had been completed, but the uncertainties were multiplying. Not only was there scant funding for the access road, but there was also no guarantee there would ever be anything at the end of it. There was still no approved project to build a dam at the Woodward site. What's more, a reorganization of federal relief programs was looming. Never intended to be more than a temporary agency, the ERA had been set to last only two years, and the clock was about to run out.

On May 6 President Roosevelt created an ambitious new agency, the Works Progress Administration (WPA), to assume most responsibility for federal work relief. Rather than functioning through grants to the states, as did the ERA, the WPA would fund projects directly, but it would also require the support of a local sponsor. Over its eight-year lifetime, the agency would devote most of its resources to such works as public buildings, parks, utilities, roads, bridges, and flood-control projects, and it's especially well remembered today for its employment of out-of-work artists and writers.[15]

As the WPA readied itself to accept project applications, frustration with the federal government boiled over in Tucson due to perceived inequities in distribution of relief funds around the state. A committee of concerned citizens organized in protest. The fiercest resentment was directed at the Regional Forester in Albuquerque and a close subordinate, both of whom had persisted in rebuffing all pleas to support Sabino Canyon projects. Al Condron proposed removing southern Arizona from Albuquerque's authority. Bill Misbaugh went further. He said the offending Forest Service employees should be replaced or fired. Isabella Greenway, ever the diplomat, replied that the agency's apparent obstinacy was merely a reflection of its limited and uncertain funding.

Arizona State Library, Archives and Public Records

During the late spring and summer of 1935, while federal relief was in transition from the ERA to the newly created WPA, ERA laborers were at work on the fourth crossing. In addition to carrying the roadway and creating a recreational pond, as had the three previous check dams, this one was meant to supply water to Lowell Ranger Station, which had been completed the previous year. It would never fulfill this function, though, and Lowell would eventually receive water from a spring near the USGS streamgage.

At the end of July 1935, with four crossings complete, the Arizona ERA ran out of funds to pay any of its enrollees, and progress on the access road came abruptly to a halt. Meanwhile, Greenway and the chamber of commerce had taken on the formidable challenge of navigating the move from the ERA to the WPA, which had come with a wholly new set of rules and procedures. By late October the new agency had approved continuation of the access road and the comptroller general, head of the General Accounting Office, had secured that project with his approval, but the large dam at Woodward's site was still seriously in doubt. A succession of seemingly insurmountable barriers had risen in its way. Only the Forest Service could apply for it, Greenway had been told. The per-man labor cost was too high. The cost of materials was too great. The local contribution was too small.

In the face of all this, Greenway pressed ahead. Marshaling her formidable powers of persuasion, she wrote directly to Harry Hopkins, powerful administrator of the WPA. Disappointingly, an assistant administrator replied, confused about the two Sabino Canyon projects, the access road and the dam. She set him straight, then she bargained. Without consulting her chamber of commerce allies, she offered, in exchange for WPA approval of the dam, to withdraw the already approved access road project from federal funding and let the locals take it over. She ended with an appeal to disregard all objections for the sake of her constituents.

> Lastly, I feel that what this dam development will mean to the present and many future generations of this desert population is such a far reaching opportunity for this Administration that it should not be measured by momentarily existing yardsticks; and that it is really so important that it merits the very serious and mutual concern and consideration of every one of us—and to this end I am hopeful of your understanding help and co-operation.[16]

Greenway's gamble caused consternation at the chamber of commerce, but the sacrifice wouldn't be necessary. By the end of the month, the WPA had consented to the dam and only approval by the comptroller general remained.

With the finish line coming into view, the supporters of the Sabino Canyon dam picked up the pace. Greenway and her secretary, Howard Caffrey, were at a ranch she owned in northern Arizona, so running the representative's Washington office fell to another assistant, Gladys Lytle. The three stayed in continual, often hectic communication, and the pressure took its toll. In a request to Caffrey, Lytle begged, "I hope you hurry with this information, if you don't I will pass out."[17] In his telegraphed reply, Caffrey commiserated, "AM IN A CONSTANT STATE OF SOMETHING BETWEEN A SWOON AND A FAINT AND MORE POWER TO YOU."[18]

At the last moment, the General Accounting Office balked when it belatedly realized that the project was on national forest land. Greenway wrote to the chief of the Forest Service, who at long last gave his agency's approval. She telegraphed Al Condron, whose brother-in-law, Frances Montgomery, by an extraordinary stroke of luck, happened to be a special assistant to the comptroller general. Condron enlisted Montgomery's help, and Gladys Lytle gained a perfectly placed ally for the final push.

The long-hoped-for moment came on the seventh of November 1935. Lytle immediately telegraphed Greenway in Arizona: "SABINO CANYON DAM WARRANT SIGNED BY COMPTROLLER JUST TWO MINUTES AGO STOP THIS IS THE FINAL APPROVAL OF THE PROJECT."[19] She followed up with a breathless letter to Caffrey.

> Just sent the grand news that the Warrant for Sabino Canyon Dam had been signed. I called Mr. Montgomery right after noon and asked if there was any news and he said no but he expected some later in the day or in the morning. I have fairly sat on the phone waiting for him to call and when he did I was in the Veterans Administration office down the hall and in running back to answer it I fell down and nearly broke my ankle to say nothing of bursting the knee out of a new pair of hoes [sic]. Nothing could make me mad now tho, even if I had both knees out.[20]

It was the happy task of William Misbaugh to make the announcement in Tucson: the comptroller general of the United States had granted $750,000, covering the entire cost of a WPA project to build the 250-foot dam in Sabino Canyon. The *Arizona Daily Star* hailed Misbaugh, chairman of the Sabino Canyon Dam Committee, as the "father" of the project, but Misbaugh graciously acknowledged that "without the constant aid of Mrs. Greenway, the project probably never would have been granted."[21]

Five weeks earlier, President Roosevelt had dedicated the 726-foot Boulder Dam (later renamed Hoover Dam) on the Colorado River near Las Vegas, Nevada. The ceremony had been front-page news in the Tucson papers. In the midst of economic hardship, the nation was flexing its creative muscle. Who could doubt that Tucson would soon have a great dam of its own? ■

Isabella Greenway

Arizona Historical Society

Isabella Selmes was just months old, living in Dakota Territory, when her rancher parents introduced her to a colorful New York politician who had come west after the deaths of his wife and mother. The infant's encounter with Theodore Roosevelt, during the summer of 1886, opened a lifelong relationship with his illustrious family.

Cancer took Isabella's father when she was nine, and a few years later she and her mother moved to New York, where, amid the aristocratic social whirl, the teenager befriended Theodore's niece, Eleanor. Isabella was a bridesmaid at Eleanor's wedding to Franklin D. Roosevelt in 1905, and months later she herself wed Robert Ferguson, a former member of Theodore's Rough Riders. Unfortunately, Robert developed tuberculosis, like too many of his comrades-in-arms (including Thomas Meagher), and he died in 1922. The next year Isabella married his friend John Campbell Greenway, another Rough Rider and a leader in Arizona's mining business. John died unexpectedly in 1926 of complications following surgery.

Isabella Greenway's second marriage had brought her to Arizona, and she soon bought a ranch near Williams, a town south of the Grand Canyon, and put down roots in Tucson. She had excelled as an organizer on the home front during the First World War and was quickly drawn into politics. Greenway served on the Democratic National Committee, seconded FDR's 1932 presidential nomination, and in 1933 won a special election to become Arizona's representative in Congress. She worked devotedly for three years on behalf of her constituents before retiring in January 1937. Greenway married her third husband, Harry Orland King, the following year. She died in Tucson in 1953.

Before embarking on her political career, Greenway had started a furniture-making business to employ disabled veterans, and when it had foundered early in the Depression, she had opened a stylish Tucson hotel featuring its products. The Arizona Inn, in operation since 1930, is perhaps Isabella Greenway's best-known legacy—but it might have been otherwise. If the Sabino Canyon project had succeeded, today there would very likely be a Greenway Dam or a Lake Greenway in the Santa Catalina Mountains.[22]

CHAPTER 17

The End of the Road

William Misbaugh's announcement that the WPA had approved the entire cost of a 250-foot dam in Sabino Canyon was a moment of both triumph and relief for everyone devoted to the cause. In celebration, the Tucson Chamber of Commerce awarded certificates of appreciation to Isabella Greenway and her two assistants. Greenway called hers "one of the finest Christmas presents that I will ever receive, and one that my children will be proud of as an heirloom."[1]

Early the next month, in December 1935, the WPA's Arizona administrator asked the Army Corps of Engineers to handle planning and construction. Major Theodore Wyman Jr., district engineer in the corps's Los Angeles office, personally inspected the dam site, sang its praises, and predicted the project would be completed within a year and a half. The road to the dam had been a rough one, literally and figuratively, but now, at long last, the way forward looked smooth.

In reality, the next pothole was just around the corner. When word of the arrangement with the Corps of Engineers reached WPA officials in Washington, one of them hit the brakes. "The possibility of completing this project in its entirety appears to be remote," he declared to the state administrator. "It appears to be wholly unsuited for inclusion in your program." He forbade him to spend anything at all on the dam until others in the WPA had studied it.[2]

The stark news reached the chamber of commerce in January 1936. "All the old skeletons that we thought buried are again rattling," wrote Howard Caffrey to Bill Misbaugh and Al Condron at the chamber.[3] The objections from the WPA's Washington office were indeed exasperatingly familiar: the costs were too high for the relief labor provided, and the local contribution—a token six hundred dollars—was shockingly low. The situation was potentially explosive, given the raised expectations in Tucson. Condron noted ominously to Greenway, "We are sitting tight trying to keep the boat from rocking so that the community does not know of the dynamite, which any public announcement that this project is in jeopardy, would set off."[4]

A report by WPA engineers, filed in February 1936, suggested a startling reconfiguration—reducing the height of the dam at Professor Woodward's site to 150 feet and adding a 50-foot dam at Calvin Elliott's old site, downstream from the Picnic Grounds. Adding to the fast-multiplying uncertainties, the WPA's authorization was set to expire on June 30, the end of the federal fiscal year, and no one knew what would happen after that. The agency had already begun cutting back enrollment nationwide.

Once again Isabella Greenway brought her powers of persuasion to bear, and once again she bargained. She met with WPA officials in Washington, then followed up with an impassioned letter, offering to relinquish other projects to compensate for Pima County's minuscule sponsor's contribution. In late February the WPA's chief engineer approved releasing limited funds to the Army Corps of Engineers—but only for surveys and plans, not for construction. It was a mere $10,000, but it was a start. Condron wired Greenway, "CONGRATULATIONS TUCSON SHOULD CALL AT LEAST A HALF HOLIDAY."[5]

Author's collection

In contrast to the anxious maneuvering outside of public view, in Sabino Canyon, work on the access road was proceeding apace. Enough equipment had been "begged, borrowed, stolen, chiseled, appropriated and high-graded" to keep things moving, and as for the WPA laborers, "they couldn't work better if you paid them $4 day," a county foreman laughed.[6] ERA workers had completed four crossings before handing off the job, and by the end of January 1936, the WPA had finished the fifth, seen here. (The slanted pathway in the background led to a restroom—since demolished.)

This postcard was produced by the prolific photographer Burton Frasher, of Pomona, California. His cards were actual photographic prints—a style popular at the time—and many of them featured scenes from the Southwest. Frasher, or perhaps one of his employees, photographed the crossing about a year after it was finished. The close-up of the WPA plaque is by the author.

While some of the men were at work on the crossings, others were well ahead of them, pushing the access road up the canyon. In this WPA photo from January 1936, the laborers are contending with a steep and unstable slope, and huge boulders are hanging precariously above their heads.

Look carefully at the much more distant slope, above center. The diagonal mark, indicated by the arrows, is the old Sabino Canyon Trail. Its fresh appearance indicates recent work, most likely by the Civil Works Administration during the winter of 1933–34 (chapter 15). By the date of this photograph, much of the newly restored trail had been obliterated by construction of the new road, but the section seen here, safely located above the canyon floor, had survived.[7]

Coronado National Forest

By late February 1936, six crossings were complete. Farther up the canyon, the road had reached the vicinity of a small recreational dam, seen right of center in this undated photograph. Plans drawn for the CWA in 1934 had called for the restored Sabino Canyon Trail to provide access to this dam, and it, too, seems to have been built by CWA laborers. The modest structure soon came to be called Anderson Dam, apparently in honor of William John Anderson, assistant supervisor of Coronado National Forest, a respected and well-liked older employee who had been deeply involved in organizing relief projects in Sabino Canyon. "Pop" Anderson died in mid-1934, a few months after the CWA expired.[8]

The prominent tree at center is an Arizona cypress, sometimes called a *Sabino* in Spanish (see preface). Today this fine example of the canyon's namesake tree is long gone, and the dam has been almost completely destroyed by floods.

I n March 1936, fueled by the WPA funding authorized the previous month,
nine men from the Army Corps of Engineers led a pack train up Sabino
Canyon to begin a fresh survey for the dam and reservoir. A few weeks later,
the comptroller general signed off on a supplemental WPA appropriation of
$25,000 for the access road. It was encouraging news. "DIRT WILL NOW FLY,"
Condron telegraphed Greenway. He was right.[9]

The rush was on to finish the road before the end of June, so that work on the
dam could start without delay if the WPA were reauthorized for the next fiscal
year. The lengthening road had left the canyon floor and begun its steep climb
toward the dam site—the last and most difficult two miles of its construction.
By early May a power scraper, an air compressor, air drills, a tractor, and a steam
shovel, all financed by the supplemental appropriation, were noisily at work in
the canyon. When these proved insufficient, Coronado National Forest offered
two more air drills, and a local WPA official asked permission to run a night
shift to speed things up. As the laborers blasted their way through bedrock, a
foreman was hit by flying fragments. He escaped with no more than bruises, but
his prized pocket watch would never tick again.

The Tucson Chamber of Commerce was pressing the WPA hard to keep on
schedule—functioning, as a local newspaper put it, as "shock troops" for Pima
County, which was keeping a healthy distance from day-to-day operations.[10]
Meanwhile, negotiations were ongoing in preparation for construction of the
great dam itself. The WPA had rejected Greenway's offer to relinquish other
projects, and it was clear that Pima County, local sponsor for the Sabino Canyon
project, would need somehow to increase its cash contribution. The dark clouds
of the Great Depression were by then starting to lift, but the county was still in
dire financial straits. Despite this, influential community members had vowed to
"do their utmost to raise a sum of possibly as much as $100,000.00 toward the
construction and completion of this wonderful project."[11] In the end, even this
enormously optimistic sum would fall short.

The seventh crossing was ready for its portrait in May 1936. Between the camera and the WPA sign in this photograph is a temporary road the workers used to bypass the dam while it was being built. That road and the tossed-aside lumber near the automobile suggest that the dam has just been completed. Visitors are already taking advantage of it, as shown in the next photo, taken the same day.

The seventh was the tallest of the nine crossings, and it created the deepest recreational pond—a refreshing place for a dip on this sunny spring afternoon. Notice the two pairs of shoes set neatly on the stone curb at the left side of the photo. Not surprisingly, the new pastime of skinny dipping above the crossings isn't pictured in any of the WPA's publicity photos.

We may wonder today how inviting these artificial swimming holes would have been once filled with cold water released from the bottom of a deep artificial lake, two miles upstream—and what the effects of that chilly flow would have been on Sabino Creek's native aquatic life.

T o the relief of the project's supporters, early in the summer of 1936, Congress reauthorized the WPA for the coming fiscal year. Then, quite unexpectedly, in August the Army Corps of Engineers announced it would hold a public hearing in Tucson to consider the Sabino Canyon dam.

The hearing would mark a crucial moment for Sabino Canyon, but it had been triggered by events far from Arizona. Earlier that year, flooding had caused severe damage and many deaths across the northeastern United States. In the District of Columbia, the Potomac had overflowed its banks, forcing CCC boys to stack sandbags around the Lincoln Memorial and the Washington Monument. Although high and dry on Capitol Hill, Congress had been well aware of the crisis that had reached nearly to its doorstep. Its response, the Flood Control Act of 1936, authorized the Army Corps of Engineers to make improvements nationwide, and it directed the corps to examine projects at several specified sites. One of these sites was Sabino Canyon.

The proceedings opened on the morning of September 10, 1936, in a crowded Tucson City Council chamber. Presiding was Major Theodore Wyman, by then an old hand in the army's Sabino Canyon investigations. After calling the meeting to order, he turned over the floor to Bill Misbaugh from the chamber of commerce. In an impressive show of community solidarity, representatives of every relevant local government and agency, the University of Arizona, and several private concerns testified unanimously in favor of the dam, without limiting their opinions to flood control, the ostensible subject of the inquiry. The army, still fixated on the two-dam notion conceived by the WPA earlier in the year, had been studying both the Woodward and the Elliott sites, but the locals made their preference clear. Fred Winn, Coronado National Forest's supervisor, pointedly noted that a dam at the Elliott site would drown tens of thousands of dollars' worth of recent improvements to the Picnic Grounds—something unlikely to please the secretary of agriculture.

The hearing concluded, and the dam's supporters held their collective breath while Major Wyman considered. The whole project was hanging in the balance. The entire route to Sabino Canyon from town had been paved by the WPA, all nine of the planned stream crossings were finished, the access road had reached within a mile of the dam site, and eager citizens were pestering Coronado National Forest about lakeside permits for everything "from private homes through dance halls and hot dog stands to hotels."[12]

Voices from the Past

Among the many who testified at the Army's Tucson hearing in 1936 were a few whose connection to the Sabino Canyon dam long predated the Depression. Frank Kelton, William B. Alexander's long-ago college chum (we saw their photo in chapter 8) bestowed the blessing of the American Society of Civil Engineers. David Cochran, who had helped build Professor Woodward's streamgage, lent his personal support. Most remarkably, William H. Daily, founding secretary of the Great Western Power Company, spoke as well. Years ago he had struggled unsuccessfully for more than a decade to bring the great dam to life, and he was still angry. One of Great Western's Chicago backers had offered to spend millions on construction, he recalled, "and a bone-headed city council turned him down."[13]

Young Research Library, UCLA

Theodore Wyman Jr.

The officer who ran the proceedings, Major Theodore Wyman Jr., was a decorated World War I veteran with an eventful career ahead. Five years after the hearing he was the army's district engineer in Honolulu when the Japanese attacked Pearl Harbor. Energetic and competent, but abrasive in personality, he became the subject of rumor and resentment when his massive postattack responsibilities inconvenienced Hawaiian civilians. Despite later honors for his service during the Second World War, he eventually fell victim to national finger-pointing surrounding the Pearl Harbor tragedy. The secretary of war absolved Wyman, by then risen to the rank of colonel, of any responsibility for the disaster.

Major Wyman's anxiously awaited report was released in January 1937. He rejected the Elliott site, called the Woodward site ideal, and raised the dam's estimated cost from $750,000 to $1,100,000. He dismissed the dam's value for flood control in the Tucson Basin, the question for which the Tucson hearing had been called. But he declared that the dam's benefits for recreation—both directly, at the lake itself, and indirectly, through flood protection for improvements downstream—made the project worthwhile. Yet his conclusions, summed up in the final paragraph, came as a shock.

> [The district engineer] recommends that the project be considered favorably as a water conservation, recreational, and flood control project, provided work relief projects are needed in the locality and local interests are willing to contribute $500,000 toward the cost.[14]

The call for a half-million-dollar sponsor's contribution stunned the dam's supporters. And as if that huge blow were not enough, it was matched by a second at nearly the same moment. The previous spring, on her fiftieth birthday, Isabella Greenway had announced that she wouldn't seek reelection to the House of Representatives. Her last day on the job was January 3. The Tucson Chamber of Commerce had seemingly lost its most powerful ally.

The outlines of the predicament soon became clear. Pima County would need to file a new WPA application for the dam, this time with a truly substantial sponsor's contribution. The county couldn't possibly get together the half million dollars specified by Major Wyman, though, just perhaps, it might be able to raise enough to fill the gap between the WPA's $750,000 allotment and Wyman's estimated $1,100,000 total cost. But did that WPA allotment even exist? The question would come to haunt the dam's supporters.[15]

After several months of uncharacteristic quiet, the Tucson Chamber's Sabino Canyon Dam Committee, led by Bill Misbaugh, launched into a series of contentious meetings with the Pima County Board of Supervisors. Unfortunately for the chamber, by this time its close ties to the supervisors were starting to fray. The committee proposed $300,000 in tax levies. The supervisors balked, and their chairman openly doubted that the WPA's $750,000 share would ever materialize. The chamber countered with a proposal for a $300,000 bond issue. The supervisors demanded that the committee first circulate a petition to prove the Tucson community's support. The chamber's representatives thanked the supervisors for "the hearty cooperation it never gave" and walked out.[16]

The supervisors were wise to be skeptical. Toward the end of May, the WPA's administrator, Harry Hopkins himself, delivered devastating clarification. There had never been a $750,000 allotment. The agency had merely given preliminary approval to the dam, adding it to a list of projects for consideration by the state administrator. "Selection of this project for operation was out of the question, due to its high man-year cost and negligible sponsor's contribution," Hopkins wrote. The WPA would consider a revised application, but only if the sponsor were willing to contribute at least half the cost—roughly the half million dollars specified in Major Wyman's report.[17]

Having come so far, having struggled so long, and with its reputation increasingly at stake, the Tucson Chamber of Commerce still refused to give up. Secretary Condron traveled to Washington to meet with Arizona's congressional delegation and to lobby the WPA. Isabella Greenway emerged from retirement in New York City and flew to Washington to help.

By this time the Pima County Board of Supervisors had come to regard the WPA with suspicion, bordering on contempt. The WPA changed its rules almost monthly, the board said, and it couldn't be trusted to finish any project it started. (Their disillusionment reflected a nationwide attitude that extended even to the WPA's enrollees. The economy was improving and so, by pernicious logic, anyone still on the WPA's rolls must be too lazy to get a real job.) Nevertheless, despite their deep misgivings, the supervisors agreed in June to file a new application for the elusive $750,000, supplemented by a $300,000 bond issue for a sponsor's contribution—but only if the WPA's involvement would be kept to a minimum after it had turned over the cash.

The WPA's chief engineer rejected the county's application out of hand. The agency would pay only for labor, not for materials or equipment, he said, and he raised the sponsor's required contribution to $600,000—fully one thousand times Pima County's original commitment.[18]

The final act played out at a meeting of the board of directors of the Tucson Chamber of Commerce. Only recently returned from Washington, Condron gave his report and encouraged his colleagues to continue their efforts. Stalwart supporter John O'Dowd, who had appointed the first Sabino Canyon Dam Committee four years earlier, moved that the chamber ask Pima County to file one more WPA application. The room fell silent. Tense minutes passed. At last the presiding officer quietly declared the motion had failed for lack of a second.

O'Dowd swore, resigned on the spot, and stormed from the room. There was a motion for adjournment, but Bill Misbaugh interrupted.

Old Pueblo is a good name for this G—damned place. I don't see how you ever expect to do anything, accomplish anything here. You shy away from anything new. Thousands of communities are getting government money for their projects and you won't even try.[19]

Pima County's most ambitious federal relief project had ended in frustration and anger. There would be no great dam in Sabino Canyon.[20]

USDA Forest Service, Southwestern Region

The access road was still a mile from the dam site when work halted. A truncated series of switchbacks had been carved into the eastern canyon wall, as seen in this photograph, taken by Forest Service employee Charles Cunningham in the spring of 1937. A few months later, the unfinished road was aptly described at a meeting of the Pima County Board of Supervisors as "ending at a point of nowhere up the canyon . . . not only an eyesore to the public but an eyesore to WPA."[21]

Eventually a turnaround was created at the foot of the switchbacks (at the left edge of the photo) and the roadbed beyond that point was abandoned. The unused segment remains today a scar on the canyon wall, eroding and increasingly overgrown, a slowly fading reminder of dashed hopes in difficult times.

Once again, as in the story of the Great Western Power Company and its rivals, a vision of a great dam in Sabino Canyon had failed. Perhaps the lake might have been a boon to Tucson's citizens, as the chamber of commerce imagined—though there's reason to question how large a boon it might have been. It would have been a relatively small lake, despite its impressive depth when filled, and with some awkwardly steep shorelines, rising and falling with the vagaries of the desert climate.[22]

The greater flaw may have been not in the vision itself, but in the pathway to its realization—the continually reconfigured maze of agencies, subagencies, regulations, and policies that was the New Deal. In the end, there was no way to fit the project into the WPA, an agency dedicated first to work relief and only second to public works. Raising a 250-foot dam, with its huge equipment and materials costs, was simply not an economical way to generate jobs. A prescient *Arizona Daily Star* editorial in June 1937 had summed it up well:

> Perhaps it is possible, if enough pressure is brought to bear, that an attempt will be made to twist the WPA idea to meet the local purposes. But let us not blink the fact that a twisted idea will remain a twisted idea with every likelihood that it will go wrong in the end.[23]

That it went so badly wrong was a personal tragedy for William Misbaugh and Albert Condron, whose tenacity eventually lost them the support not only of the community but also—and perhaps most painfully—of their colleagues in the Tucson Chamber of Commerce.

Yet something significant had been accomplished. Men had been given paid employment during years of desperate hardship. And what those men created had value. Before the Great Depression, few visitors to Sabino Canyon had ventured much farther upstream than the old Picnic Grounds. The new road, even unfinished as it was, opened up miles of beautiful canyon to everyone. The nine stone crossings have become the most treasured of all the artifacts of the Great Depression in Sabino Canyon.

If the Tucson Chamber of Commerce had succeeded in its efforts, the road in Upper Sabino Canyon, so popular today among hikers, bicyclists, and nature lovers, would have become a busy thoroughfare to a crowded recreational lake. Many would say we're better off with a road to nowhere. ■

Albert H. Condron

Lured by former high-school classmates singing the praises of Tucson, Albert Harlan Condron moved to the city from Los Angeles in 1912, enrolled in the University of Arizona, and joined the football team. He made an early impression on his adopted town when, in celebration of his team's victories over a rival college, he suggested that a large letter *A* be installed on Sentinel Peak near downtown. Completed in 1916, the *A* of "A Mountain" remains a landmark today, just down the hill from where Carleton Watkins set his tripod in 1880.

Condron graduated in 1917 with a degree in civil engineering, then worked several years in other states for the USGS on hydrological matters. He returned to Tucson in 1920 and two years later became secretary of the Tucson Chamber of Commerce. His tireless efforts on behalf of the city earned him respect during the twenties, when this portrait was made by the Buehman studio.

Primed by his experience with the USGS, and with a deep affection for his college town and an expansive view of its future, Al Condron seems almost to have been predestined to play a major role in the saga of the Sabino Canyon dam. When the project collapsed at a chamber of commerce meeting in August 1937, he held his tongue. But the next day, in a letter blasting the Pima County Board of Supervisors for "wilful, malicious, and 'fifth-ace-in-the-deck' tactics to forestall acceptance of federal funds," he resigned.[24] Several months later he left town to become secretary of the Nogales chamber, but he was soon back in Tucson, where he accepted a prestigious new position as field representative for the United States Chamber of Commerce.

CHAPTER 18

A Lake at Last

Scarcity was a hallmark of the Great Depression, but there was no shortage of misery. Among those who suffered most were men, women, and children who had been forced to abandon their homes. Many took to the roads and the rails and headed for the lush (if largely illusory) promised land of California. Along the way, some passed through communities in the deserts of Arizona. Some chose to stay.

The attitude of Tucsonans toward the homeless among them was an uneasy blend of compassion and resentment. The outsiders, though in dire need, were competing with the locals for both relief funds and jobs. It was the same almost everywhere; vagrancy was an interstate problem and it cried out for federal remedies. The ERA took action early with its Transient Division, which established camps providing housing, food, work, recreation, and job training. In November 1933 one such camp opened a few miles from downtown Tucson.

When the ERA passed its expiration date in the spring of 1935, it didn't immediately sell the furniture and burn the stationery. Instead it received a temporary reprieve while most of its functions moved to other agencies, including the newly created WPA. Many transient workers stayed with the ERA, though, and that summer the Tucson Transient Camp opened a side camp in Sabino Canyon, about three-quarters of a mile above the Picnic Grounds. The Sabino Canyon Camp would outlast the agency that founded it, and it would remain a lively little community between the canyon walls until 1939. We'll spend some time there in the next chapter.

At first the camp's residents labored on the new road in the upper canyon, but when the WPA took over that task in late 1935, the men were free to take their shovels elsewhere. Forest Service officials seized the opportunity to draw up plans for the broad canyon floor south of the old Elliott dam site. It was an open and sunny place that had long been relatively neglected in favor of the popular Picnic Grounds farther upstream, though the flat terrain had served nicely as a campsite for military cadets earlier in the century (chapter 9). By early 1937 an attractive if unexceptional recreation site was taking shape. Then Forest Supervisor Fred Winn proposed a substantial change of plans.

In March Winn led a group of local officials and chamber of commerce members into the canyon to pitch his idea: a small recreational dam to be installed downstream from the USGS streamgage. If the city and county would contribute a few thousand dollars for materials, Winn promised, the Forest Service would take care of the rest. The worthy residents of the Sabino Canyon Camp would have a project to keep them employed a bit longer, and, after years of incomprehensible government twists and turns, the people of Tucson would at last have a lake in Sabino Canyon.[1]

The forest supervisor's proposal came shortly after the one-two punch of Major Theodore Wyman's report and Isabella Greenway's retirement, at a moment when, for many in Tucson, the long-sought dam at Professor Woodward's site seemed to be receding into myth. Winn's dam would be far less grandiose—and vastly less expensive—than any of the conflict-plagued schemes that had attached themselves over the decades to the Elliott and Woodward sites. As it would turn out, it differed from them all in another crucial respect. This dam would actually be built.

The place Forest Supervisor Winn chose for his dam was a series of ledges that crossed the creek about a thousand feet downstream from Calvin Elliott's site. Engineers had previously passed over the spot because the low canyon walls there made it unsuitable for a deep storage reservoir, but it seemed ideal for a shallow recreational lake.[2]

Not many surviving photographs show the site before the dam was built. Here, University of Arizona faculty and family members have gathered on one of the ledges, perhaps during the 1920s. At far left is botanist J. J. Thornber, who earlier accompanied R. S. Kellogg during his exploration of the Santa Catalinas in 1902 (chapter 7). Seated at right, looking toward a child in the background, is microbiologist Mary Estill Caldwell. Her aunt, Alice Estill, is sitting next to her, and her mother, Ella Estill, is standing nearby, in the dark dress. We'll see all three family members again, in the last chapter.

Does this scene seem familiar? A group of pioneer picnickers posed nearby for one of the earliest dated photographs of Sabino Canyon (chapter 2).

Cline Library, Northern Arizona University

Cline Library, Northern Arizona University

In June 1937, while Chamber of Commerce Secretary Al Condron was in Washington making a last-ditch effort to save the great WPA dam at the Woodward site, men from the Sabino Canyon Camp began work on the much more modest structure in the lower canyon.[3] By this time Coronado National Forest had managed to secure ERA funds for materials, leaving the citizens of Tucson entirely off the financial hook.

The workers began by erecting a wooden scaffold with a plank runway along its top. As the scaffold was extended across the ledge, an open framework was attached on its downstream side, defining the space to be filled by the masonry dam. The future lakebed, at right, had already been stripped of vegetation, leaving mostly sawed-off tree stumps and clumps of grass.

Work went quickly despite the summer heat, and by mid-July an impressive number of stones had been laid. The shape of the dam was emerging, including two triangular buttresses on the downstream side to give it additional strength. The section between the buttresses, marked by a lower segment of the plank runway, would become the spillway.

Compare this photograph to those in chapter 16 showing ERA laborers at work on the first crossing in Upper Sabino in 1934. In building the dam in 1937, the men were using the same techniques as their predecessors, but on a larger scale.

W orkers from the Sabino Canyon Camp cemented the last stone in place on October 6, 1937, but there was still work to be done. Parts of the lakebed needed to be carefully sculpted to make it safe for the feet of swimmers and waders. Fortunately, sparse summer rains had reduced Sabino Creek to a trickle, and the weather stayed dry through the fall, adding welcome weeks for the work. By early January 1938, the men were rushing to finish before the creek rose.

"Rain glorius rain," penciled the work supervisor in his journal on January 20, capturing the excitement with some creative spelling. Water was spotted making its way down the upper canyon, and he put nearly the entire camp to work finishing the lakebed. When they wrapped up the job on the twenty-eighth, the water was still coming, "but OH, so slow."[4] It rained again, and on February 2 the stream picked up speed. It passed the workers' camp an hour before midnight, it reached the dam after sunrise the next morning, and the lake began to fill.

Someone must have kept watch though the following night, because we know that water first trickled over the spillway at 1:35 a.m. on February 4, 1938. It was a proud day for the men of the Sabino Canyon Camp. The sheet of water crossing the spillway varied in depth by no more than an inch from one side to the other. The dam was the largest structure that anyone had created, or would create, in Sabino Canyon during the New Deal years, and here it was at last, performing to perfection.

A celebration was clearly in order, and within a week one was in the works. Supervisor Winn attended a preliminary discussion during which, according to the *Arizona Daily Star*, an intriguing proposal was made.

> "Why," someone asked, in the midst of suggestions about having the mayor and governor and council and supervisors and things attend the ceremonies, "why don't we have a bathing beauty contest?"[5]

It was noted that, in publicity photos from other proud localities, pulchritudinous models sometimes wore costumes fashioned from the local flora—a hackneyed gimmick, to which objection was immediately raised.

"These gals in the picture here—look at 'em. They're wearing spinach and lettuce and stuff like that. Why, one of 'em's even wearing water lily leaves. We haven't got any water lilies around here!"

"Hell! They could wear cactus, couldn't they?" proposed an optimist.

"Sure," contributed Winn, who theretofore had been looking askance, "and you could have a jury of doctors do the judging. The entrant who had the fewest needles to be picked out of her hide when the show was over would get the prize!"[6]

The beauty contest would persist in the plans for weeks, though without botanical enhancement. Unfortunately for Sabino Canyon's visual record, it would be dropped before the ceremony.

Coronado National Forest

About six weeks after the lake filled, on an afternoon in mid-March, Forest Service employee Charles H. Cunningham visited the area with his camera. Cunningham was one of the most skilled of the agency photographers documenting changes to Sabino Canyon during the Great Depression. He took the photo of the unfinished switchbacks in the previous chapter, and he also may have taken the construction photos we've just seen.

This particular photograph is among the best to show us the dam when it was new and the lake when it was still an open body of water, free of aquatic weeds, cattails, and trees. It also demonstrates that in 1938, just as now, some people were capable of selective illiteracy. The sign near the boys reads, "DANGER KEEP OFF."

Coronado National Forest

Just below the dam, Cunningham found a group of teenagers enjoying some new play equipment. Fortunately for the photographer, they were in a cheerful and cooperative mood—and remarkably agile, as well. The swings had been made to order by a blacksmith and cemented in place in January, along with at least two pairs of seesaws. These features, which had been in the plans drawn back in 1935, as well as the lake that had been added later, encouraged quite a different style of use from what went on in the more traditional Picnic Grounds farther up the canyon. "Lower Sabino Recreational Area" was the title inscribed on the original plans, and it was apt.[7] The name also marked the beginning of the way we speak of the canyon today, dividing it into Lower Sabino, in the canyon mouth, and Upper Sabino, from the old Picnic Grounds upstream.

Cunningham climbed a steep, rocky hillside a short distance down the canyon to snap this overview. Uncharacteristically, he held the camera off kilter, probably due to the precarious footing, but he captured the pristine recreational developments in remarkable detail.

The cars at lower right are at the end of a parking loop the transient workers had created in 1936. Between the play equipment and the dam is a stone diversion wall the men had built that same year to protect downstream developments from flood damage. Notice the solitary saguaro cactus on the sandbar in the lake. We'll see it again in a moment.

The workers had quit for the day when Cunningham took these pictures, but the next few weeks would be busy ones. The lake needed to be drained and cleaned, new signs needed to be installed, a speakers' platform needed to be built—all to make ready for the dedication of the dam. The big day was less than a month away.

It's Sunday, April 10, 1938, and we've arrived in time to join nearly two thousand citizens who've turned out for the dedication of the new dam in Lower Sabino. A combined junior high school band has been assembled for the festivities. Can you spot the round bass drum right of center? The kids aren't playing right now (fortunately) and instead we hear the amplified voice of one of the dignitaries. Tucson's movers and shakers have collected on the platform—Mayor Henry Jaastad, Ed Goyette from the Welfare Board, and John Reilly, president of the Chamber of Commerce, among other notables—and a Forest Service representative has come all the way from Albuquerque to address the crowd.[8]

Despite the formality of the ceremony, it's a come-as-you-are occasion for the onlookers. Some are formally dressed, while others are in their swimsuits. A few are standing on the new dam in the background, and still others can be heard splashing in the lake, ignoring the proceedings entirely. The dam may be small consolation for the loss of the much greater one, miles upstream, but Sabino Canyon has a lake at last and it's something to celebrate.

Coronado National Forest

It didn't take long for the lake to fill with swimmers in the spring of 1938, and the most popular place to get wet was this cove on the western shore. It had taken many truckloads of sand to line this shallow area so children could safely wade and swim, and still more sand to cover the peninsula that set it apart from the lake's deeper sections.

A lone saguaro had been transplanted onto the peninsula to serve as a picturesque accent to the scene, as can be seen in this photograph by the prolific Charles Cunningham. (It was less likely a remnant of the natural vegetation.) Needless to say, the water-soaked sand was terrible habitat for a cactus. The plant was gone within a year.

Coronado National Forest

Cunningham wasn't the only one in Lower Sabino with a camera on that pleasant day in May 1938, as is evident in his delightful photograph of a photograph being taken.

Early on, men from the Sabino Canyon Camp had installed about two dozen concrete tables in Lower Sabino Canyon. Only a few were upstream from the eventual site of the dam, and one of these had to be removed when the lake was grafted onto the plans. The rest, including this one, remained along the western shore, where they were prime real estate for hungry swimmers. The doomed saguaro is barely visible through the branches of a mesquite, and though that cactus is now long gone, both the tree and the table are still there today.

abino Lake's heyday as a swimming hole was surprisingly brief. In the pre-dawn hours of June 2, two young men set out swimming from the shore to the sandbar where the lone saguaro stood. Partway across the water, one swimmer shouted that he couldn't make it, sank beneath the dark surface, and failed to reappear. Sheriff's deputies arrived before sunrise and residents of the Sabino Canyon Camp assisted in the search for the body, but it wasn't recovered until late in the morning, when the lake was partially drained.[9]

Two days later Coronado National Forest's assistant supervisor was quoted in the *Arizona Daily Star*. "The lake in lower Sabino canyon was designed as a landscape addition to the picnic area," he claimed. "It never was intended as a swimming pool." It was a sad misrepresentation of the facts. The official went on to discourage the public from swimming in the lake, citing the lack of a lifeguard or water sanitation, but some visitors continued to take a dip despite the risk.[10]

Sabino Canyon's visitors were soon offered a safer way to use the lake, how-ever. In August the Arizona Game and Fish Department planted eight thousand bass and bluegill in its waters. For many months the fish remained tantalizingly off-limits to fishermen. The wait ended the following spring.

Not many reached the six-fish limit on the inaugural day of fishing at Sabino Lake, but it was a great occasion. The day's catch was reported the next morning by *Star* sportswriter George Hall. Some of what he wrote was true.

> There were a lot of fish caught yesterday in Lower Sabino Canyon lake. Some were right big, some were not so big and some were so small they had to yawn to get hold of a hook. . . . There were more gadgets designed to lure the finny inhabitants to shore cast into the lake than Mr. Woolworth could possibly crowd into one store window. There were plugs of every description, flies that defy description, grass-hoppers, crickets, and worms, and it was even whispered about that one fisherman whistled to lure his bass into shallow water where he could hit them with a club. . . . No one was pulled into the lake by a fish.[11] ■

Arizona Historical Society

When the long-anticipated first day for fishing was set for May 27, 1939, eager sportsmen, sportswomen, and sportskids camped out overnight in hopes of scoring prime spots in the morning. Opening time was 4:00 a.m., but at about 3:50 someone adjusting his gear in the dark "accidentally" dropped his lure into the water, where it was snapped up by a bass. It seemed an unlikely story, but the fisherman in question was a sheriff's deputy, so who could doubt it?

At daybreak anglers were lined up across the dam and around the shore, risking flying hooks and tangled lines, while a well-prepared few had floated out onto the lake in a boat. It was a scene to remember, and *Arizona Daily Star* photographer J. Robert Burns recorded it admirably.

Fred Winn

Born in Wisconsin in 1880, Frederic Hinsdale Winn enjoyed a luxurious childhood in China, where his father was personal physician to a powerful statesman. Later, back in the United States, he was educated in eastern prep schools, attended Princeton and Rutgers, and after graduation spent several years studying art in New York. In 1903 he put privilege behind him, answered a hankering for the wide-open spaces, and headed for the Southwest, where he tried on roles as a cowboy, a prospector, and a mounted mail carrier.

Arizona Historical Society

By 1907 even the Southwest was becoming too civilized for him, so he sold his horse, his pack mules, and his gear and got ready to move to Argentina. By chance, just as he was about to leave, he learned of an assistant ranger position opening up in a newly created national forest in New Mexico. He got the job, rose quickly through the ranks, and served in several forests before landing as supervisor of the Coronado in 1925. He had found his calling—and along the way a lifelong companion, his wife, Ada.

A tall man with a ranch hand's slow way of speaking and a disarming wit, Fred Winn made friends easily. He was an accomplished raconteur, and, despite being deaf in one ear, a good listener—a quality that served him well in resolving disputes. Like Tom Meagher before him, Winn sometimes found himself at odds with westerners accustomed to unrestrained use of federal lands. Once, early in his career, he came across a cattleman named Pat Dobson, herding livestock where they shouldn't have been.

> I told him the land was now part of the national forest and asked to see his permit. Dobson looked at me for a minute and then tapped the large .38 revolver in his holster. "This here's my permit," he drawled. "Well, Pat," I replied, "I guess that's a good enough permit for me," and I rode off.[12]

Winn might never have retired had regulations not required it on his sixty-second birthday. Even then he didn't quite leave. He moved into a space in the Coronado's offices and went to work on a history of the national forests of Arizona and New Mexico. Sadly, he died in 1945 before he could complete the task.

CHAPTER 19

Camping Out

I t was well over a century ago that curious Tucsonans first saddled up their horses, climbed into their wagons, and set off to explore a little-known canyon northeast of town. Since those early days, a great many people have had the pleasure of visiting Sabino Canyon, but only a few have had the privilege of living there. Yet for several years during the Great Depression, the canyon was both a haven and a workplace for men uprooted by the nation's economic upheaval.

As we've seen, the idea of a camp in Sabino Canyon for transient workers arose during one of the periodic restructurings that marked the progress of the New Deal. In the spring of 1935, the ERA was trucking in men to build the road to Professor Woodward's dam site. The agency had been granted an extension while it transferred projects to the newly created WPA, but the WPA still wasn't up and running in Arizona. At this unsettled moment, the Arizona ERA devised a plan to speed up work on the road: the Tucson Transient Camp would open a satellite camp in Sabino Canyon to supplement the men already on the job.

It didn't work out quite as planned. In August the ERA laid off its regular workers, so when the camp opened soon afterward, its residents had the road-building task entirely to themselves. Toward the end of the year the WPA belatedly took over, freeing the transient laborers to work on a newly planned recreation area in Lower Sabino Canyon (chapter 18).

By midsummer 1936 the Sabino Canyon Camp, too, was being funded by the WPA, and the transition to the newer agency was nearly complete. The final step came in August, a year after the camp had opened, when the WPA officially recognized camp residents as no longer transient workers but as rightful citizens of Pima County, Arizona. That was an affirmation in itself, but what probably mattered more to the workers was what came with it: a raise in take-home pay from $17 to $24 per month.[1]

These were, after all, ordinary men with ordinary hopes under extraordinary circumstances—economic refugees from all across the country, of varying backgrounds and races, who by sheer chance found themselves thrown together in an unfamiliar canyon in the desert Southwest. In their tiny, short-lived community, they experienced hard work, humor, conflict, companionship, pain, and pride.

Because the first job of the men in the Sabino Canyon Camp was to extend the access road toward the hoped-for dam at the Woodward site, it made sense to stake their tents as far up the canyon as possible. The site chosen was a small terrace just beyond the fourth crossing—the last one that had had been finished by the summer of 1935. The pyramidal roofs of the tent cabins can be seen in the background of this photo, taken for the ERA.

At the time the Sabino Canyon camp was founded, its parent facility, the Tucson Transient Camp, was publishing an occasional newsletter called *The Oasis*. Some of the earliest accounts of the lives of Sabino Canyon's transient laborers come from that lively periodical. This whimsical drawing of Sabino Canyon Camp residents hard at work appeared in the October 1, 1935, issue. The artist isn't identified.

The setting of the Sabino Canyon camp was fit for a travel brochure, but the accommodations were something less than five-star, as described by resident Bill Griffin in *The Oasis*.

Rain! "When you gonna rain again—Rain!" For some unknown reason that seems to be the most popular song going around camp. . . . In some of the tents we had all of an inch of water on the floor and two inches on the beds with a continual promise of more to come. I was warned not to put my hand on the wet canvas as that would cause it to leak. Leak? I came dern near drowning—and I didn't touch the d——d canvas. It's fun to lie on one's bed and look up at the water streaming down the outside (and inside) of the tent, and to count the tadpoles and pollywogs, along with fish worms, and wondering whether the next fish to slide down will be a trout or a perch.[2]

The project superintendent was living on-site, and according to Griffin, his experience of camp life was no less than total immersion.

The other morning C. M. Brady reclined in yaller pajamas and a languid mood, when Chedester and Morrison burst rudely into his sanctum. . . . They laid gentle but firm hands upon C. M. and to the bridge they carried him. Then with a one—two—allez-oop they initiated him into the Ancient and Royal Order of Fisheries. C. M. evened up with Chedester—now for Morrison.[3]

Despite the hijinks, there was serious work to be done. By the beginning of November 1935, the men were nailing wooden roofs onto the cabins to get ready for the coming winter and to make room for an expanded crew. Nearly the entire membership of the Tucson Transient Camp, with their equipment, had just been moved to Sabino Canyon, raising the resident population from fewer than fifty to eighty-four. Correspondent Griffin wondered whether the camp dogs would show up next.

All this seemed threatened on the morning of June 10, 1936, when camp residents spotted a wildfire burning on the steep western slope of the canyon. In short order a crew of transient workers was dispatched to the fire, where they joined Forest Service personnel, CCC boys, and WPA men in battling the blaze into the night. At midnight the worst seemed over, but during the morning the wind rose and drove the flames to within four hundred yards of camp. Forest Service officials called in reinforcements, and by the end of the day, several hundred men had joined the battle.

Meanwhile the camp had become headquarters for the firefighters. Residents set up a first-aid station to care for overheated, sunburned, and injured personnel. They prepared rations in the mess hall, and late in the day they cooked 150 steaks to be packed up the canyon by horse and mule—which they were, along with canteens filled with ice. The ground was so rough that the animals had to be reshoed after two trips. By the second morning, the fire was under control. The instant army disbanded and life in camp settled back into its workaday routine.[4]

Two weeks later eight camp residents, flush with extra firefighting pay, spent a warm afternoon holed up in a hotel room in town, enjoying beer, whisky, and watermelon. That night a few of the men crossed the street to cool off in a city park, where, asleep in the dark, they were attacked and robbed. One of them, a fifty-one-year-old cook, had just quit his job in camp and was set to catch a bus to California the next morning. He was killed. Suspicion at first fell on certain of his camp-mates, who had been too drunk to give a coherent account of events, but three local youths were soon arrested and confessed to the crime.[5]

Coronado National Forest

A month or so after the fire, the canyon was still hot and dry and waiting for the monsoon rains. An unidentified photographer climbed a short distance up the slope opposite the camp to take its picture. By this time the self-contained little community seems to have comprised not only the residential cabins but also an office, a mess hall, a commissary, a latrine, and a shed for an electric generator—though it's hard to tell which is which in this photo. Notice how carefully the structures have been arranged to avoid removing trees and cacti. Camp enrollees would later need ropes and chains to guide a falling saguaro between two of the close-set buildings.

On the road at the extreme right is a cement mixer and a chute extending down to the streambed. The workers were finishing a small concrete dam to collect water for the camp. The catchment would prove helpful, but water would still need to be trucked in during the driest months.

C. M. Brady was still in charge the next year when camp residents began work on the dam in Lower Sabino Canyon, and in late June 1937, Charles Cunningham photographed him at an early inspection. Brady is the wiry man in dark work clothes, flanked by heftier VIPs. Immediately left of him is C. Edgar Goyette, secretary of the Pima County Board of Social Security and Public Welfare. Once Al Condron's high school buddy in Los Angeles, he had been at the hectic center of local relief efforts since the earliest days of the Depression. Right of Brady is Robert C. Baker, director for the local WPA district. Earlier, as an ERA project engineer, he had planned both the dam at the Woodward site and its access road.[6] At far left is Pima County Supervisor Richard H. Martin, looking as cheerful as might be expected for a man caught in the bitter dispute between the supervisors and the chamber of commerce over the much larger proposed dam four miles upstream.

In the background the men are tending the cement mixer that will shuttle back and forth along the plank runway as the masonry dam rises.

Not long after the inspection Mr. Brady moved on, and Edgar B. Raudebaugh (pronounced RAW-da-baw) took his place as camp superintendent and project supervisor. A lean six-footer and a seasoned outdoorsman, fresh from several years supervising construction on national forests in northern Arizona, Raudebaugh was eight days short of his fifty-sixth birthday—experienced, mature, and well suited to the demanding responsibilities he was taking on.

Edgar Raudebaugh kept a work diary throughout his time with the Forest Service. His Sabino Canyon entries, hastily written, unfussy about spelling, and enlivened by straight talk, give an unvarnished view of life in camp and on the job. (It was he who celebrated the arrival of "rain glorius rain" when the lake in Lower Sabino Canyon was about to fill for the first time.)

The new superintendent dealt with a tricky question on his very first day, July 16, 1937.

> During Noon Meal told men they could have beer in comissary or store as long as they helped take care of each other and mantained order and if they did not coperate in this Beer would be taken away.[7]

Ten days later Raudebaugh delivered paychecks in the morning. "All fine boys having lots of fun," he wrote in his diary, but the mix of money and beer was trouble on a delayed fuse. That evening there was gambling. One of the men got drunk and started a fight, and Raudebaugh, who lived in town, was forced to return to camp to calm things down.[8]

It wouldn't be the last such incident. The canteen was later closed for a time, and when the operator sought to reopen it Raudebaugh stated his objections in person and in writing to the forest supervisor, Fred Winn. Winn disagreed, but he visited the camp, spoke to its residents, and held a vote. To their credit, the men chose to allow the store but to banish the alcohol. The vote should have been no surprise. A majority of the residents had already petitioned the Pima County Board of Supervisors to deny the canteen a liquor license. Beer, they had written, would be "a detriment to ourselves and a nuisance to the camp."[9]

Despite occasional outbreaks of democracy, Raudebaugh ran the little outpost with a firm hand, and he didn't hesitate to fire troublemakers. Fortunately, most of the time the men got along reasonably well, but living in a desert canyon could be a challenge. The month after Raudebaugh took over, the camp's water supply ran so low that he banned baths and laundry until the situation could be resolved. The men were working eight-hour shifts in August, so the potential consequences to pleasant cohabitation are easy to imagine. The next day he relented: "gave orders of bath every other day if men will not waste water."[10]

When the problem wasn't too little water, it was too much. Late the next winter, in March 1938, Sabino Creek flooded during a rainstorm and took out the pump at the camp's water-supply catchment. Because the camp was sandwiched between two crossings, both submerged, for a day or so there was no way out in either direction. A bit later another pump, farther downstream, turned uncooperative. When a worker tried to start it, the gasoline engine "back fired and Crank knocked out a mans false tuth and broke out 5 teeth."[11]

Regardless of the weather, isolation from the city's varied amenities could take a toll, and it occasionally led to trouble during time off in town. In September 1937 Tucson police swept up a forty-three-year-old camp resident during a raid on "a disorderly house" in Tucson. En route to jail, packed into a police car with seven other men and women, he somehow broke loose and dove to the street. He was recaptured and, after a brief detour to a hospital, he made it to jail, where he was booked on a drunkenness charge.[12]

Incidents like this, and the alcohol-soaked afternoon that had led to tragedy the previous year, could hardly have benefited the camp's reputation, but they were far outweighed by reports of helpful behavior. In May 1936, before Raudebaugh took over at the camp, a woman wandered away from a late-evening picnic and disappeared into the dark. About forty camp residents and a camp dog, Oscar, searched through the night. It was Oscar who found the lost and terrified woman early the next morning, and according to the *Arizona Daily Star*, the heroic canine "got a double portion of breakfast for his good work."[13] Two years later another woman set off alone up the canyon floor in Upper Sabino Canyon. The next day, camp residents noticed her parked car at the end of the road and reported it to the sheriff. Nearly the entire camp then joined a well-publicized search, ending several days later when the woman's body was found floating in a deep pool at the Woodward dam site. A one-armed transient laborer swam out to the body and brought it to shore, earning praise from the undersheriff leading the search.

That tragic event, in July 1938, was the second of three drownings in Sabino Canyon during a ten-week span. Raudebaugh had recorded the first in June, less than two months after the dedication of the dam in Lower Sabino: "Young man drowned in lake about 2 am this morning Sheriff etc out after body. . . . drained lake and found body by 11 am."[14] (We heard about that sad incident in chapter 18.) The third drowning, in August, was in one of the swimming holes created by the crossings in Upper Sabino. It was a camp resident who pulled the body from the pond. Ironically, the same recreational developments that brought new opportunities for fun also created new ways to get hurt. The men of the Sabino Canyon Camp were caught in the middle of this reality, and when needed they stepped up and helped.

Raudebaugh, outdoorsman that he was, took special interest in the canyon's more sport-worthy inhabitants. Soon after the lake filled in early 1938, the *Star* reported that "a flock of 20 wild ducks had alighted on the lake behind the lower Sabino canyon dam, paused in flight northward on the wane of winter"—a "news exclusive" courtesy of the camp superintendent himself. There was pleasure in living amid the changing seasons of Sabino Canyon. One fall day camp residents took a long horseback ride and "saw 12 does 3 Fawns." The following spring they "caught Hela M [Gila monster] and brought him into camp to get picture." Descriptions like these, scattered through the routine work records that crowd the pages of Raudebaugh's diary, hint at the importance of such occasions to Raudebaugh and the hard-working men under his charge.[15]

Fortunately, the camp's occupants had more than ducks, deer, and poisonous lizards to entertain them. From time to time the "show boat" truck rolled into camp, bringing a government-sponsored program of movies and live demonstrations. One Thanksgiving, Forest Service employees treated the men to an extra load of firewood for the holiday. Though the hungry residents of the little camp in Upper Sabino Canyon weren't always thrilled with the grub, there were no complaints that night, according to Mr. Raudebaugh: "Men in camp say swell dinner and all they could eat."[16]

During the entire lifetime of the Sabino Canyon Camp, and indeed through all the New Deal years, the canyon rarely if ever closed completely for construction, so visitors were often to be seen enjoying themselves in the vicinity of work sites. Here a family is wading in a swimming hole in Lower Sabino Canyon while the dam is being built just upstream. The unfinished masonry is visible, as is the wooden scaffold installed to aid the work. The photographer is Charles Cunningham once again and the date is July 16, 1937—by coincidence, the day Edgar Raudebaugh took over at the camp.

By the time Ed Raudebaugh showed up in Sabino Canyon, the camp had spilled down the road nearly to the fourth crossing. During his second month on the job, he had the men install a gasoline tank for the camp's vehicles. The towerlike gas pump is seen here near the first buildings above the crossing. Its presence tells us the photo was taken no earlier than August 1937, but the exact date is unknown, as is the photographer.

Unfortunately, the precious fuel was an irresistible temptation in those lean times. The year after the pump went into operation, the watchman turned in one of his camp-mates for giving away government fuel, and he later had to chase off nonresident gas thieves during the night.

Cline Library, Northern Arizona University

Shortly after the lake in Lower Sabino first filled, the Sabino Canyon Camp began another project. For about a week in February 1938, Edgar Raudebaugh and a small contingent of camp residents traveled almost daily to Tucson to work on a float for the Rodeo Parade. This popular event, held since the mid-1920s, was (and still is) a beloved Tucson institution—a colorful occasion in itself as well as a prelude to the annual rodeo, the Fiesta de los Vaqueros.

On the day of the parade, the simple float, a decorated wagon titled "Bury Your Camp Fire," was driven proudly through downtown Tucson. The men on board, most likely workers from the camp, were dressed to represent the many users of national forests, such as "the hunter, the hiker and the fisher." The entry won the prize for best float in the parade.[17]

Toward the end of May 1939, a visitor to Upper Sabino Canyon climbed 250 feet up a cliff, took off his boots for better purchase, and stepped on a cactus. He was trapped on a ledge for two hours until a man from the Sabino Canyon Camp helped him down. It would be the last of the publicized good deeds by camp residents.

"No work except Cleanup & Checkers," Edgar Raudebaugh wrote on the third of June. With the dam and most other projects in Lower Sabino finished, he was running out of things for the men to do. Three days later Raudebaugh was called to Lowell Ranger Station, where he was shown a telegram ordering that the camp be closed at the end of the month. He posted a copy the next morning. "Men in camp very quiet about it," he wrote. Everyone seemed stunned.[18]

By the twenty-third all the men were leaving except the cook. Raudebaugh's diary entry was brief.

Out to Camp to bid gang good by but met last of them going out

Chucked Fritz out and took him to town

Things are a mess[19]

Raudebaugh spent a frustrating week with an inexperienced crew from the city, wrapping up jobs as best he could. On Friday, the last day of June, he dropped by the ranger station and signed one final government form. Then he "told men at office So Long and called it a day." With that laconic entry, the era of New Deal construction in Sabino Canyon came quietly to an end.[20]

It had all happened in a rush: from the day the CCC boys had begun molding adobe bricks for Lowell Ranger Station to the moment Edgar Raudebaugh walked out its door for the last time, fewer than six years had passed. ∎

Edgar Raudebaugh

Born in Kansas in 1881, Edgar Black Raudebaugh was destined for a vigorous life in the outdoors, despite ill health in his youth. According to family legend, he became a crack shot with a rifle when he was bedridden as a teenager and his brothers set up a target outside his window. Unfortunately, not everyone was as skilled with firearms as he. In his early twenties he came to northern Arizona, where he worked as a carpenter until his employer's son accidentally shot him in the leg at the Grand Canyon. He cast away his crutches within a week, but he would forever carry a .25-caliber souvenir in his left ankle.

Courtesy Mary Lou Raudebaugh Morrow

Raudebaugh returned to Kansas and married his sweetheart, Abbie Harriett Wright, the next year. By 1911 they were back in northern Arizona with three children, and Ed had found a niche replacing Flagstaff's boardwalks with concrete sidewalks. Tragically, their youngest child, born a few years later, died in a polio epidemic at the age of thirteen.

Ed Raudebaugh remained a well-known Flagstaff cement contractor until the economy unraveled. His construction skills would be his family's meal ticket during the Great Depression. In 1933 the Forest Service hired him as a foreman, and for several years he supervised CCC boys and other relief workers building campgrounds, bridges, cabins, and other improvements in the Coconino and Kaibab National Forests. In 1937, when he came to Tucson to run the Sabino Canyon Camp, he was primed for the job.

Ed returned to Flagstaff not long after leaving Sabino Canyon in 1939. During the war he helped to construct the Navajo Ordnance Depot outside of town, and later served there as a guard. The huge army installation helped lift Flagstaff out of the Depression, and Ed later went into business with his son, building houses for the burgeoning population. He died in retirement in 1962.

Author photograph

After the Sabino Canyon Camp shut down, the buildings, the water tank, and the gas pump were all dismantled and carted away, and the site was thoroughly cleaned up. Today almost nothing remains, but in the nearby streambed, the concrete water catchment can still be spotted by sharp-eyed passersby.

In 2019, eighty years after the camp's closing, a rusted artifact unexpectedly appeared in the channel of Sabino Creek. The robust crankshaft showed it to be part of an automobile engine, eroded out of the slope above the stream, where it seemed to have been dumped to reinforce the bank. Details encoded on the cast iron block helped to identify it as part of a 1934 Stovebolt engine from a Chevrolet pickup—one of the hard-working trucks driven by the hard-working residents of the Sabino Canyon Camp.

CHAPTER 20

Getting There, Great Depression

I n the early summer of 1936, the reimagined Sabino Canyon was still a work in progress, but the modernization of the route to the canyon was complete. The old Rillito crossing—by turns easy, challenging, or terrifying, depending on the water level—had long since become routine and unremarkable thanks to a wooden bridge, and a recently finished WPA paving project had made possible a pleasant, dust-free ride all the way from downtown to the Picnic Grounds.[1] To the people driving their sleek automobiles to Sabino Canyon, the sight of a horse and buggy moving slowly up the road would have seemed as quaint and surprising as it would to us today. The years of the pioneer picnickers were only memories in the minds of a dwindling number of old-timers—and fading photos in family albums.

By 1936 the American economy was well along its own road to recovery (though unemployment was still a nagging problem), and people looking for fun were showing up at Sabino Canyon in unprecedented numbers. The men of the Sabino Canyon Camp were keeping count. In May 1937, the month before they began work on the dam in the lower canyon, they recorded over 18,000 people arriving in over 4,800 cars from all forty-eight states plus the District of Columbia and Mexico. The dedication of the dam in April 1938 boosted Sabino Canyon into the recreational big time. In that year, by Forest Service estimate, 125,000 people descended upon the little canyon in the Santa Catalinas—more than a third the number who visited the Grand Canyon the same year.[2]

The local newspapers gave the canyon's new amenities their enthusiastic endorsement, and many citizens voted positively with their steering wheels, but not everyone was pleased. Ethel Stiffler Carpenter had enjoyed the beauty and challenge of Sabino Canyon many times since becoming acquainted with it in the 1920s as a young University of Arizona faculty member. In March 1938 she and her husband, astronomer Edwin Carpenter, drove out toward nearby Bear Canyon but found automobile access cut off by a property owner below the national forest boundary. There had been too many wild parties, day and night. "Now there's no place left to go, where there's water," she lamented, "except that very public and crowded Sabino Canyon."[3]

No doubt there were others saddened by the changes to Tucson's canyon oasis, but their opinions, too, were mostly voiced in private. Whatever one's feelings about it, there was a brave new Sabino Canyon and no going back. ■

Author's collection

For people on their way to Upper Sabino, the first view into the canyon comes at a high point on the road, just before it begins its descent toward the canyon floor. Many have stopped to take out their cameras at that spot, including, around the end of the Great Depression, a postcard photographer for the L. L. Cook Company of Milwaukee.

The road long predates the 1930s, of course. It shows up in George Roskruge's 1893 map of Pima County, as we've seen (chapter 5), and by the early twentieth century, it was carrying traffic to Sabino Canyon's most popular destination, the Picnic Grounds at Rattlesnake Canyon. The steep stretch in the photo was much steeper then—enough so to cause a problem for automobile drivers on their way home. In those days cars with gravity-fed fuel lines had to be backed up the hill in reverse gear to deliver gas to their engines. By the time of the photograph, the grade had been reduced and the road had been surfaced as far as the Picnic Grounds. Beyond there, perhaps surprisingly, it would remain unpaved until the mid-1950s.

USDA Forest Service, Southwestern Region

In his final days with Coronado National Forest, Edgar Raudebaugh had supervised work on a small trailer campground in Lower Sabino Canyon, just north of the national forest boundary, and before long families were regularly hauling their camping rigs along the roads to Sabino Canyon. Earlier facilities had been designed to serve both picnickers and campers, though picnicking had always been their main use. This later installation, completed during the waning years of the Great Depression, was a dedicated campground, and it would serve that function for more than two decades.[4]

Forest Service employee Bailey F. Kerr took this photo at one of the campsites in early spring 1941. Coats are airing out in the sun, towels are drying on the line, and the campers are enjoying an outdoor meal together—all except for the smallest family member, who seems to be blissfully asleep.

(*following pages*) When the Tucson Chamber of Commerce and the Sunshine Climate Club joined forces in 1936 to publish this map of "Points of Interest of Tucson and Vicinity," the transportation grid had marched eastward from downtown nearly halfway across the Tucson Basin. Sentinel Peak, where Carleton Watkins had unpacked his camera more than a half century earlier, had been rechristened "A Mountain," and the melting adobe ruins of Fort Lowell, though still interesting to see, were no longer a routine stop for picnickers on their way to or from Sabino Canyon.

As the map suggests, many of the major routes in the basin had been paved, including, by July of 1936, Sabino Canyon Road all the way to the entrance to the canyon. But beyond there the map takes a turn into fantasy. The "Sabino Canyon Dam and Recreation Area" isn't the small dam and lake in Lower Sabino Canyon. In 1936 those had yet even to be proposed. Instead it represents the ambitious development at the old Woodward dam site, an idea that was still being pushed by the chamber of commerce and studied by the WPA. The map was designed to promote tourism and growth, and the prominent lake was one of its most tempting features. No matter that it didn't exist—the chamber of commerce was determined that someday it would.

Better grounded in reality is the "Mt. Lemmon Road," which is shown accurately as "under construction." (It would be completed about fifteen years later.) By 1936 a link between the big dam and the future highway had been proposed, and if that had ever materialized, the narrow road up Sabino Canyon would have become a very busy route indeed.

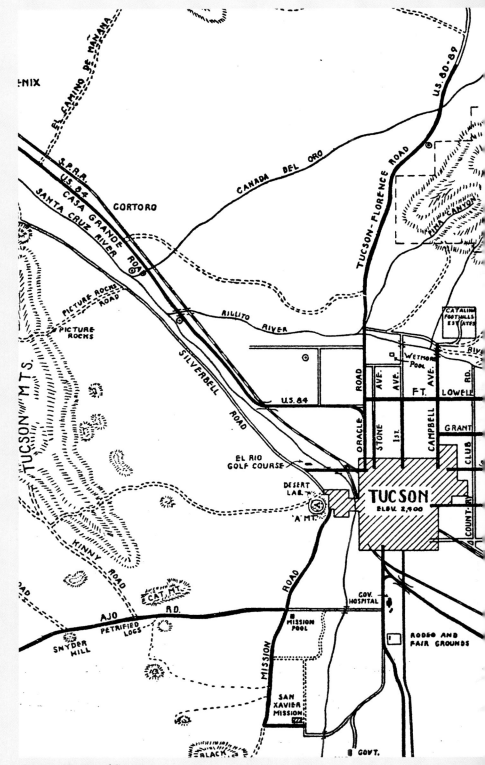

Arizona Historical Society

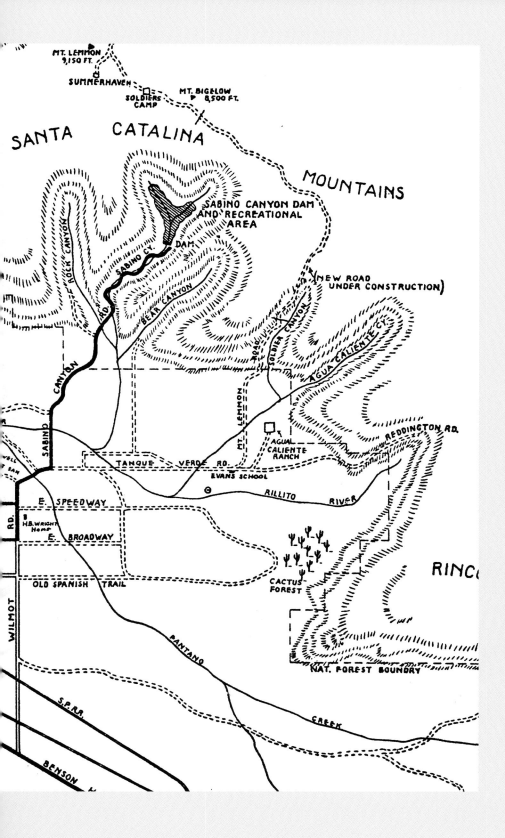

MT. LEMMON
9,150 FT.

SUMMERHAVEN
SOLDIERS
CAMP
MT. BIGELOW
8,500 FT.

SANTA CATALINA MOUNTAINS

ROCK CANYON

SABINO CANYON DAM
AND RECREATIONAL
AREA

SABINO CY. DAM

SABINO CY. RD.

BEAR CANYON

(NEW ROAD
UNDER CONSTRUCTION)

SOLDIER CANYON ROAD

AGUA CALIENTE CY.

CANYON

MT. LEMMON RD.

REDDINGTON RD.

SABINO RD.

WELL
SAN

TANQUE VERDE RD.

AGUA
CALIENTE
RANCH

EVANS SCHOOL

RILLITO RIVER

E. SPEEDWAY

H.B. WRIGHT
Home

E. BROADWAY

RINCO

OLD SPANISH TRAIL

CACTUS
FOREST

WILMOT RD.

PANTANO

NAT. FOREST BOUNDRY

S.P.R.R.

CREEK

BENSON

Tucson Daily Citizen

PART IV
Growing Pains and Pleasures
1940–1985

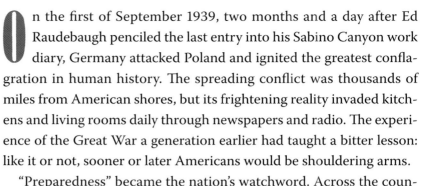

On the first of September 1939, two months and a day after Ed
Raudebaugh penciled the last entry into his Sabino Canyon work
diary, Germany attacked Poland and ignited the greatest confla-
gration in human history. The spreading conflict was thousands of
miles from American shores, but its frightening reality invaded kitch-
ens and living rooms daily through newspapers and radio. The experience of the Great War a generation earlier had taught a bitter lesson:
like it or not, sooner or later Americans would be shouldering arms.

"Preparedness" became the nation's watchword. Across the country, men toughened by service in the CCC put on U.S. Army uniforms, factories rolled out tanks instead of automobiles, and new air-
planes were riveted together by the thousands. At Tucson the army
took over the municipal airport, Davis-Monthan Field, and soldiers
poured in for training. The American war machine was already in
gear when Japan attacked Pearl Harbor in 1941, plunging the United
States directly into the conflict.

The battles overseas were horrific, but the military's need for men
at last solved the stubborn problem of unemployment and provided
the final push needed to free the country from the Great Depression.
Inspired by Rosie the Riveter, women stepped into traditionally male
industrial roles—at least temporarily. Ironically, men and women
with welcome cash in their pockets were forced to carry ration books,
too, thanks to shortages caused by the shift to military production.

If the First World War had barely made itself felt in Sabino Canyon,
the second was a different story. Visits dropped by about a third the
year after Pearl Harbor, then, defying expectation, began to recover.
"The lure of Sabino canyon apparently is stronger than the government's appeal for conservation of gasoline and rubber," observed a
Coronado National Forest official.[1] In fact, the crowds kept coming
partly because of those very federal restrictions. Tucsonans were driving to the nearby canyon rather than expending more gas and tire
tread by traveling farther afield. The law abiding among them were
taking their time getting there, too, observing the wartime speed limit
of 35 miles per hour.[2]

Those who had known Sabino Canyon before the war couldn't help
but notice a new kind of visitor there. Adding to the usual small col-

Defense was the focus of the Red Cross float in Tucson's 1941 Rodeo Parade, about nine months before Pearl Harbor.

lections of family and friends were large groups of soldiers and war workers—often showing up on their own, but occasionally accompanied by young women called junior hostesses in outings organized by the United Services Organizations (USO). In its small way, Sabino Canyon was making a contribution to the war effort.

After the dual triumphs of V-E Day and V-J Day in 1945, the canyon quietly returned to its prewar routines of fun and picnics. Then, a few years later, a tragic event briefly put Sabino Canyon in the public eye nationwide. ∎

CHAPTER 21

Incident at the Old Dam Site

On an August Sunday in 1948, Guy Rockefeller dropped off his fifteen-year-old son, Guy Jr., along with six friends from George Roskruge Junior High, at the third stream crossing in Upper Sabino Canyon. He left the boys ample provisions for a picnic, then departed for Tucson, planning to return in the evening to drive everyone home.

It was a warm afternoon and Sabino Creek was flowing nicely, filled by monsoon rains. Adventure beckoned. After their meal the boys began working their way up the canyon. About three quarters of a mile beyond the last crossing, the canyon's walls drew closer together and its floor became choked with gigantic boulders. Despite the difficulty—or perhaps because of it—the teenagers pushed on. After another three quarters of a mile, the walls suddenly steepened and closed in further. The boys had reached the narrows that had caught the imagination of Professor Sherman Woodward a half century earlier. By 1948 it had come to be called the "old dam site," as it sometimes is today.

Blocking the entrance to the gorge was a wide and deep pool, shimmering between the stone walls. Seeing there was no way to continue up the canyon floor on foot, six of the boys stripped down and went in for a swim. The seventh, Guy Rockefeller, decided instead to bypass the pool by climbing the imposing cliff to its left. It took about a half hour for him to appreciate the seriousness of his mistake. By then Guy was well past the pool where his friends were swimming, and he was perched on a narrow ledge high above the stream. He could go no farther. Having dislodged footholds on the way up, neither could he return the way he had come. This time he made a sensible choice: he stayed put.

Guy shouted down to his friends. Though they could barely make out his voice over the rush of the creek through the gorge, his predicament was unmistakable. After an anxious discussion, one of the boys took off down the rugged canyon for help. He reached Lowell Ranger Station shortly after sunset and phoned the Pima County Sheriff.

It was well after dark when several deputies reached the old dam site. There they were joined by Guy Rockefeller Sr., who had showed up in Sabino Canyon that evening, as promised. The men agreed that it would be too dangerous to attempt a rescue before morning. Above them, the ledge where Guy Jr. was trapped was so narrow he couldn't safely lie down. Frightened and cold, he sat through the night with his feet dangling over the edge, the ceaseless noise of the stream far below him, and every so often the voices of the deputies and his friends calling out to keep him awake.

At daybreak several of the deputies climbed the slope upstream from the gorge and made their way down the canyon. With difficulty, they reached a point at the top of the cliff, about fifty feet above the trapped teenager. Frustratingly, they could neither see him nor throw him a rope.

Among the deputies on the brink of the precipice was thirty-three-year-old investigator John Dodge Anderson, a good climber despite an artificial lower leg he wore due to a motorcycle accident in his youth. Anderson bravely volunteered to take the rope to the boy. Tying one end around his waist, with his fellow deputies holding on above, he descended until he reached a ledge midway between his fellow rescuers and the boy. Then he untied the rope from himself and dropped the end of it down the cliff.

Guy was still sitting on his ledge when the rope appeared from above. Following shouted instructions, he stood and tied it around his own waist. The men at the top of the cliff began pulling him upward. When he reached Anderson, the deputy climbed on ahead of him, holding the rope in one hand and grasping the rocks with the other. Watching, Guy was terrified. At each step, Anderson needed to use his free hand to position his artificial leg. Then, in a terrible instant, Anderson lost both his footing and his grip on the rope. A witness at the foot of the cliff described what happened next.

> Anderson clutched frantically for the rope for an instant and then started to fall. His body struck three or four ledges on its way down, each time with a sickening thud that sounded above the noise made by the rapids in the creek at that point.

The body struck the last ledge about 75 or 80 feet above the pool and then plunged directly into the water.[1]

All this was out of view of the deputies at the top of the cliff. They imagined they had heard a boulder falling. Only once they had hauled up Guy did they learn the truth.

After plunging into the creek, Anderson's body surfaced once, then disappeared. Reinforcements were called in. Divers and men with grappling hooks worked the creek at the dam site while personnel dispatched from Davis-Monthan Air Force Base searched farther downstream. Nearly seven hours after Anderson had fallen, his body was discovered wedged under rocks in the pool where Guy Rockefeller's friends had been swimming the previous day.

It wasn't the first time death had visited that pool. A decade earlier, in July 1938, the body of Mrs. Lucille Randall had been found there after an intensive search joined by the workers from the Sabino Canyon Camp (chapter 19). Two years after that, in August 1940, the body of an eighteen-year-old man, Ray Dougherty Jr., had been recovered from its dark waters. These two deaths may have resulted from falls, too, but it's impossible to know. Both victims died without witnesses.[2]

The pool is still there, chilly and serene, at the lower end of the gorge. Its part in these incidents has been largely forgotten, as has the deeper role of the dam site in Sabino Canyon's past. Despite the difficulty of access, over the years the site has been visited from time to time by adventurous hikers, many of whom have misinterpreted the Great Western Power Company's unfinished diversion tunnel, just up the canyon. Thanks to this confusion, the lonely water hole, scene of repeated tragedies, is known today by the innocent and misleading name "Miner's Pool."[3] ■

Arizona Daily Star

The witness who vividly described Deputy John Anderson's fall was Sam Levitz, a staff photographer for the *Arizona Daily Star*. He had stayed with the rescuers through the night, and in the morning he had stationed himself in the bottom of the gorge with a clear view of the stranded teenager, Guy Rockefeller. Levitz was photographing the unfolding rescue above him when the unthinkable happened, and he was able to snap the shutter only once as the deputy fell. He didn't know what he had captured until he later developed his film.

The shocking photograph dominated the front page of the *Star* on August 10, 1948, the morning after Anderson's death. It was distributed nationwide by the Associated Press, and it was published in *Life* magazine about two weeks later, with other photos by Mr. Levitz of events surrounding the rescue.[4]

Sam Levitz left the newspaper a few years later to join his family's furniture and appliance business. His popular "direct-to-you" warehouses soon became Tucson fixtures. He died in 2005 at the age of 91.

CHAPTER 22

≡ 🍃 ≡

Keeping Up

After the Second World War, change blew through Tucson like a whirlwind. Soldiers who had trained at Davis-Monthan and other nearby military bases remembered Tucson's warm winters and friendly ways, and many returned to make the city their home. They were participants in a massive immigration into the Southwest, fueled by economic growth and a sunny view of the future. Tucson didn't just expand in the postwar years; it burst its boundaries and spilled across the surrounding desert. In a single decade, the count of Tucson's inhabitants multiplied nearly five times, from fewer than fifty thousand in 1950 to well over two hundred thousand in 1960—a growth unmatched before or since. The city's population boom echoed through Sabino Canyon as seekers of refuge and relaxation showed up in larger and larger numbers.

Meanwhile, the stone-and-cement artifacts so painstakingly installed during the Great Depression were showing their age. An unspoken goal of the miles-long recreational complex conceived by the Tucson Chamber of Commerce had been the taming of Sabino Creek—the transformation of a wild mountain stream into a watercourse thoroughly altered for the convenience of people. The dam at Professor Woodward's site was to have released water at regulated rates to the developments downstream. The nine crossings (check dams) in Upper Sabino Canyon, as well as the extremely popular dam in Lower Sabino, featured gates to further control the flow. The great dam at the top would have protected the many improvements below it, products of years of effort and expense, from destructive flooding. What's more, it would have captured sediments and slowed siltation of the canyon's multiple artificial ponds. The failure to install this key element exposed all the rest to conditions never intended by planners.[1]

In particular, the little lake in Lower Sabino, once the canyon's showpiece, was suffering the inevitable consequences of this failure. It had begun to silt in even before it was dedicated. During the Depression years, residents of the Sabino Canyon Camp had drained it several times to clean it out, but after the camp had closed in 1939, ending this ready source of labor, the lake hadn't been drained again until 1941. The attack on Pearl Harbor had come just a few months later, and during the war years the lake had been dredged just once more, in 1944. After that Sabino Creek had been left to do its relentless work, unimpeded.

Arizona Daily Star

By 1951 the once-popular fishing spot had shrunk to a shallow pond. That spring the Arizona Game and Fish Department sent in men and heavy equipment to dig out the lakebed. Water-logged leaf mold was offered gratis to anyone willing to cart it away, and grateful Tucsonans shoveled the fertile bounty of Sabino Creek into their flowerbeds and vegetable gardens.

The excavation of the lakebed briefly exposed long-hidden features of Sabino Canyon's historical landscape. Notice the bedrock ledge beyond the water, right of center. We saw it in chapter 2. (Look for three barefoot boys and a man in a top hat.) The photographer in 1951 is Thomas R. Ellinwood of the *Arizona Daily Star*.

Arizona Daily Star

Once the dredging was done, the lake was refilled and restocked, this time with trout rather than the bass and bluegill of earlier years—or for that matter the outlaw catfish, smuggled in by fishermen, that had sometimes outnumbered the officially planted species. When fishing resumed on May 5, 1951, anglers sat and stood shoulder to shoulder on the dam in a déjà vu replay of opening day 1939. Compare this photograph, taken by *Star* photographer Bernie Roth, to the strikingly similar one taken on that earlier occasion (chapter 18). Tucson's postwar population explosion was already underway in 1951, and it was making itself felt in Sabino Canyon.[2]

ame and Fish and the Forest Service had granted Sabino Lake a new lease on life, but Sabino Creek wasn't party to the agreement. Less than three years later, on March 23, 1954, the stream overflowed its banks in the most powerful flood since the construction of the USGS streamgage in 1932. Persistent rains were the cause, and the sights and sounds of the storm and the flood were alarming in the extreme. Noises like gunshots, perhaps caused by boulders rolling down the steep slopes, resounded through the upper canyon. In the stone house at the old Picnic Grounds, Sabino Canyon's live-in caretaker, Pierre Early, was kept awake by the crashing during the night. By daylight the installations of the Great Depression—dams, roads, picnic tables, and the rest—were seen to be inundated as never before. Nearly everyone assumed the worst. "Flood Water Ruins Sabino Picnic Area," ran the front-page headline in the *Arizona Daily Star*. "Landslides of house-size boulders obliterated sections of the high road in upper Sabino. In some spots, the two days and nights of rain simply peeled the road off the face of the cliffs. With incredible force, debris-laden flood waters smashed through some of the nine stone and concrete bridges. In low areas, the torrent swept over the road and blasted it into an oblivion of creek-bottom boulders and pits."[3]

But when the water eventually receded, reports of Sabino Canyon's demise proved greatly exaggerated. Sections of road had badly eroded and soil had washed away in the Picnic Grounds, but the stone crossings and the hand-built tables had held firm. Repairs began almost immediately. Within a week and a half, the Forest Service was admitting automobiles as far as the first crossing in Upper Sabino and promising to open the entire canyon by summer.

Sabino Lake was another story, though: it had silted in all over again. It was a lesson not quite learned. The lake would be dredged at least one more time, in 1959, before being abandoned to the elements—this time permanently.

While fishing seemed to be coming to an end in Sabino Canyon, another sport had been revived and was going strong. In 1953, under a Forest Service permit, the Tucson Rod and Gun Club had opened a rifle range north of the entrance. The echo of gunfire, absent since 1919, was back—and with greater insistence than before. It was inescapable every day of the week along the road to Upper Sabino, and when not covered by traffic noise on crowded weekends, it could be heard in the canyon, as well.[4]

Author photograph

Federal prisoners, bussed downhill from a minimum-security camp in the Santa Catalinas, did most of the work of rehabilitating Sabino Canyon after the flood of March 1954. Among them were Mexican nationals serving time for violating American immigration laws. Three such prisoners seem to have signed their work in February 1955.

The prison camp had opened in early 1939 to house convicts constructing the Catalina Highway. When the road was done, they began working with Coronado National Forest on cleanup, maintenance, and construction—a fruitful partnership that would last until the camp's closing in 1967.[5]

Photographic postcards picturing Sabino Canyon in full and natural color began showing up in stores and mailboxes in the early 1950s. This was one of the first. The sunny image shows several people relaxing near Anderson Dam—but we're limited to monochrome reproduction here, so the green trees and the blue sky are for the reader to imagine. Later versions of the card added bright red lettering, "Sabino Canyon," in one corner.

Color itself was nothing new to Sabino Canyon postcards. Many of the most beautiful of Rudolph Rasmessen's cards (chapter 13) were artfully hand tinted. Later, during the 1940s, some cards featured bright (and sometimes garish) hues added in other ways. By then color photography had been practical for decades, but the early processes involved complicated materials, specialized cameras, or both. A breakthrough came during the Great Depression, when easy-to-use color films, including the very popular Kodachrome (used for this postcard), appeared on the market. Color films would eventually take over amateur photography, too, but not until prices dropped during the 1960s and 1970s.

Arizona Daily Star

By the mid-1950s the Second World War was a decade in the past, but a new kind of international conflict, less overtly violent but of even more deadly potential, was underway, with the United States and the Soviet Union as chief antagonists.

On June 15, 1955, the Cold War paid a visit to Sabino Canyon. By order of President Dwight D. Eisenhower, military bases across the country carried out Operation Alert 1955, a rehearsal for defense against thermonuclear attack. Beginning at 9:12 am, when the civil defense alarm sounded over Davis-Monthan Air Force Base, some five thousand civilian dependents, almost all women and children, left their homes, drove out the gate, and proceeded in an orderly caravan to Sabino Canyon. Informed in advance of the drill, mothers had packed sandwiches and sodas, and on that memorable day, in the shadow of an imaginary mushroom cloud, Sabino Canyon hosted the greatest picnic in its history. It was a quasi-military invasion on a scale far surpassing the cadet campouts of earlier in the century. The next morning, the *Arizona Daily Star* featured photographs of the feast and the officials who directed the arriving traffic.[6]

abino Canyon had suffered neglect during World War II, but it was far from alone among American parklands in that respect. After the war problems of aging infrastructure were magnified coast to coast as happily mobile citizens, freed from restrictions on automobile manufacturing, gasoline, and rubber, began driving through park gates in unprecedented numbers. In 1956 the Department of the Interior launched Mission 66, a ten-year effort to update facilities in national parks and monuments in time for the fiftieth anniversary of the National Park Service. Not to be outdone, the Department of Agriculture followed suit the next year with Operation Outdoors, a five-year program to improve facilities in national forests. The stage was set for a Sabino Canyon upgrade, but it might have been no more than a token production if not for the fortuitous availability of local funds and labor.

Several years earlier, in 1951, Coronado National Forest had been so financially strapped that the forest supervisor had been ready to lease Sabino Canyon to Pima County, which had proposed taking it over and charging admission fees. That notion didn't take hold, though, and the following year the forest supervisor announced a different plan—handing off Sabino Canyon to a private concessioner and letting the concessioner charge the fees.

If the supervisor had intended to provoke public outrage, he could hardly have found a better way to do it. The cherished tradition of free access for everyone, rich and poor, to Tucson's most beloved natural retreat seemed suddenly under threat. Fortunately, the county supervisors saved the day by pledging to contribute annually to the canyon's operation, supplementing the Forest Service allotment. "Old Picnicking Spot to Become Pima County's Newest Park," was the celebratory, if misleading, headline in the *Arizona Daily Star*. Coronado National Forest would still be in charge.[7]

That was the local source of funds for Sabino Canyon's postwar upgrade. The source of labor was of course the federal prison camp, whose supervisor had promised that inmates would continue helping out at Sabino Canyon no matter who was running the show.

The burst of building at the canyon during the early decades after the Second World War paralleled the wave of construction that swept across the Tucson Basin, and it would continue well past the planned expiration of Operation Outdoors in 1962. Surprisingly, though, the first project of consequence wasn't in Sabino Canyon.

Arizona Historical Society

Bear Canyon, once the object of intense interest for the Great Western Power Company and its rivals, had long served ordinary Tucsonans as a less-crowded alternative to Sabino Canyon—slightly farther from town but similarly beautiful, and with its own refreshing mountain stream. Like Sabino Canyon, it was a fine place for a picnic, a swim, or other outdoor amusements. In this photographic tableau, arranged on a bank of Bear Creek in 1914, a woman is aiming her rifle at a feathered hat held out by another. (No need for alarm. The hat almost certainly survived.)

Both: Coronado National Forest

By midcentury it had become hard to reach Bear Canyon from outside the National Forest due to intervening private land. In 1957, the first year of Operation Outdoors, Coronado National Forest began planning a new recreation site in Bear Canyon to relieve increasingly troublesome overcrowding in Sabino Canyon. Work began two years later on a short road to the site from Lower Sabino, and in the spring of 1960, the Lower Bear Canyon Picnic Ground opened for public use—a joint project of Coronado National Forest and Pima County. In effect, Bear Canyon had become an extension of Sabino Canyon, and families were soon hauling their ice chests a bit farther to take advantage of the new picnic tables.[8]

In early planning the road was to have been extended beyond the picnic ground and far up Bear Canyon, mirroring the earlier developments in Upper Sabino. Fortunately for hikers, an old pathway was later improved instead—the Bear Canyon Trail, today a very popular route to the photogenic cascade called Seven Falls.

Coronado National Forest

Most later projects were of course in or near Sabino Canyon itself. Many involved simply adding tables and retaining walls to older picnic grounds, but several entirely new sites were created. This one, overlooking Lower Sabino Canyon, was finished in fall 1963. Caretaker Pierre Early, who supervised the prisoners during construction, is at one of the tables, and in the background is what's left of Sabino Lake—already silting in, sprouting a fringe of cattails, and growing a forest of willows after being dredged for the last time a few years earlier.[9]

Notice the style of the picnic table. Unlike Depression-era tables, which had been individually crafted on site, tables emplaced during the postwar years were all alike, assembled from precast concrete parts. These utilitarian objects, Sabino Canyon's version of midcentury-modern furniture, make it easy to recognize picnic installations from the 1950s and 1960s.

Coronado National Forest

On June 13, 1964, Sabino Canyon's postwar upgrade culminated in the official dedication of the Sabino Canyon Visitor Center. By then the center had already been open for several months, but the big event had been delayed to accommodate the crowded schedules of Washington dignitaries. Perhaps two hundred people showed up for the speeches and a military presentation of the colors, while a ceremonial guard of mounted deputies looked on. The pomp suited the historical circumstance: this was only the fourth visitor center to be opened by the Department of Agriculture, and the very first in the Southwest.[10]

Designed and built by local companies, the new center was a compact and efficient building whose architecture looked both to the past and to the future. Dark wooden posts and beams at the entrance evoked Forest Service structures of earlier times, but the materials and simple shape of the building itself reflected contemporary tastes.

USDA Forest Service, Southwestern Region

Despite its name, the Sabino Canyon Visitor Center had a broader purpose—to serve as a center for visitors to the Santa Catalina Mountains and to Coronado National Forest as a whole. People touring the lobby after the dedication ceremony admired a colorful relief map of the Santa Catalinas, and they looked out through floor-to-ceiling windows past Sabino Canyon to the mountains beyond. The center's main exhibits illustrated the array of plant and animal communities that clothe the range from desert foothills to forested summits, complementing signs installed the previous year along the Catalina Highway. It was a coherent plan, drawing on contemporary scientific work in the Santa Catalinas.

Coronado National Forest

With the new visitor center came a small cadre of employees dedicated to informing the public about Sabino Canyon through nature trails, talks, and guided walks. All this encouraged a different way of thinking about the canyon, not only as a venue for the traditional outdoor pastimes of picnicking, hiking, swimming, and fishing, but also as a place to be appreciated for its natural beauty and diversity of life. The new emphasis reflected a growing environmental awareness across the country—a cultural shift that would lead to the signing of the Wilderness Preservation Act the year the visitor center opened, and later to the creation of the Environmental Protection Agency and the passage of the Endangered Species Act.

In this photo the visitor center's chief naturalist, Leland Singer, is drawing attention to desert life in the foothills west of Rattlesnake Canyon—though one member of his audience seems more interested in the person with the camera.

While all this was happening, Tucson's expansion was being reliably propelled by social and economic forces, but civic boosters were making it their business to help it along. Among their best tools for attracting immigrants and tourists was the glossy publicity photo, typically featuring a sunny landscape inhabited by exotic cacti and happy westerners. Sabino Canyon, with its enticing desert stream, offered something extra to the propagandists, but it scarcely mattered—the center of attention seemed always to be either handsome mounted cowboys or shapely Arizona girls.

The two visual clichés, cowpoke and cheesecake, converge in this carefully staged scene in the old Picnic Grounds. Sue Rowton and Bob Tenney are the human models (the horse is anonymous) and the photographer is Robert Riddell of the Sunshine Climate Club. Ironically, this appealing example of the publicist's art depicts a Sabino Canyon that didn't exist and never had.

"HELLER IN PINK TIGHTS"

TECHNICOLOR® • A Paramount Picture

60/52

Paramount Pictures Corporation; author's collection

Sabino Canyon had long been providing settings for moving pictures as well as stills. Most of the films had been period westerns, as we might expect, many firmly in the B-movie category, and the canyon was also showing up in the newer medium of television. The haste with which many of the early films and TV episodes were turned out adds to the fun of watching them today, because the makers didn't always bother to edit out water tanks and picnic tables in the background. (See the filmography at the back of this book.)

The lobby card shown here, originally in color, advertised one of the better efforts, *Heller in Pink Tights*, released in 1960, featuring international stars Sophia Loren and Anthony Quinn. The picture is from a sequence filmed on the ledges below Anderson Dam. Loren, glamorous member of a traveling drama troupe, has bet herself in a poker game and lost to disreputable admirer Steve Forrest. He's about to collect his winnings—discretely off camera, of course—but all will eventually end happily, with Loren and Quinn, the good-hearted leader of the troupe, on the cusp of matrimony.

While Tucson and Sabino Canyon were busily growing, a timeworn idea, so long dormant it might have been taken for dead, unexpectedly stirred. In 1957, the inaugural year for Operation Outdoors, a sportswriter for the *Tucson Daily Citizen* lamented the lack of local fishing holes. "There are some diehard fishermen," he wrote, "who will tell you bluntly that Tucson and its metropolitan population of some 200,000 are 'suckers' for being caught in such a predicament." The ideal solution, in their opinion, would be a dam at Professor Woodward's site.[11]

Despite the instructive history of similar proposals, the Pima County Board of Supervisors, the Arizona Game and Fish Commission, Coronado National Forest, and the Tucson Chamber of Commerce all joined in support. The hoary litany of imagined benefits—water sports, flood control, lucrative concessions, water storage, lakeside camping—was eagerly resurrected. The editors of the *Arizona Daily Star* called for caution. Evaporation from the lake "would amount to wasting a precious natural resource," they wrote.[12] In the end, as in the past, expense was the scheme's undoing. A report prepared for the Arizona Game and Fish Department estimated the cost at nearly $2.5 million and the coalition evaporated, not the water.

Unfortunately for fishermen, by this time the little lake in Lower Sabino was nearing the end of its useful life. Undeterred, in April 1962, the Arizona Game and Fish Department planted rainbow trout in Upper Sabino Canyon instead. The experiment was judged so successful that the department planted more rainbows in Lower Sabino two weeks later. Springtime put-and-take trout fishing became an annual event in Sabino Canyon, until Game and Fish called a halt a few years later. The *Star* explained why.

> Last year traffic in the narrow canyon was something fierce. At one point there were so many cars on the road rangers had to start stopping people at the entrance. It's a wonder someone wasn't killed, if not in an automobile accident, in a squabble over who had the first fishing rights in one of the tiny potholes.[13]

The newspaper gave another reason, too. There were too few places to put the fish. Not only had Sabino Lake mostly silted in, so had all the artificial ponds above the crossings in Upper Sabino. Just a few decades after the Great Depression, the vision of a manmade aquatic paradise along Sabino Creek was buried under sand.[14] ∎

Courtesy Donald and Betty Early

On the tenth of August 1966, Sabino Creek overflowed its banks again in a deluge even more powerful than the one that had inundated the canyon in 1954. The violent current tore up pavement, yanked stones from the crossings, and demolished a three-year-old nature trail at the old Picnic Grounds. A month later a second flood set back the repairs. No one could know it then, but the floods of the 1950s and 1960s marked the beginning of a trend. The relatively well-behaved stream of the Depression years, when federal relief agencies could build with confidence on the canyon floor, was starting to change its character. Scenes like this would be repeated multiple times in the coming decades—and with increasing destruction.

Caretaker Early took this photo just a few months before his retirement. That's his wife, Hazel, standing just below the second crossing in Upper Sabino. In a moment we'll pay the Early family a visit at their home in the old Picnic Grounds.

Dodging Ecological Bullets

Professor Sherman Woodward's idea, pursued early in the twentieth century by the Great Western Power Company and its rivals, would have drained every drop from Sabino Creek. Except during rare years of extreme rainfall, when water might have overflowed the spillway at the professor's site, the stream below it would have been almost entirely dry. It would have been lined

Author photograph

(*continued*)

(continued)

with the skeletons of dead trees, wildlife would have been devastated, families would have taken their picnic baskets elsewhere, and this book would have been many chapters shorter. When the project failed, Sabino Canyon dodged a bullet.

The canyon dodged another bullet during the Great Depression. Every flood in Sabino Canyon delivers nutrient-bearing sediments, and fresh sandbars, exposed when the water retreats, become important seedbeds for renewed plant life. If the reimagined dam had been built at Woodward's site, stabilizing streamflow, the vegetation on the canyon floor would have become less vigorous, and older, dying trees would have been more slowly replaced. The decline would have unfolded insidiously, over decades. To resist it we might have become locked in a never-ending program of artificial flooding, much like the one now in force on the Colorado River in the Grand Canyon—a tricky proposition at best, given the need to protect Sabino Canyon's historic stonework.[15]

When the notion of the great dam briefly revived in the 1950s, Sabino Canyon dodged a bullet once more, though this time it wasn't a near miss. Since then the old idea has occasionally resurfaced, but the ecological bullets have ceased to fly. In 1978 Congress established the Pusch Ridge Wilderness in the southern Santa Catalina Mountains. The heavily visited lower reaches of Sabino and Bear Canyons were excluded, but the professor's dam site today rests safely within that wilderness—still tempting, perhaps, but protected at last from would-be dam builders, private and public.[16]

CHAPTER 23

Caretakers

Throughout the years of postwar expansion, the face of the Forest Service in Sabino Canyon was the rugged and genial visage of its live-in caretaker, Pierre Early. Everything in Sabino Canyon seemed to be in his bailiwick, and every problem his to solve. Whether you were the parent of a missing toddler, a coed abandoned by her boyfriend, a kid with a kneeful of cactus spines, or a picnic cook who had forgotten the ketchup, it didn't matter—Early was the go-to guy.[1]

As one might suppose, an important part of Pierre Early's work was patrolling, cleaning up, and checking that everything was in good repair. Being out and about made him a familiar figure, and a trusted one as well. It led to many pleasant exchanges with visitors, some of whom became instant friends. It also occasionally landed him in the middle of a fracas. Fortunately, Early was a master at defusing confrontations. Even after many years on the job he was able cheerfully to report, "I haven't been slugged by anyone—yet."[2]

Early was often called upon in moments of crisis, much as residents of the Sabino Canyon Camp had been during the Great Depression (chapter 19). During the monsoon of 1955, a flash flood in Sabino Creek washed downstream two terrified sisters, ages sixteen and twenty-two, when they attempted to cross to a friend stranded on the opposite bank. They reached their friend, but when they tried to get back they became stranded on a small island, surrounded by the torrent. Pierre Early and a sheriff's deputy swam out with a rope and tied it to trees on the island, enabling rescuers to bring the girls safely to shore. Yet the incident wasn't quite over. The older sister had lost her treasured engagement ring, so Early and the deputy returned to the island, found the ring, and rescued it, too.[3]

Early wasn't just witness to Sabino Canyon's postwar construction; he helped make it happen. In 1957, by coincidence the inaugural year for Operation Outdoors, the federal prison camp in the Santa Catalinas began a transition to a facility for youthful offenders. It became Early's job to supervise these young men in upgrading the canyon's picnic areas and creating new ones. Early insisted on high standards—he was known to kick over fresh stonework that wasn't good enough—but he had compassion for the youths under his charge, and he taught them more than construction skills. After their release some showed up at his home in Sabino Canyon to thank him for helping set them straight.

Over the years Pierre Early came to know the canyon and its visitors as few have, before or since, and he noticed things that others missed. In 1962, while looking over a new group picnic area in Lower Sabino, he came across a handful of rifle and revolver shells, marked with dates from 1870 through 1887. Nearby, partly buried in the desert soil, was a brass army telescope, its old lenses still intact. These seemed to be links to a much earlier time, before picnic tables or caretakers, when the mouth of Sabino Canyon had been an annex of the Fort Lowell Military Reservation (chapter 1). Had soldiers practiced their shooting skills in Sabino Canyon? Had they used the scope to spot bullet holes in a target? Such was the speculation, but no one could say for sure.[4]

Pierre Early retired in 1966 after sixteen years in Sabino Canyon. Clyde Doran, Coronado National Forest's supervisor, summed up the feelings of many. "We'll miss that guy," he said. It was an understatement.[5] ■

Courtesy Donald and Betty Early

It was late 1949 or early 1950 when the Early family moved into the stone house at Rattlesnake Canyon. Several caretakers had lived in the tiny building since 1934, when federal relief workers had raised its walls (chapter 15), and a previous resident had enclosed the porch to create more living space. There in the photo is the relocated front door, where visitors might knock at any hour of the day or night. It was the fate of the caretaker to be always on duty, officially or not.

A family member seems to have taken this photograph not long after the Earlys moved in. During their stay a small room was added to the rear, electricity was delivered for the first time, and eventually, as in households everywhere, a television set arrived. Pierre set an antenna in the rocks above the house and it worked fine—except when javelinas chewed up the wire.

Shall we say hello to the family? They won't mind if we drop in unannounced. They're used to that sort of thing.

It looks like they already have a visitor. Hazel Early is relaxing with her husband, Pierre, here in front of the house, and a friend has joined them (at left).[6] As the caretaker's wife, Hazel was a part-time, unpaid, bonus employee. She patched up skinned elbows, sometimes joined Pierre on his routine patrols, and was his invaluable partner in emergencies.

One of Pierre Early's many responsibilities was to watch the weather and to sense when the creek might rise. When high water threatened, he drove through the upper canyon, warned picnickers to leave, then closed a gate to keep anyone else from entering. (The "flood gate" is now gone, but the pillars that once supported it remain, below the first crossing.)

Despite Early's best efforts, motorists were occasionally trapped when flood waters submerged the crossings. If he could, Pierre ferried them out in a high-clearance truck, and Hazel warmed the storm-soaked refugees with hot soup.

Courtesy Donald and Betty Early

Here's Mr. Early again, with his ever-present cowboy hat, relaxing next to the house in 1952. A writer for the *Arizona Daily Star* would later describe him as "a short wiry man with a friendly twinkle in his eyes."[7]

Pierre Early had a special affinity for children. Sometimes, with their parents' permission, youngsters camped out in the canyon. He didn't mind when the parents phoned, asking for a status report, and he cheerfully risked the consequences when the kids offered a sample of their outdoor cuisine. "You'd be surprised," he said, "by the outlandish hamburgers and potatoes I've eaten when invited to join them for a meal."[8]

Would you like to meet Pierre and Hazel's daughter? She's just around the back.

Courtesy Donald and Betty Early

Pierre and Hazel Early had four children. Three sons were already grown by the time the family came to Sabino Canyon, and only Karen became a Sabino Canyon resident. Karen was about six years old when the family moved into the stone house. She grew up with Sabino Canyon as her front yard.

Wild creatures, from lizards to bobcats, were part of Karen's everyday world. She loved seeing the deer and javelina that wandered through the canyon and the ringtail that hung around the house in the evening. For a while, with the approval of the Arizona Game and Fish Department, the family cared for a pair of whitetail fawns. One failed to thrive but the other did well. It made itself at home, hopping up on the couch and stealing grapes from the kitchen table.

Over the years the family kept several pets, including the dachshunds in the photo, but Karen's favorite animal, by far, was the one we're about to meet.

Courtesy Donald and Betty Early

This is Karen's horse, Sabino. He's in a playful mood. Sabino enjoys it when hikers (or photographers) stop by his corral to chat, but smokers need to watch out: given the chance, Sabino will snatch a pack of cigarettes from a shirt pocket. He likes the taste of tobacco.

Karen's horse brings to mind an old story about the naming of Sabino Canyon. The word "sabino" is sometimes used to describe a horse with a particular pattern of white markings, especially on the face, legs, and belly. Might the canyon have been named for a sabino horse that once grazed there? Some have suggested so, though the notion is likely no more than speculation based on a coincidence of words.

Karen's horse wasn't a sabino. Her father named it for where it lived—and thereby created a neat historical twist. While Sabino Canyon was probably not named after a horse that once lived there, a horse that once lived there was named after Sabino Canyon.

Courtesy Donald and Betty Early

Pierre Early, who loved horses himself, was the one who usually took care of Sabino, but it was understood that Sabino belonged to Karen. The fondest dream of many girls then and now, to have a horse of their own, came true for Karen Early. When she was quite young, she rode Sabino only under her father's supervision, and Pierre himself rode the horse up and down the canyon for exercise. Later, Sabino was Karen's mount in Tucson's Rodeo Parade, and by the time she was a teenager, she was taking long rides by herself, wherever she wished, on the trails in Sabino Canyon and in Bear Canyon.

The two photos of Karen were taken in the early 1950s by journalist Edwin M. Hunt, a University of Arizona graduate who had returned to Tucson after serving as an air force information specialist in Japan during the Korean War.

Courtesy Donald and Betty Early

In 1964 Karen Early left Sabino Canyon to be married. Pierre retired from the Forest Service two years later, and he and Hazel moved north to raise racehorses near Phoenix. Not long after that, in the early 1970s, the Forest Service dynamited the house. No longer occupied, it had been attracting drunken party-goers and vandals. The old stone stairway is still there today, but of the house itself no more than rubble remains. Karen later revisited the site, and she cried.

One day during Karen's childhood in Sabino Canyon, a family member stood near the foot of the stairway and snapped this photograph. Looking at it in her later years, Karen recalled with pleasure the ever-changing view from her childhood home, past the mesquites in the picnic grounds and up the long canyon toward Thimble Peak—in the bright sun, shadowed by clouds, draped with snow, bathed in warm evening light.

CHAPTER 24

Troubled Times

Numerous complaints are being made against the action of picnic parties who
go to Sabino canyon for the day and throw the remains of their luncheons in the
stream at the canyon, thus polluting the water supply of residents lower down.[1]

It was the spring of 1912 when that report appeared in the *Arizona Daily
Star*. Littering, picnicking's unsavory companion, was an unwelcome visitor
to Sabino Canyon even in the horse-and-buggy days. For many years Forest
Service employees merely issued occasional warnings to those who left their
trash in the canyon, but toward the end of the Great Depression, the growing
numbers of recreationists, drawn to the canyon's many New Deal improvements,
prompted the agency to begin taking offenders to court.

Unfortunately, enforcement of regulations was uneven at best during the
Second World War. A young Katie Lee, who had grown to love Sabino Canyon
during the Depression, found the deterioration so disturbing that the thought of
it still rankled decades later. The well-known singer and environmental activist
described it for *The Journal of Arizona History*.

How clearly I remember the sight, the shock, and the anger that followed, the day
I brought two Shavetails from Davis Monthan Airbase to the canyon for a swim,
to find our ledges near the bridge and the sandy bottom of the pool strewn with
glass and broken beer bottles. Drunk or sober, *how could anyone be that stupid,
careless, thoughtless, downright evil.*[2]

The editors of the *Arizona Daily Star* expressed similar outrage a few years after the war.

> There is hardly a place around one of the camping spots but what is littered with broken glass from beer or soft drink bottles which have been emptied and then tossed against a rock. In order for some out sized mental infant to enjoy the tinkle of breaking glass on stone, all actual children who visit the canyon for the remainder of the summer will either have to wear shoes or risk being cut by glass.[3]

Sabino Canyon wasn't alone. The situation was similar elsewhere in the nation's parks and forests.

Coronado National Forest

In 1951 a Forest Service cameraman set up his gear in Lower Sabino Canyon for a film production called *Forest Manners*. Caretaker Pierre Early played himself, performing what was all too often his real-life role: cleaning up after careless picnickers. The scene in this still photograph was staged but realistic, except for a leg of the movie camera's tripod, intruding into the frame at far right.

Notice the rock at left. Before there were manmade tables in Sabino Canyon, picnickers often sought out large, flat stones to serve the same purpose. Clara Fish and her friends spread their meal across that very rock a half century before this photo was taken (chapter 2). Did they take the remnants home in their carriage, or toss them into the creek?

Entered as second-class matter,
Post Office. Tucson, Arizona.

TUCSON, ARIZONA, MONDAY MORNING, APRIL 26, 1954

Saturday Night Party Clutters up Picnic Area

Assistant ranger William Hughes points to the wide-spread litter of beer cans, cartons, and party litter left by an estimated 100 persons who partied in the Sabino Canyon picnic area late last night after sheriff's deputies had locked the entrance gates. It took a maintenance crew more than an hour to clean up for Sunday picnickers. "It must have been a whale of a party," Hughes sighed. (Wong-Sutton photo)

Arizona Daily Star

Life regularly imitated the filmmaker's art in later years, and it could make the 1951 production seem tame by comparison. During a Saturday night in April 1954, an unidentified collection of beer-soaked party-goers so thoroughly trashed an area in Lower Sabino that the aftermath made the front page of the *Star*. In the photograph Forest Service employee William Hughes is seen surveying the mess, but it was Pierre Early who led the cleanup, as usual.[4]

Something had changed since Katie Lee's infuriating experience a decade or so earlier. The broken bottle had given way to the empty beer can, and it was no accident. Beer cans had been introduced to America during the Great Depression, after the repeal of Prohibition, but they had disappeared from store shelves during the war, to save metal for the military. By 1948 they were back, and on this morning in 1954, Early's crew picked up nearly three hundred of them.

If we had to choose an icon for Sabino Canyon during the 1950s and 1960s, it wouldn't be a cottonwood or Thimble Peak. It would be a beer can. In early 1959 a travel editor for the *San Francisco Chronicle* spent a week in the Tucson area as a guest of the Sunshine Climate Club. Among her impressions: "Frankly, I was shocked over all the beer cans in Sabino Canyon. And you can quote me." The *Arizona Daily Star* obliged.[5]

A few weeks later, a group of young people calling themselves University of Arizona students asked caretaker Early for directions to the local Forest Service dump. Suspecting nothing, he pointed them in the right direction. The next morning a truckload of beer cans, pilfered from the dump and neatly bagged, appeared at a roadside in Sabino Canyon. As if that weren't odd enough, by the end of the following day, the cans had mysteriously returned to the dump. "Someone did a lot of work getting those things in and out of here," said Early. "I still don't know why!"[6]

In 1962 a *Star* staff writer summed up Sabino Canyon's astonishing "beer can blight" with some telling questions: "Remember the last time you went to Sabino Canyon? Take a moment to recall what it looked like. What stands out most in your mind's eye? The dam? The stream? The cliffs rising above the tree-lined valley? Or the beer cans?"[7] The *Tucson Daily Citizen* called it "Slobbovia in Sabino."[8]

Coronado National Forest

Appeals to the better nature of visitors had limited effect. Editorials and letters in the newspapers decried the litter problem and implored picnickers to mend their ways, but not everyone took it seriously. In the spring of 1962, a statue of "Big Litterbug," the endearingly sinister emblem of a national antilittering campaign, was bugnapped from near the caretaker's home. Eight weeks later, acting on an anonymous tip, the University of Arizona police recovered it from a fraternity house. According to the *Citizen*, the oversized insect "showed some of the wear and tear of being a fraternity brother." Plans were to replace its missing nose, repair its dented cheek, and return it to duty—a monument to the art of plastic surgery.[9]

I f trash occasionally showed a comic side in Sabino Canyon, traffic was nothing but trouble. On busy weekends the luxuriously enlarged cars of the fifties and sixties rumbled up and down the canyon, trailing exhaust and jamming the narrow roads. People parked wherever they could and some entertained (or irritated) everyone within earshot by turning up their car radios full blast. Frustrated motorists leaned on their horns in disputes over the right of way. Engines overheated; drivers, even more. Accidents were inevitable.

The narrow stone crossings were especially hazardous. During the spring of 1955, in two incidents less than three weeks apart, motorists intending to cross the creek ended up in it instead. In May 1963 a driver just entering the fifth crossing was startled to find himself closing fast with a car coming from the opposite direction. Instinctively he veered to one side, but then the laws of motion took over. His sedan ricocheted off one curb, rolled over the other, and landed upside down in the stream with only its wheels above water. Fortunately, he was able to crawl out a window and go for help. Unfortunately, when he returned twenty minutes later, three tires had been stolen.[10]

Theft, in fact, was another perennial problem at Sabino Canyon—though tires were unusual loot. Wallets, purses, and other things of value, left unattended in the numerous parked cars, were the favored targets, and the perpetrators were seldom caught. A rare exception occurred in 1957. After a series of auto break-ins, deputies baited a car with a movie camera, a portable radio, and other tempting items, then sat back and watched. When the expected occurred, the deputies radioed fellow officers, who were waiting at the entrance to nab the thieves as they drove out. The stolen objects had been dusted with an invisible, moisture-sensitive powder, and the miscreants, three teenage boys, were caught "purple-handed."[11]

Arizona Historical Society

Coronado National Forest

Fortunately, Sabino Canyon wasn't always a host for automotive chaos. This peaceful scene captures an uncrowded canyon, most likely within a decade after the war's end. A lone, late-1940s Dodge is safely negotiating the fifth crossing—by coincidence the same crossing where years later another car would take an unplanned detour into the creek. A leisurely drive through the canyon had become a popular pastime after the roads had been improved and lengthened during the Great Depression. The trick was to avoid weekends—holiday weekends above all. If you timed it right, you just might be able to motor clear to the end of the road in Upper Sabino without seeing another soul.

Notice the cattails bordering the pond above the crossing—a sign that it's silting in.

Of course, rather than taking nonstop drives to admire the scenery, many more motorists set the brakes and stepped out of their cars. The photographer for this 1958 picture seems to have been driven to the Picnic Grounds in the two-tone Chevrolet with the space-age tail fins—a Forest Service vehicle, judging by an insignia barely visible on the original print. As the shutter snaps, a boy is about to jump into the creek from the same ledge where Muriel Upham posed in 1904, playfully waving a stick after a long ride from town in a horse-drawn carriage (chapter 10). Sabino Canyon had changed during the intervening half century, and the experience of visiting it had changed even more.

Despite the serious nuisances of trash, traffic, and petty thieves, the venerable tradition of the Sabino Canyon picnic, shared among family and friends, flourished during the early postwar years. The plentiful tables near Rattlesnake Canyon and in Lower Sabino Canyon were prime picnic territory, but there were a few tables farther up the canyon as well, and two families have found an inviting one here, in the cool shade of an oak tree near the seventh crossing. Soda pop, ketchup, thermos, ice chest, parents chatting, kids on the loose—it could be last week, but Forest Service photographer Bluford W. Muir snapped this picture in June 1959.

If days at Sabino Canyon belonged to everyone, of every age, nights increasingly belonged to the youth, and the scene could be freewheeling, destructive, exhilarating, dangerous—or all these at once. By the early 1960s the situation was nearly out of control, but some liked it that way. Writer Charles Bowden later described the thrill of driving up the wide-open canyon after dark.

> We'd hit the bridges with a yell. Cars would be parked here and there as we went up the road. People would be down along the creek drinking and partying. If the night was warm, they might dive into one of the water holes.
>
> We'd leave a trail of beer cans bouncing off the pavement as we climbed. Our cigarettes hit the road with a red smack and then flashed a star of embers. It was good to be alive drinking and smoking and pitching empties into Sabino Canyon. There was nothing out there at night. No cops. Just kids. Sabino was no hassle. You could howl at the moon and nobody cared.[12]

Unfortunately, some of the revelers did more than scatter cigarette butts and beer cans. Rocks and walls were spray-painted with graffiti. Branches were torn off trees, doors ripped off restrooms, wooden signs broken up—to fuel bonfires or just for the wild rush of destruction itself. It took determination to demolish the old hand-built picnic tables, two of which met their end on Halloween night 1963, as reported by the *Arizona Daily Star*.

> The vandals used auto jacks to break the table tops, each weighing over 1,000 pounds, from their foundations. The concrete benches were loosened the same way except the vandals smashed the reinforced steel concrete over rocks and then dragged them onto the road to form a barricade. At least one car is believed to have struck the concrete during the dark hours.[13]

Dark hours. The newspaper's words were well chosen. So were these: "Some of the vandalism there has exceeded the bounds of belief."[14]

On Christmas Eve 1963, following the focused destruction on Halloween, vandals tossed rocks through a picture window at the rear of the Sabino Canyon Visitor Center. The building had been completed several months earlier and was still awaiting its first exhibits. The disheartening incident capped what may have been Sabino Canyon's peak year for vandalism.

Coronado National Forest

A distressing type of agency photograph becomes significant in Sabino Canyon's visual record during the early postwar decades. To the many photos showing construction of recreational improvements are added images showing their destruction by vandals. This is the second in a series of at least forty, all taken more or less at once in 1963, documenting willful damage to and defacement of both manmade structures and natural features. Here the top of one of the original, Depression-era tables has been torn from its pedestals and dropped upside down at left, and one of the bench tops has been wrenched free as well. Rather than repairing this badly damaged picnic set, Forest Service personnel substituted a prefabricated unit like those being installed elsewhere at the time. The replacement is still in use today.

Coronado National Forest

Of the many varieties of vandalism revealed when the sun rose after a raucous night in Sabino Canyon, incidents of graffiti were perhaps most common. A Forest Service employee stood in the bed of a pickup to snap this photo of an exasperated coworker near a newly decorated wall at the end of the road in Upper Sabino. Black-and-white photography fails to do justice to the brightly painted words, including this pithy expression of car culture: "T-BIRD SUCKS CANAL WATER."

Many years later the entire structure would be demolished by a flow of mud and rocks during a summer rainstorm, permanently removing one canvas for spray-painted commentary.

With or without picnic benches repurposed as barricades, Sabino Canyon
could be a dangerous place to drive after dark. You never knew what you
might run into. One night in 1957, a peculiar-looking vehicle tore through
the canyon at breakneck speed with a sheriff's deputy in hot pursuit. The chase
ended when the deputy blocked the car's exit from Upper Sabino. The driver
turned out to be a seventeen-year-old boy, and the automobile a 1948 Ford.
Or so it had been, once. The *Citizen* described it this way: "Body removed, no
windshield, steering wheel sawed in half, no floor boards, no speedometer, no
fenders, no hood, no registration. The seat was attached to the frame with bolts,
the gas tank with bailing [*sic*] wire."[15] The vehicle, such as it was, was impounded
and its driver cited.

The narrow stone crossings in Upper Sabino were even trickier to negotiate
by headlights than by the light of day, but the most dangerous stretch of road
was farther up the canyon. Youthful drivers seem to have made it a practice to
show off by driving fast down the high, winding pavement below the road's end,
occasionally with disastrous results.

On a night in late April 1963, a nineteen-year-old boy lost control of a small
sports car on a curve below the end of the road. The car skidded off the pavement, fell about 150 feet down the slope below, and landed against a tree just
above Sabino Creek. The driver, thrown from the car during its downward
plunge, crawled back up to the road, where he was encountered by a pair of air-
men from Davis-Monthan Air Force Base. Hearing the boy's desperate words,
"Car down in the canyon . . . girl down there," the men left him in the care of
teenage passersby and drove to the caretaker's house for help. Sheriff's deputies
later found a semiconscious seventeen-year-old girl near the car. Both passenger
and driver survived.[16]

Less than a week later, amazingly, it happened again. A freshman from the
University of Arizona sped down the same stretch of road in his Volvo, a wheel
went over the edge, and the sedan rolled side over side down the slope. Two passengers in the back seat, a female university student and her boyfriend, remained
in the vehicle and survived. The driver was thrown from the car and pinned
under it in the creek. He later died of his injuries.[17]

For young couples in Sabino Canyon at night, it could be more dangerous to park than to drive. A frightening scenario played out repeatedly over several years. On three occasions, in 1959, 1961, and 1962, a couple in a parked car was confronted during the early hours of the morning by a pair of men and the woman was sexually assaulted.

This alarming series of events culminated in a startlingly violent incident on January 11, 1964. That night, twenty-year-old friends William Bailey and Karen Boettcher were parked at the end-of-road turnaround in Upper Sabino, innocently laughing and talking. Bill was at the steering wheel, Karen in the passenger's seat. At about 10:00 p.m., a second car pulled up with its driver's window next to theirs. The intruder then leveled a high-powered rifle at Bill and ordered the couple out of the car. Bill quickly rolled up his window and pushed Karen downward, out of harm's way. At that moment the gun discharged. The bullet shattered the window, passed through Bill's body, killing him, and lodged above Karen in the passenger's door.

Karen started to flee but the gunman threatened, "If you don't want the same thing he got, get in my car!" She complied. As the vehicle left Sabino Canyon, Karen told herself not to panic. She studied her abductor's face, clothing, and voice, as well as the car's interior. About a half hour after the shooting, they slowed at an intersection, where Karen spotted a highway patrolman and jumped from the moving car. The gunman escaped.[18]

Karen had received only bruises and scrapes, and the information she provided to police eventually helped bring the murderer to justice. Just over two weeks after the incident, a twenty-one-year-old man was arrested in Globe, Arizona. In his confession he described how on the night of the crime he had visited his estranged wife in Tucson, hoping to reconcile. When she had refused, he had gone to Sabino Canyon to "find a woman."[19]

No Clues In Sight On Sabino Slayer

By TOM KASER and
ACE BUSHNELL

Straw - grasping sheriff's detectives today searched vainly for the slightest clue or even a warped motive in the Upper Sabino Canyon slaying Saturday night of a 20-year-old Tucson youth.

They also continued to question the murdered boy's hospitalized girl friend, an eyewitness to the shooting who remained in a near-hysterical state after jumping from the soft-spoken killer's car after a brief abduction.

It was a 1964 version of last January's senseless Rickel Hanson murder under similar circumstances about 12 air miles away at the edge of the Rincon Mountains.

BOTH THE victim's date and her abductor were reported to be total strangers, so investigators i m m e d i a tely speculated that it was the grim work of a twisted mind rather than a man with a logical motive.

Detectives instituted an all-out hunt for suspects meeting

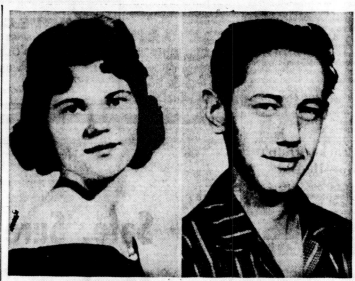

STUDENT AND SLAIN YOUTH

Karen Marie Boettcher, 20, of Coolidge, was abducted Saturday night after her boy friend of three months, William Bruce Bailey, also 20, of 6221 E. Oak St., was shot to death by a black-haired killer in Sabino Canyon. The girl, still in a state of severe shock, escaped from a moving car 17 miles from the remote scene. These photos were taken in 1960 (Bailey) and 1961 (Miss Boettcher).

Arizona Daily Star

After the murder of William Bailey and the abduction of Karen Boettcher, Tucson newspapers followed the case closely. This article, with photographs of the victims, appeared on January 13, 1964, two days after the incident.[20] A suspect was arrested later the same month. He pleaded guilty before going to trial, and on June 11, after calls for mercy by his parents, he was sentenced to life imprisonment for the murder, plus up to thirty-one years for the kidnapping.

The dedication of the Sabino Canyon Visitor Center, two days after the sentencing, was pale news in the wake of these troubling events.

Throughout the early postwar decades, as Tucson's population doubled, then more than doubled again, Sabino Canyon's managers struggled to deal with the sometimes dangerous goings-on after dark. Beginning in 1951, for several years they closed the recreation area to cars at night. It was the first such curfew not only in Sabino Canyon but anywhere in Coronado National Forest, and it worked—so long as the gate held. One after another, four gates were torn down before a more robust model, framed with railroad tracks, was installed in 1953. The headline-grabbing three-hundred-can beer bash the next year happened when the gate was left unsecured because of a missing lock.

It was after that curfew was lifted, around mid-decade, that the plague of automobile accidents and violent crimes began, along with a surge of vandalism. After the shocking murder and abduction in 1964, Forest Service employees began closing Upper Sabino Canyon each night, but this was only a partial remedy, lasting just a few months and leaving the rest of the recreation area still open to cars.

It wasn't until two years after William Bailey's murder that Coronado National Forest was again willing to risk public objection and close the entire canyon overnight, to combat the continuing problems of partying and vandalism. The entrance gate was first locked in the evening of May 9, 1966. As during the 1950s, it was attacked by furious motorists—both those wanting to get in after hours and those wanting to get out after failing to leave in time. But the gate held and so did the closure. At long last, the night's natural quiet returned to Sabino Canyon, this time to stay. ■

Coronado National Forest

The automobile curfew that began in May 1966 brought to a close years of wild nights in Sabino Canyon. Pierre Early and his family had experienced the best and the worst of it, living as they did in the stone house at the old Picnic Grounds. The man at the gate in this Forest Service photograph seems to be the well-respected caretaker himself, wearing his signature cowboy hat. If so, it's one of the last photos of Early in Sabino Canyon. He would resign later that year.

CHAPTER 25

On the Mend

Things were looking up at Sabino Canyon in 1967. Picnic areas had been spruced up and expanded. There was a new visitor center, with a staff of naturalists. Put-and-take fishing, with its epic traffic jams, had ended for good. A car curfew had at last restored serenity to the canyon at night, while during the day the canyon was open for everyone's enjoyment—by midyear fully repaired after the previous summer's record flood.

The improving situation was due in no small part to an evolution in philosophy among Sabino Canyon's managers. A few years earlier, a *Tucson Daily Citizen* reader had made an interesting suggestion: "How about fixing up a place at Sabino Canyon just for swimming with sand on the bottom and a screen upstream to keep out the beer cans and other debris?"[1] There once had been exactly such a swimming pool, of course. It had been created in Lower Sabino during the Great Depression, before the need for a beer-can filter. In replying to the reader's query, Forest Supervisor Clyde Doran cited the needs for lifeguards and sanitation—the same issues that had eventually moved managers to discourage swimming in Sabino Lake. But he went further, according to the *Citizen*.

The Coronado supervisor explains first of all that the national forest service tries, and does, create the wilder, outdoor, more rugged type of developments. They develop areas more for camping, fishing, hunting, hiking, horseback riding and other such activities. They are not in the business of developing recreational facilities along the lines of a city park. They don't create swimming pools . . . and small fry playing equipment.[2]

It was a striking repudiation of the very attractions that had once made Lower Sabino, with its artificial lake, its swings, and its seesaws, by far the most popular place in the canyon.

Another significant change had come to Sabino Canyon as well. On the same momentous day in 1964 that President Lyndon B. Johnson had signed into law the Wilderness Preservation Act, he had also put his signature on the Land and Water Conservation Fund Act, allowing recreation fees in national forests, national parks, and certain other federal areas. The carefree years of free admission to Sabino Canyon came to an end on the first day of July 1965, when the first visitor paid twenty-five cents for the privilege of picnicking.

The new state of affairs never provoked anything like the outpouring of protest triggered by the mere threat of fees during the previous decade (chapter 22). For one thing, few supposed that complaints concerning a single canyon in southeastern Arizona could affect a nationwide policy. For another, it was clear that the funds collected would have real benefits—though not, unfortunately, at Sabino Canyon. Most of the money would go toward acquiring new recreational lands and facilities elsewhere.[3]

No One-Armed Bandit

A Sabino Canyon visitor, Peter Jordan, 2643 E. 20th St., tries out one of three new coin-operated vending machines installed at the popular picnic area yesterday in connection with the U.S. Forest Service fee program. A quarter will get a ticket, good for admission to the recreation site. The Sabino Canyon machines will go into operation this weekend.

—Citizen Photo

Tucson Daily Citizen

By the end of 1965, Tucsonans were dropping quarters into ticket-vending machines in the picnic grounds, as seen in this photo from the *Tucson Daily Citizen*. Incongruous as the gadgets may have appeared, they were an efficient way to collect cash.

At least they seemed so at first. The following January, Coronado National Forest had to send them all back to the factory. The fee was changing from twenty-five cents per picnicker to a dollar per car, and the mechanisms needed to be modified to take a pair of fifty-cent pieces. Unfortunately, at that moment there happened to be a shortage of half-dollar coins, so some hungry picnickers had to drive to the visitor center to buy their tickets before unwrapping their sandwiches.

s the decade's end approached, weekday visitors to Sabino Canyon were still paying a dollar per vehicle to stay and picnic, but nothing at all just to drive on through, enjoying the changing view through their car windows. On weekends, though, every arriving car and truck was being stopped near the entrance while its impatient occupants paid the fee or showed a pass. (A seven-dollar Golden Eagle Passport, good for a year in any national park or forest, was an alternative to daily fees.) The queue of waiting vehicles lengthened while hapless employees, cash and tickets in hand, stood in the road as departing cars raced past a few feet behind them. A tollbooth eventually fixed the safety issue, but not the fee-collection bottleneck.

Even if no longer entirely free, Sabino Canyon was still available to everyone—though not everyone appreciated everyone else. In March 1970 a couple revisiting from out of state was annoyed to find the canyon occupied by "an assortment of hippies, beatniks, long-hairs, creeps and motorcycle thugs."[4] It was the year after Woodstock, and the vigorous counterculture flourishing nationwide, partly in response to the deeply divisive war in Vietnam, was reaching into Sabino Canyon and carrying its controversies with it.

In 1969 a Forest Service employee had come across about ninety "hippies" encamped in Sabino Basin, well beyond the end of the paved road. Some seemed to be involved in spiritual ceremonies; others were sunbathing in the nude. The officer ordered them all to leave—and to take their dogs and goats with them. The next day he returned by helicopter to make sure they were gone. A *Citizen* reader objected.

> Does the Forest Service have nothing better to do than fly up Sabino Canyon ogling the naked girls camped below? . . . Certainly the Forest Service could find better use for one of its expensive helicopters than cruising, at the taxpayers' expense, in search of the unwashed members of our society . . . Has the U.S. Forest Service, in a burst of bureaucratic righteousness, violated the hippies [*sic*] constitutional rights to free assembly and freedom of worship?[5]

Despite the agency's efforts, the little community waxed and waned for years. It was an odd historical first. Its members briefly made real what previously had been only imagined—a mountain resort above Professor Woodward's dam site—and they didn't need a lake to do so.

Public nudity was among the most provocative expressions of the counter-culture, and though it seldom caused serious trouble in Sabino Canyon, events there revealed the depth of the community's ambivalence toward it. In April 1970 a crew showed up in Lower Sabino to record scenes for a low-budget biker film. One of the stars was football quarterback Joe Namath, cashing in on his fame after a Super Bowl victory the previous year. Newly repackaged as an actor, he performed in a nocturnal nude scene on what was by then the forested bed of Sabino Lake. The experience left him unfazed. "Hell, I enjoyed it," he declared afterward.[6] But the very idea of Broadway Joe's performance was enough to prompt a negative review.

> The first sight-seeing trip our family made on arriving in Tucson was Sabino Canyon. . . . We have returned there many times, enjoying each visit. However, now the desire to return has been stunted. This place, we are told, is where "God's gift to women" was unwrapped. On Arizona maps, the name will still appear as Sabino Canyon, but in the minds of Tucsonans, it's Nude Namath's Netherland, consequently, the canyon will suffer from thought-pollution.[7]

Almost exactly a year after the scene in question was committed to celluloid, two men found sunbathing in the nude in Upper Sabino Canyon were arrested and hauled off naked to the Pima County jail. It was evidently their misfortune not to be celebrities.

Tucson Daily Citizen; *author's collection*

Joe Namath, New York Jets quarterback and costar with actress Ann-Margret in the film *C. C. and Company*, obliges *Tucson Daily Citizen* photographer Art Grasberger by taking a spin beneath the willows at Sabino Lake. The movie's working title when it was filmed, *C. C. Ryder and Company*, was a parody of the much-better-remembered *Easy Rider*, which had been released to theaters the previous year.

M eanwhile, surprisingly, there were encouraging signs on Sabino Canyon's litter front. Dealing with the perpetually replenished debris had been an endlessly frustrating task for Forest Service employees, even with the regular help of inmates from the minimum-security prison camp in the Santa Catalinas. After the camp had closed in 1967, the job had become even more difficult—and more expensive. In 1969 Ray Roser, Pierre Early's successor as caretaker, pegged the cost at $10,000 per annum. "It's unbelievable," he said, "but it's a fact."[8] That same year a visitor reported spotting seventy-six beer cans during a one-mile walk in the canyon. He had made similar counts elsewhere, he said, "but, why oh why in Sabino Canyon?"[9]

By the end of 1971, the hard work seemed to be paying off. Pete Cowgill, a popular outdoor columnist for the *Arizona Daily Star*, was one who noticed. After years of litter-related laments in the newspaper, his opening sentence was deliberately startling.

> Sabino Canyon has not been ruined. In fact, during the week when the hoards [*sic*] are working or in school, the canyon is nearly pristine. The only sounds heard are the rushing of water, the rustling of leaves and the songs of birds. . . . Beer cans and pop bottles are nowhere in evidence, and even paper napkins and gum wrappers are scarce.[10]

Cowgill's closing, however, was sobering.

> This is Sabino on a weekday. On a weekend it is a different story. Men and woman swarm like locusts; they bring noise and leave litter. Sabino becomes a Coney Island or a Randolph Park.[11]

Coronado National Forest

A healthy share of the credit for cleaning up Sabino Canyon was due to dedicated Tucsonans, moved to action by pride in their beloved but beleaguered oasis. Women's groups, scout troops, and other community organizations pitched in—so many, in fact, that it was sometimes tricky to coordinate their work. During a single fall day, the Tucson Varmint Callers pulled eight pickup-truck loads of trash from the canyon—two hundred pounds of it from around a single tree—but believed they had left at least that much behind. Despite all the volunteer help, it would be years before the litter problem would be fully under control.

In this photo, most likely taken by a Forest Service employee, members of a University of Arizona fraternity are helping to clean up not only Sabino Canyon but also the well-earned reputation of college students as prolific contributors to the beer-can count.

y this time it had dawned on visitors and managers alike that the fundamental problem at Sabino Canyon might not be too many people; it might be too many automobiles. Two hundred vehicles were being admitted to the canyon at a time, and once that number was reached, others were being turned away at the tollbooth. The pressure on Sabino Canyon's managers to raise the limit was fierce. For Easter 1971 they more than doubled it. A long line of vehicles was waiting when the gate opened at 7:00 a.m. More than thirteen hundred cars made it in that Sunday, and two hundred others were turned away.

A year earlier, in the spring of 1970, Coronado National Forest had let it be known it was weighing a ban on private cars at Sabino Canyon in favor of public transportation—an idea already being considered in certain national parks. Cowgill, at the *Star*, had stated his own position immediately and succinctly: "My vote goes for mass transit. Sabino Canyon is for people, not cars."[12] The seeds of a crucial conversation had been planted, and a series of apparently unrelated events would help them grow and bear fruit.

That summer Sabino Creek overflowed its banks, exceeding even the record deluge of four years earlier. Roads and picnic areas were badly damaged again, and parts of the canyon were closed to cars for more than a month. Some saw the flood not as a disaster but as an opportunity, and they called for an immediate shift to public transportation. Forest officials assured Tucsonans that the change was under study, but still years in the future—that is, if it were feasible at all.

In 1972 Congress declined to renew the national recreation fee program. To the relief of visitors, after seven confusing years of tickets and passes, once again everyone could drive into Sabino Canyon for free. It soon became clear, though, that the program had been an unappreciated ally to the volunteer cleanup brigades. Not only had fees reduced weekend crowding, but they had also lowered the proportion of can tossers and petty vandals in the crowds. The resurgent problems bolstered the idea of eliminating cars altogether.

But in the end it was something quite unexpected that persuaded many Tucsonans to embrace public transportation in Sabino Canyon. On October 1, 1973, Coronado National Forest closed the canyon temporarily to automobiles for long-overdue improvements to the canyon's sanitation system. While workers buried new pipelines and replaced Depression-era stone restrooms, healthy and well-motivated citizens were free to enter the canyon under their own power. For eleven eye-opening and ear-soothing months, they experienced a Sabino Canyon free of automobiles.

It wasn't the Sabino Canyon the pioneer picnickers had known, of course. Over the decades roads, trails, restrooms, picnic tables, and dams—the multiplying accoutrements of a modern recreation area—had infiltrated the landscape. Yet the canyon's natural beauty largely remained, and it was no longer masked by rumbling engines, exhaust fumes, and cluttered parking lots. The wildlife seemed to notice, too, shedding some of its shyness, to the delight of visitors. It was a revelation: Sabino Canyon as it once had been, and as it might be again.

Many visitors were thrilled by the transformation and hoped it would last. Others were outraged to be prevented from driving to their favorite picnic spots. By early 1974 the controversy was spilling onto the pages of Tucson's newspapers. Editors unanimously praised the move to make the automobile ban permanent. Letter-writers, though, were vehemently divided.[13]

> February 16, *Arizona Daily Star*
> Perhaps some of those who take self-satisfaction in such a move have never been in the position of a young mother with three (or maybe 5) preschool children. . . . Even if a shuttle bus would pick them up and then drop them off, would it have room for the extra diapers, blankets, pillows, sweaters, cooking and eating equipment, food, etc. for the family that are usually kept handy in the car?

> February 19, *Tucson Daily Citizen*
> Not only would it make the canyon more serene, but it would help to alleviate some of the problems that the forest service encounters. Auto accidents would be no more. Vandalism, theft and rowdyism would be reduced. Something happens to people when they are denied the sanctuary and anonymity of their automobiles.

> February 22, *Arizona Daily Star*
> How in the hell can these irresponsible and inconsiderate officials expect the elderly, some incapacitated, to walk or bicycle—especially those without bicycles—to reach their favorite area carrying picnic paraphernalia?

March 1, *Tucson Daily Citizen*

I don't think the Sierra Club or the hiking club should dominate. As to the solitude for deer, etc., they are not afraid of people. One hippie couple and a dog will chase deer for miles. . . . So why turn it over to hikers and hippies?

March 4, *Arizona Daily Star*

We don't need to use our cars once inside the park gates. Maybe we're just afraid to be told so.

Tucson Daily Citizen

While arguments raged, people adapted. Visitors undeterred by the closure made their way into Sabino Canyon without the aid of internal-combustion engines. The great swarm of automobiles that had plagued the canyon retreated outside the gate and settled onto roadsides to the north, south, and west.

On some weekends an almost festive spirit prevailed. Adults and kids walked confidently up the road without fear of dangerous automobile traffic. Parents lifted strollers over the gate to bring the youngest children with them. Bicycles became so popular that an enterprising college student began renting them out of the bed of his pickup. Inside the gate, the change was striking. One woman remarked that without cars and motorcycles the canyon seemed to have doubled in size.

P. K. Weis, a staff photographer for the *Tucson Daily Citizen*, snapped these pictures in March 1974.[14]

People boom afoot in Sabino

Bikers and hikers are sampling the sunny skies, clean air and empty roads of Sabino Canyon in ever-increasing numbers since the Coronado National Forest banned cars in October.

College students, families and retirees were in evidence yesterday when more than 750 Tucsonians left their motor vehicles and walked or rode their bicycles more than a mile into the canyon.

"We've had a good cross-section of age groups," said Douglas Salyer, Catalina District ranger.

The canyon was closed to vehicles temporarily to permit construction of a sewer system. But forest officials now are considering a permanent ban on cars.

The only people who seem to be staying home so far are those who drove through the canyon but never got out of their cars, Salyer added.

Although cars are now left at the gates, Sabino Canyon is still open to bicycles, and Salyer said the number of cyclists riding to the canyon has "mushroomed since the closure."

The canyon is a lot cleaner this year too, he noted. Each visitor now can carry in only an arm-load of supplies, limiting the amount of litter that could be left behind, Salyer said. Visitors seem to be more conscious of the canyon's natural beauty now that cars are left outside the gates, and this may encourage them to do a better job of cleaning up, he added.

With less litter and no reckless drivers to warn, the rangers have only one law enforcement problem left — dogs.

All dogs must be on leashes while in the canyon, but many owners have been ignoring warnings, leaving their pets to run wild, Salyer said.

"We're starting to crack down and anyone with a dog better have it on a leash or be prepared to pay a $10 fine," he warned.

Story by Edward Stiles
Photos by P. K. Weis

'Stroller'

Kenny Quail's year-old legs are too rubbery to negotiate the mile into Sabino Canyon, so he got a push (above) from his 4-year-old brother Isaac, sons of Mr. and Mrs. Kenneth Quail, of 8570 E. Vicksburg. At left, John Piri, 5, of 2670 N. Fontana Ave., puffs up the canyon road on his minibicycle. However, most of the canyon visitors are legging it (below) since the canyon was closed to motor vehicles in October.

Tucson Daily Citizen

B y May 1974 Vern Zarlingo, the district ranger responsible for Sabino Canyon, was convinced. "To return to the old transportation system in the canyon—almost unlimited numbers of private cars, trucks and motorcycles—would be disastrous," he declared, and he promised progress in planning over the coming months.[15] With the eventual outcome seemingly a near certainty, the argument's temperature dropped several degrees and public attention turned to unexpected issues brought on by the closure: too many cyclists speeding dangerously down the road in Upper Sabino, and too many pedestrians failing to leash their dogs.

Before the first shuttle could run, there was a multistage federal planning process to be navigated—one that might stretch out for years—but the construction work that had closed Sabino Canyon's gate was wrapped up before the end of the summer. Beginning on Labor Day, September 2, 1974, in what the *Citizen* called "an unhappy compromise," Coronado National Forest reopened parts of the canyon three days a week to private cars.[16] Over the following months, restrictions were relaxed until only the narrow stretch of Upper Sabino Canyon, with its historic stone crossings, remained closed. Two years passed before Forest Service officials announced their expected decision in favor of public transportation, then one more before they issued a permit to a private company for operating a shuttle.[17]

Suddenly, public transportation in Sabino Canyon was nearing reality, and the long-simmering passions surrounding it returned to a boil. By this time memories of the halcyon days of the full closure had lost their freshness. In the spring of 1978, three hundred citizens signed a petition demanding continued access by private cars. The *Tucson Daily Citizen* ran a straw poll in its pages. Of the nearly eight hundred readers who responded, more than two-thirds opposed the shuttle. The editors endorsed the shuttle anyway. The decision, for better or worse, had been made.

The first commercial shuttle carried curious passengers into Upper Sabino Canyon at the start of June 1978. *Citizen* photographer H. Darr Beiser snapped its portrait at the fifth crossing on its way up the canyon. From the start, a shuttle ride was more than transportation. Drivers delivered a live and electronically amplified commentary on the passing scenery—for riders a popular extra, for pedestrians a distraction at best.[18]

By fall the verdict was in. Despite the furious disagreements of the past, nearly everyone liked the shuttle—ninety-nine percent, according to District Ranger Zarlingo. The fares were so cheap, almost anyone could afford the scenic ride into Upper Sabino: eighty-five cents for adults, fifty cents for children, and, in a gesture to those who might find even these amounts a hardship, only forty cents for everyone on Wednesday mornings. It was a promising beginning, but there were no guarantees for the long haul. In December Sabino Creek flooded again, and the shuttle shut down for a month. A year and a half later, the owner abandoned the business, unable to make a profit. Another company took over and more than doubled the fares.

As the 1980s opened, Sabino Canyon was still stuck in the awkward transition between private and public transportation. A large, new entrance parking lot was accommodating visitors riding the shuttle into Upper Sabino, while others continued to drive themselves into Lower Sabino and Bear Canyon. If psychiatrists treated recreation areas, Sabino Canyon might have been diagnosed with a split personality. A refreshing calm reigned in Upper Sabino, where walkers and cyclists shared the road with the shuttle. Lower Sabino, by contrast, remained the epicenter of a vastly different style of outdoor fun. At worst, automobiles of all sorts jammed the parking areas below Sabino Lake, and families were forced to retreat from deafening radios, shouted profanity, drunken fights, and flying bottles. More often, fortunately, the area was crowded but conflict free.

In this laid-back weekend scene in Lower Sabino Canyon, youthful visitors have set a volleyball net in the lake while others are soaking up sunshine on the dam's spillway and the rocks below it. It's late summer 1981, and while a commercial shuttle has been ferrying visitors into Upper Sabino for several years, private cars are still allowed into Lower Sabino—an uncomfortable compromise soon to end, and with it gatherings like this one. Twenty-two years after Sabino Lake was dredged for the last time, it has been reduced to a shallow pond, narrowed by encroaching willow forests on its banks.

Peter Weinberger of the *Tucson Citizen* took this picture and the next, both on the same afternoon.[19]

Tucson Citizen

We've moved farther upstream to just above the lake, where young swimmers are launching themselves into the air from a streamside cliff. Unbeknownst to the daredevils, they are at Calvin Elliott's dam site, long ago the favorite getaway for Sabino Canyon's pioneer picnickers. It's also exactly the same place where a few decades earlier another youngster had been photographed dangling from the cable at the United States Geological Service streamgage (chapter 15). By the time of this photo, both the streamgage and the cable had been removed, but the risk-taking impulse had found a new outlet.[20]

On October, 1, 1981, three years after the Forest Service's decision in favor of the shuttle, the entire recreation area—Upper Sabino Canyon, Lower Sabino Canyon, and Bear Canyon—was finally and permanently closed to private cars. The long-anticipated day, a turning point in Sabino Canyon's history, passed without fuss or fanfare. Tucsonans had been both actors and audience in a long-running civic drama, but most seemed to doze off during the finale.

That afternoon a reporter from the *Citizen* drove out to see what was going on. Not much, as it turned out. In the entrance parking lot, he couldn't help but notice a small group of youthful visitors. "The doors to their pickup were open, the sounds of heavy metal rock 'n' roll blasting neurons at 50 paces," he wrote. Why were these people hanging out at the entrance? The walk to Lower Sabino was too long and the shuttle was too expensive, one of them said. Besides, they complained, "going down without their car stereo would be boring."[21]

Ninety-six years had passed since the pioneer picnickers had begun Tucson's long love affair with Sabino Canyon. An important anniversary was near. ∎

CHAPTER 26

Being There, Late Twentieth Century

T he year 1985 was the centennial for Sabino Canyon's discovery by adventurous townsfolk, but the historical milestone passed unnoticed. Over ten memorable decades, the canyon had evolved from a near wilderness, a long carriage ride from a small western town, into a thoroughly developed recreation area in a bustling city's backyard.

For a privileged few, "backyard" had become more than a metaphor: they could walk out their doors and into Sabino Canyon in a matter of minutes. Tucson's growth had slowed after the early postwar decades but it had never stopped, and by 1985 the advance colonists of suburbia were settling near the boundaries of the Sabino Canyon Recreation Area. Transportation planners sensed the day coming when the old road to Sabino Canyon might need to be widened to four lanes, but the canyon's new neighbors resisted and that never came to pass.

Inside the gate, lovers of Sabino Canyon were still adjusting to the new, car-free reality. The situation was both bright with hope and tinged with loss. There were things people could no longer do. Among these, the pleasure of a leisurely drive through the scenic canyon, in one's own car and on one's own schedule, was especially missed.

Certain other pastimes, while still allowed, had become markedly less convenient. Predictions of the decline of one of Sabino Canyon's most time-honored and cherished experiences—the family picnic—were coming true. It was indeed awkward to carry in everything needed for an elaborate meal, either on the shuttle or on foot. The handcrafted tables from the Great Depression and the prefab furniture of the postwar years, once in such enormous demand, were mostly standing unused. It was a striking change from preshuttle times, when on a spring weekend a family had needed to arrive in their car by midmorning to claim a table for lunch.[1]

Unfortunately, another undeniably popular activity at Sabino Canyon—getting drunk and raising hell—hadn't quite gone the way of the picnic. While it had become a serious chore to carry in hot dogs, lemonade, chips, charcoal, cups, plates, forks, and a tablecloth, it was still an easy task to import a six-pack of beer. Thankfully, empty cans were no longer a defining feature of the landscape, but the perennial problems of litter and vandalism had been only half solved by banishing automobiles. It would take an alcohol ban to bring those under control. That would come, but it was still nearly a decade in the future.

Author photograph

The arrival of the shuttle and the departure of private cars transformed the experience of being in Sabino Canyon. Many people welcomed the change, but some lamented the passing of an era.

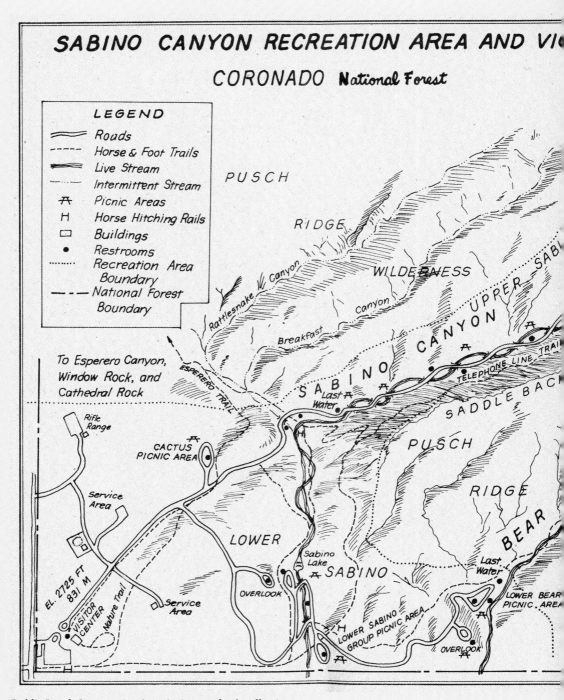

SABINO CANYON RECREATION AREA AND VIC

CORONADO National Forest

LEGEND

Roads	
Horse & Foot Trails	
Live Stream	
Intermittent Stream	
Picnic Areas	
Horse Hitching Rails	
Buildings	
Restrooms	
Recreation Area Boundary	
National Forest Boundary	

PUSCH

RIDGE

WILDERNESS

Rattlesnake Canyon

Breakfast Canyon

To Esperero Canyon,
Window Rock, and
Cathedral Rock

ESPERERO TRAIL

SABINO CANYON

UPPER SAB

TELEPHONE LINE TRAIL

SADDLE BACK

Last Water

Rifle Range

CACTUS PICNIC AREA

Service Area

PUSCH

RIDGE

BEAR

LOWER

Sabino Lake

SABINO

Last Water

LOWER BEAR PICNIC AREA

EL. 2725 FT 831 M

VISITOR CENTER

Nature Trail

Service Area

OVERLOOK

Lower Sabino Group Picnic Area

OVERLOOK

Public Lands Interpretive Association; author's collection

MT. LEMMON
El. 9152 FT - 2790 M
20 Miles - 32 Km.

MT. BIGELOW
El. 8550 FT - 2606 M
18 Miles - 29 Km.

To Sabino Basin,
Palisades Admin. Site,
Mt. Bigelow, Romero
Pass, Marshall Gulch,
and Mt. Lemmon

EL. 3334 FT
1016 M

THIMBLE PEAK
EL. 5323 FT
1622 M

To Sycamore
Basin and
Sabino Basin

Seven
Falls

N

FOREST SERVICE
U S
DEPARTMENT OF AGRICULTURE

W — — E

S

RNESS

1/2   1
Miles
        1   2
meters

P. Eisenberg

In 1985 a new map appeared in a brochure at the Sabino Canyon Visitor Center.[2] Drawn by Tucson artist Patricia Eisenberg, it's an information-packed snapshot of the canyon during its centennial year.

Little on the map recalls the years before the Great Depression. Calvin Elliott's dam site, where pioneer picnickers parked their carriages, is unmarked and long forgotten. Not even the old Picnic Grounds at Rattlesnake Canyon, setting of so many outings early in the twentieth century, rate a label. Only the Phoneline Trail is shown, though by 1985 almost no one remembers the ambitious company that created it.

The legacy of the Great Depression, though, is everywhere—especially the never-finished road in Upper Sabino, with its iconic stream crossings, and the tangle of roads in Lower Sabino. Sabino Lake (what's left of it) is named, but Lowell Ranger Station, east of the visitor center, has been demoted to "Service Area."

Overlaid on all these are the products of postwar expansion—the rifle range and the picnic grounds at Cactus, the two Overlooks, and in Bear Canyon. The visitor center is still there, too, though mostly converted to office space a few years earlier—a painful consequence of federal budget cutting. Fortunately, able volunteers have taken over its educational efforts.

Embracing the Sabino Canyon Recreation Area since 1978 is the Pusch Ridge Wilderness, in which Professor Woodward's dam site sits north of the map, off-limits to hydraulic engineers. Just south of the boundary, and also off the map, new housing developments are pressing against the fence.

The map barely hints at the epochal change a few years before it was drawn. The road into Sabino Canyon, traveled by generations of visitors, has been cut near the entrance, and some are boarding the shuttle for a ride into the canyon.

While some once-popular activities of earlier times were on their way out by 1985, certain others were newly coming into their own. Many visitors to Sabino Canyon seemed to have rediscovered their own feet. Hikers and walkers made their way up and down the roads, while runners raced past them, pounding the pavement. Across the nation, fitness had become fashionable, and Sabino Canyon was gaining a reputation as a prime venue for outdoor exercise.

Bicycling was still enjoying the uphill climb in popularity begun when the canyon had closed for upgrades in 1973. Much had changed, of course, since Professor G. E. P. Smith's intimate encounter with chollas during his bike ride to Sabino Canyon, early in the century. Cyclists in 1985 approached the entrance along a cactus-free route, and once in the canyon they pedaled at high speed along pavement cleared of traffic jams. Unfortunately, sharing the roads with slower hikers and shuttles led inevitably to conflicts and collisions, and toward the end of the year, District Ranger Steve Plevel closed the canyon entirely to bicycles. The closure was only temporary, but it would take more time to reach a compromise acceptable to Sabino Canyon's cyclists.

Meanwhile, the Sabino Canyon shuttle, originally conceived as a convenient and affordable alternative to private cars, was undergoing a metamorphosis. With its narration by the driver, it was no longer considered simply transportation; it was increasingly viewed as a recreational ride to be experienced for its own sake, especially by tourists. Fares were rising accordingly, with no end in sight, and some people were feeling the pinch. A few years earlier, an *Arizona Daily Star* reader had worried that Sabino Canyon was becoming "the preserve of the wealthy."[3] By mid-1985 adults were paying four dollars each to ride the shuttle into Upper Sabino—nearly quintuple the original fare.[4]

Author photograph

The New Deal had left Sabino Canyon with a road to nowhere, but for thousands of visitors every year, "nowhere" seemed the perfect destination. Families and small groups of friends regularly took advantage of the broad pavement, walking side by side, chatting while taking in the sights. It was a relaxed, shared experience quite different from hiking the trails.

Author photographs

By the 1980s the pools above the historic stone crossings were mostly filled with sand. As a result, Sabino Creek sometimes spilled across the roadway even at times of moderate flow, adding to the pleasures of a walk—or a dash—through Sabino Canyon.

Author photographs

Flood-borne sediments had transformed Sabino Lake, once a broad body of water filled with swimmers or ringed by anglers, into a narrow pond bordered by a forest of willows. The lush and shady environment had become a nationally known hot spot for birders. Below the pond, the falls at the spillway were a favorite destination for families with children.

Author photograph

There had been many changes at Sabino Canyon over the decades; generations of people had come and gone, but some things had remained the same. The combination of warm days, cool water, and polished stone was as irresistible as it always had been—and will be as long as the sun shines and the creek flows.

A year before Sabino Canyon's unmarked centennial, Coronado National Forest had updated the many regulations that had accumulated at the canyon since the creation of the Santa Catalina Forest Reserve. The new "special order" read like a review of Sabino Canyon's many problems over the years. Private cars topped the list of prohibited items. Katie Lee's despised glass containers were there, too, and so were pets and public nudity. Guns could be fired only at the shooting range. The native wildlife was not to be harassed, harmed, or removed. Not quite two decades after the last squirming trout had been dropped into the creek, all introductions of animals and plants were forbidden.[5] The reformulated rules were the latest chapter in a long story, one that had been well underway during Sabino Canyon's Depression-era transformation.

On April 2, 1938, the small dam in Lower Sabino Canyon had been finished and the lake had filled, but the official dedication was still more than a week away. Ed Raudebaugh, supervisor of the WPA workers' camp, paid a routine visit to Lower Sabino, where the men were getting ready for the big day. He found a few youngsters there, and his work diary tells what happened.

> Boy scouts out having a good time. Men took Fish hooks away from them and cautioned them about fishing in lake also I asked them not to throw rocks in wading pool.[6]

Before there was a lake for wading and swimming, kids could toss stones into the creek wherever they liked and no one cared. Before the lake was stocked with fish, there was no way to break rules for catching them. Developing Sabino Canyon for recreation multiplied the ways in which recreationists might transgress. The hidden cost of a new facility was often a small contraction of a visitor's freedom.[7]

As the years had passed, visitors to Sabino Canyon had accepted much greater restrictions on their freedom to do what they pleased. They had, for a time, lost the right to enjoy a picnic without paying a fee. They had surrendered the choice to drive their own cars into the canyon at any time of day or night. By 1985 they also had been forbidden to camp, to hunt or fish, to skinny-dip, to drink from a glass bottle, to walk their dogs, or to release their unwanted pets. If some people resented these constraints, that was hardly surprising.

And yet, remarkably, what most people seemed to feel most deeply in Sabino Canyon wasn't a loss of freedom. It was a gain in possibility. After years of crowding and conflict, it was possible to stroll along a historic road without dodging modern automobiles. It was possible to enjoy a canyon wren's song without an accompaniment of car radios. It was possible for a child to wade in the creek and feel only sand between her toes, not broken glass. It was as though, by relinquishing a bit of their own freedom, people had freed Sabino Canyon to be itself. One had only to sit a moment near the creek, take a breath, open one's eyes, and listen to know it was a fair trade. Most would call it a bargain.

Tucsonans were renewing their century-long love affair with Sabino Canyon, even if they had forgotten the anniversary. No matter. Perhaps after the next hundred years they would remember to celebrate. ■

Author photograph

Author photograph

CHAPTER 27

=== ◆ ===

Before We Go

That's it. We've come to the end of this century-long story. But, as generations of visitors have discovered, Sabino Canyon can be a very hard place to leave. What's the hurry? Shall we stay just a few minutes longer?

Before we go, let's enjoy one last look at the time-honored tradition of the Sabino Canyon picnic—how it has changed and how it has stayed delightfully the same. We'll reconnect with a few recent acquaintances along the way. ■

This wonderful picture is the earliest known dated photograph of a picnic in Sabino Canyon. It's June 11, 1890, and several pioneer picnickers are sharing an afternoon meal just where we'd expect: at Calvin Elliott's dam site, Sabino Canyon's informal first picnic ground. We met this hardy group in chapter 2, among the boulders a few miles farther up the canyon. Did they work up an appetite during their explorations? No picnic cloth here, but notice the basket, the jug, the teakettle, the cups and saucers, and the rifle—standard equipment for early picnics in the canyon. Watch how these props change over the years.

That's the eminent surveyor George Roskruge seated at right, with three of his assistants at Elliott's dam site in about 1899. They were posing with their technical instruments when we met them in chapter 4—all but the man standing in the center, whom we're seeing here for the first time. Notice the wooden equipment case in the foreground. That's probably where the photographer was sitting before he got up to take the picture. If there's a rifle, it's outside the frame, but cups, saucers, and teakettle are all here again, and a picnic cloth has been added to the kit. No sense roughing it any more than necessary.

Arizona Historical Society

Arizona Historical Society

It's about 1907, and the action has shifted a half mile upstream to the Picnic Grounds, the fashionable destination for outings after the turn of the century. Unlike Roskruge and his crew, this impeccably dressed group has nothing to do but enjoy themselves. We first saw them in chapter 6, lounging at Professor Woodward's streamgage. The woman offering a plate was about to startle the horses with a gunshot when we ran into her again in chapter 11. Other photographs suggest that some of these people have come from other states. No surprise there—Sabino Canyon has long been high on the list of places for Tucsonans to take out-of-town visitors.

The photographer is probably the talented Gaius Upham. A label on the print places this pleasant scene in the Santa Rita Mountains, but we know better.

Another polite meal has been served a little farther up the canyon, where the sand makes for especially comfortable alfresco dining. We can name several of the picnickers this time: at left, Mary Estill with her brother, Edward; at right, seated back to back, Mary's parents, Ella and John Estill; and at the rear, her face in shadow but with light reflected in her eyeglasses, John's sister, Alice Estill. We last saw Mary, Ella, and Alice in chapter 18, on a ledge where the dam in Lower Sabino would eventually be built.

It's no later than 1912. How can we tell? The professor's streamgage was demolished by a flood during the summer of that year, and we can spot the instrument cabinet in the background.

Arizona Historical Society

The abundance of cloche hats places this cheerful gathering in the 1920s—early 1930s at the latest. We're just yards away from the previous picnic. This attractive area, near what was then the far end of the road in the Picnic Grounds, was one of the best loved spots in Sabino Canyon in the early twentieth century.

Before the canyon was closed to private cars, many picnics there were scheduled affairs hosted by employers, civic organizations, and social clubs, and that seems to be what's going on here. This well-organized group has brought with it not only several communal jugs but even a few stools for comfort. But we seem to have arrived late. The abandoned picnic cloths and the woman with the dishes suggest the meal has ended, and it's now time for picture taking. The box cameras at left may yet be put to use.

USDA Forest Service, Southwestern Region

No one is too young for a picnic in Sabino Canyon.

Now we're in Lower Sabino in the spring of 1938, shortly after the dedication of Sabino Lake, and there's no longer any need to bring one's own furniture: government-issue tables have appeared. This time we've arrived early. A small family has claimed a table south of the dam and, judging by another picture taken the same day, others will later join them. The photographer isn't another family member, though. It's Forest Service employee Charles Cunningham, several of whose fine snapshots we've seen in earlier chapters.

This particular table had been installed the previous year by workers from the Sabino Canyon Camp. It's still there in the twenty-first century, little the worse for wear, and visited yearly by many children on educational field trips.

USDA Forest Service, Southwestern Region

Old-style picnicking, with the ground as one's table, didn't end with the arrival of furniture. This family has spread its meal across a boulder just below Anderson Dam in Upper Sabino—an area made conveniently accessible by the road and stone crossings finished a few years earlier. Notice the iconic bottles—unbroken, and may they stay that way. Recall the elegant folk dining in Sabino Canyon at the dawn of the century, then consider the bathing suits here. Picnic dress can't get much more informal than this.

Forest Service employee Bailey F. Kerr snapped this photo in March 1941, about eight months before the United States entered World War II. Although little remains of Anderson Dam today, the nearby rocks are still choice spots for sunbathing, swimming, and, of course, picnicking.

National Archives

We'll end our good-bye tour in 1959, at the height of Sabino Canyon's golden age of picnicking during the early postwar decades. It's only fitting that we've returned to the historic Picnic Grounds at Rattlesnake Canyon, where this happy bunch has squeezed onto the benches of one of the very first concrete tables to be installed at Sabino Canyon—during the winter of 1933–34 by employees of the CWA. Starr Jenkins, a Forest Service photographer and writer, snapped this picture on a cool January day in 1959.

We've arrived at just the right moment. The fixings are on the table. The plates are ready. It's time to eat. Can you smell the braised chicken? Is that Perry Como on the radio?

Epilogue

The rising sun is brushing the tips of nearby saguaros when a woman pulls into the parking lot at the Sabino Canyon Visitor Center, hangs a Senior Pass from her rearview mirror, and steps from her car, grateful to be able to avoid the entry fee. It's a cool, clear December morning, early in the twenty-first century. The visitor center has sprouted a new exhibits wing, but it isn't her destination. She's a Sabino Canyon regular and she's here for her daily walk.

As she starts up the road toward Upper Sabino, she hears little but her own footsteps, the companionable voices of other walkers, and the questioning notes of phainopeplas, calling from the mesquites. ("What? What?") The noise of gunfire has been banished by the closure of the shooting range, and the quiet is something she treasures.

Before long the road begins its steep descent into Sabino Canyon, and she moves from the brightening sunlight into the gray shade of the canyon walls. A cyclist passes by, pedaling slowly uphill. He needs to be off the road before the first shuttle run, but he'll reach the entrance with plenty of time to spare.

At the foot of the slope, the broad, shadowed floor of Sabino Canyon spreads out below the pavement. The tall trees, though in fall foliage, are subdued in color, lit dimly by the sky. Had Calvin Elliott built his dam back in the 1880s, all this would now be underwater. Instead, there's a sound resembling distant applause: the rush of Sabino Creek, invigorated by autumn rains. The stream's boulder-strewn channel has come into view. Increasingly violent floods have eroded its banks in recent decades, widening its channel. Paradoxically, the creek has also been dry for longer and longer stretches of the year. Climate change is writing its signature on Sabino Creek as clearly as on a receding glacier in the arctic.

Now the road descends again, this time onto the broad terrace near Rattlesnake Canyon, and the temperature drops. The woman zips up her jacket. She has waded into the river of cold air that drained down the canyon overnight. Far ahead and high above, Thimble Peak is brightly rimmed by sunlight. Nearby, hidden among the dark mesquites, are the tables crafted during the Great Depression. The old Picnic Grounds, once Sabino Canyon's recreational metropolis, are this morning as still as a ghost town.

The woman rounds a corner and comes to a halt. She has reached the first of the nine stone stream crossings, and its downcurved center is under several inches of water. Unsure whether to proceed, she takes in the scene while she considers.

The old structure wears its age well. It seems little changed since the day it was finished, more than eight decades earlier, but it has been altered in subtle ways. Floods have repeatedly knocked out the "dragon's teeth" lining the roadway, and only periodic dental work has preserved its aging smile.

Another walker, wearing the uniform of the Santa Catalina Volunteer Patrol, has arrived at the crossing. The two chat while he unties his shoes. In these times of fickle federal budgets, volunteers are essential partners to the Forest Service. Later this morning, a yellow bus will pull into Lower Sabino. The Friends of Sabino Canyon will help pay the driver, and the Sabino Canyon Volunteer Naturalists will lead fifty eager children on a field trip.

Shoes in hand, the volunteer steps gingerly through the icy water. Watching this, the woman decides. The miles of canyon beyond the crossing are tempting; wet feet on a cold morning are not. It's time to head back.

When she again passes Rattlesnake Canyon, the sun is just rising above the canyon walls, and its angled light is streaking the stone stairway that once led to the caretaker's house. Farther up the road, two women are approaching, in lively conversation, pushing strollers. The small passengers, bundled up and wide-eyed, are in training to join the next generation of Sabino Canyon regulars.

As she walks, the woman unzips her jacket. She has climbed out of the canyon's chilly exhalation and into the welcome warmth of the morning sun. Ahead, the pavement leads steeply upward, out of the canyon.

She stops, transfixed. Sunlight is spilling over the ridge onto the canyon floor. The autumn trees, earlier so modestly in shadow, are now aglow. Before she leaves, she has one more thing to do.

She pulls a phone from her pocket and holds it up. On the glass is an image of a place she loves. It's bright, focused, colorful, and right side up. It fills the screen. This beautiful canyon, once nearly invisible to Tucsonans, is to her as familiar and welcoming as an old friend. She taps the glass.

Carleton Watkins would be astonished. ■

Acknowledgments

The author is grateful to the many skilled and dedicated archivists who assisted him in his research: at the Arizona Historical Society in Tucson, Lisa Aguilera, Russ Andaloro, Rachael Black, Alexandria Caster, Sandy Chan, Kate Fitzpatrick, Mary Flynn, Kim Frontz, Laura Hoff, Valerie Kittell, Caitlin Lampman, Griselda Loreto, Carlos Lozano, Jill McCleary, Perri Pyle, Robert Orser, Katherine Reeve, Christine Seliga, Nancy Siner, Kate Stewart, Rebekah Tabah, David Tackenberg, Alexa Tulk, Erin Wahl, and Lizeth Zepeda; at Special Collections, University of Arizona Libraries, Mona Ammon, Patricia Ballesteros, Bob Diaz, Scott Cossel, Libby Funk, Carrie Larson, Cleo Marmion, Michelle Monroe-Menjugas, Mina Parish, Elizabeth Perumala, and Charles Wommack; at the Cline Library, Northern Arizona University, Peter Runge, Cindy Summers, and Jess Vogelsang; at the Bancroft Library, University of California, Berkeley, Susan Snyder; at the Oklahoma Historical Society, Mallory Covington; at the Wisconsin Historical Society, Lisa Marine; at the Arizona State Library, Archives and Public Records, Wendy Goen and Julie Hoff; and at the National Archives in Washington and in College Park, Arthur House, Andrew Knight, Holly Reed, and Carla Simms.

Many others were generous with their help: at the office of the Pima County Recorder, Veronica Galley, Vanessa Grimaldo, and Kevin Lopez; at the Desert Laboratory in Tucson (USGS), Diane Boyer, Ray Turner, and Robert Webb; with the Forest Service (USDA), Jeff Klas, Sheila Poole, and Rod Replogle at the Southwestern Regional Office, as well as Sarah Davis, Bill Gillespie, and Kathy Makansi at Coronado National Forest. Special thanks to Anne Harrison, who served as a naturalist at the Sabino Canyon Visitor Center during its early years, for her wonderful reminiscences; and to my former colleague at the Santa Catalina Ranger District, Bob Barnacastle, for introducing me to Sabino Canyon on my first day of work there in January 1977 and for his insights and his friendship ever since.

Many thanks as well to historians Constance Altshuler, David Faust, and Kieran McCarty; to Bobbie Jo Buel, Jill Jorden Spitz, and Rick Wiley at the Arizona Daily Star; to Michelle Gullett at Lee Enterprises; to Amanda Keith at the Public Lands Interpretive Association; to Robert Cronan of Lucidity Information Design; to Larry McCallister at Paramount Pictures; to Terry DeWald of the Friends of Sabino Canyon; to Sabino Canyon Volunteer Naturalists Phil Bentley, Dan Granger, Bill Kaufman, Brian Mathie, and Lindy Sheehy; to Bob Stewart of the Tucson Rodeo Committee; to antique auto aficionados Ernie Adams, Jim Hulse, Dave Parker, and Floyd Perrin; to Christopher Frasher, grandson of photographer Burton Frasher; to the good people at the University of Arizona Press, especially Kathryn Conrad, Alana Enriquez, Mari Herreras, Amanda Krause, Leigh McDonald, Abby Mogollón, Sara Thaxton, and Elizabeth Wilder; to copyeditor Amy K. Maddox; to Fred and Ann Boice, Tom Dudley, Paul LaFrance, Katie Lee, John Madden, Ed Ronstadt, and Peg Weber; and to Steve Phillips, who has offered valuable help and advice throughout the life of this project.

It was my great privilege to learn from individuals with strong family ties to Sabino Canyon's past: John T. and Mary Knagge, concerning the storied burro train early in the twentieth century; Mary Lou Morrow and Ray Raudebaugh, grandchildren of the WPA camp's director during the Great Depression; and Donald and Betty Early, Tom Early, and Karen Hans, descendants of Pierre Early, Sabino Canyon's caretaker during the early years after the Second World War.

Finally, I'm deeply grateful to four people without whose continued support this project might not have come to fruition: to Bill Mueller, Member Emeritus of the Sabino Canyon Volunteer Naturalists, whose generosity made possible years of research into this fascinating canyon, including travel to distant archives and the acquisition of many illustrations; to Joe Wilder, former director of the University of Arizona's Southwest Center; to Allyson Carter, extraordinarily patient senior editor at the University of Arizona Press; and, above all, to my wife, Cherie, cherished companion in discovery over these many years.

My heartfelt thanks to all. ■

Timeline

1880   Southern Pacific Railroad track under construction, reaches Tucson from California

1883   Calvin A. Elliott files claim to waters of Sabino Creek

1884   Elliott and associates form Sabino Cañon Water Company, plan to dam Sabino Creek near canyon mouth for irrigation and municipal water supply

1885   "Discovery" of Sabino Canyon as a recreational retreat for Tucsonans; Elliott's dam site rapidly gains popularity

        University of Arizona established by state legislature (classes will begin 1891)

1886   Elliott's dam site annexed to Fort Lowell Military Reservation for post's water supply (both Elliott and army will later abandon plans for Sabino Creek)

1887   Earthquake centered in northern Mexico causes rockfalls and wildfires in Santa Catalina Mountains; effects in Sabino Canyon uncertain

1891   Fort Lowell closed and vacated by army

1892   Charles P. Sykes and associates establish mining claims at Sabino Canyon

1893   George W. Roskruge publishes *Official Map of Pima County*, first generally available map identifying Sabino Canyon by name

1895   Sabino Gold Mining Company incorporated by Sykes and associates (claims will never be developed)

1898   Spanish-American War; American forces, including Theodore Roosevelt's Rough Riders, fight in Cuba

1901   Sherman M. Woodward, University of Arizona professor, leads survey of new dam site four miles above canyon mouth

        T. Roosevelt assumes presidency after assassination of William McKinley

1902   T. Roosevelt creates Santa Catalina Forest Reserve by presidential proclamation; reserve to be managed by USDI

1903   Canyon's first streamgage constructed by Professor Woodward and contractor David S. Cochran (will function until 1912)

       First University of Arizona cadet battalion encampment in Sabino Canyon (last will be ca. 1911)

1905   Forest Reserves transferred from USDI to USDA; USDA's Bureau of Forestry renamed Forest Service

       Thomas F. Meagher, supervisor of the Santa Catalina and Santa Rita Forest Reserves, constructs cabin west of canyon mouth; structure will become known as Lowell Ranger Station

       Picnic Grounds at Rattlesnake Canyon identified by name on USGS map; have replaced Elliott's dam site as Sabino Canyon's most-visited area

1906   Great Western Power Company incorporates; plans dams at Woodward's site and in neighboring Bear Canyon for hydroelectric power and water supply

       Sabino Canyon Trail, primary southern route into Santa Catalina Mountains, improved under orders of Supervisor Meagher

1907   Santa Catalina Forest Reserve renamed Santa Catalina National Forest

1908   Santa Catalina National Forest merged with others to create Coronado National Forest

1909   Great Western Power Company receives Forest Service permit for dams in Sabino Canyon and Bear Canyon

1911   Federal Power and Water Company incorporates; first rival to Great Western Power Company

1912   Arizona becomes forty-eighth state

       New trail (later called Plate Rail Trail, Phoneline Trail) opened by Coronado National Forest and Great Western Power Company; supersedes Sabino Canyon Trail as primary southern route into Santa Catalina Mountains

       New State Development Company incorporates; second rival to Great Western Power Company

1913   Great Western Power Company's Forest Service permit expires with dams unbuilt; City of Tucson immediately claims, later relinquishes water rights

New State Development Company, Federal Power and Water Company, and
John W. Daily apply to Forest Service for permits, competing for rights
formerly claimed by Great Western Power Company

1914   World War I begins in Europe

1917   United States enters World War I

Last of the rivals competing to build dams in Sabino Canyon and Bear Canyon
abandons effort; dams remain unbuilt

1918   Armistice effectively ends World War I

1919   Catalina Mountains State Game Preserve established; possession of firearms prohibited without permit, ending legal recreational shooting at Sabino Canyon

1926   Joseph Wittman applies to FPC for permit to build power-generation dam at
Woodward's site (will later amend, adding second dam in Bear Canyon)

1929   Stock market crash; Great Depression begins

1931   Coronado National Forest, Pima County, and Tucson Chamber of Commerce
cooperate in road improvements; first federally funded work relief program
at Sabino Canyon during Great Depression

1932   Canyon's second streamgage installed by USGS at Calvin Elliot's dam site (will
function until 1974)

1933   President Franklin D. Roosevelt inaugurated

CCC (then officially called ECW) and ERA created by legislation during Hundred Days, CWA by executive order later in year

Tucson Chamber of Commerce begins advocacy for large recreational dam at
Woodward's site

CCC enrollees begin work on new Lowell Ranger Station, successor to Supervisor Meagher's 1905 structure

CWA laborers begin improvements at Picnic Grounds near Rattlesnake Canyon, to include Sabino Canyon's first concrete picnic tables; will also restore
parts of Sabino Canyon Trail and possibly construct Anderson Dam (work
will continue into early 1934)

1934   CCC enrollees complete new Lowell Ranger Station

After termination of CWA, CCC enrollees continue improvements at Picnic
Grounds while living in temporary "fly camp" at Sabino Canyon (work will
continue into early 1935)

Wittman's 1926 FPC permit application belatedly denied, clearing way for
recreational dam at Woodward's site

ERA laborers begin constructing road from Picnic Grounds to Woodward's dam site (road will cross Sabino Creek over small stone dams and eventually destroy much of previously restored Sabino Canyon Trail)

1935   WPA created by executive order

ERA laborers cease work in Upper Sabino Canyon, as responsibility for construction in canyon begins shift to WPA; four stream crossings have been completed

ERA establishes camp in Sabino Canyon for transient workers, who temporarily resume roadwork in Upper Sabino Canyon

Tucson Chamber of Commerce erroneously announces final WPA approval of dam construction at Woodward's site

1936   WPA takes over road work in Upper Sabino Canyon; ERA transient camp residents turn to recreational improvements in Lower Sabino Canyon

Wildfire near ERA transient camp; camp residents support firefighting efforts

Camp residents recognized as nontransient citizens, begin receiving WPA wages; transition from ERA to WPA at Sabino Canyon complete

Army Corps of Engineers holds public hearing in Tucson on dam at Woodward's site; road construction in Upper Sabino Canyon has halted a mile short of dam site, with all nine stream crossings completed

1937   Army Corps of Engineers releases report recommending approval of dam at Woodward's site, conditioned upon half-million-dollar contribution by local community

WPA Administrator Harry Hopkins declares that dam at Woodward's site has never received more than preliminary approval; final approval would require new application with promise of large local contribution

Residents of WPA workers' camp begin constructing small recreational dam in Lower Sabino Canyon

Tucson Chamber of Commerce abandons efforts to gain final approval for dam at Woodward's site

1938   Sabino Dam and Lake dedicated in Lower Sabino Canyon

Drowning in Sabino Lake; Coronado National Forest begins discouraging swimming there

1939   Sabino Lake opened to fishing for stocked bass and bluegill

WPA workers' camp closes, ending intensive Depression-era improvements at Sabino Canyon

World War II begins in Europe

1941   Pearl Harbor attacked by Japan; United States enters World War II

1945   Germany and Japan surrender, ending World War II

1948   Deputy Sheriff John D. Anderson dies while rescuing boy at Woodward's dam site

1950   War begins in Korea

1951   Sabino Lake drained and cleaned out for first time since World War II; stocked with trout and reopened for fishing (flood will refill it with sediments in 1954)

       First automobile curfew begins, in response to nocturnal vandalism; entrance gate installed (curfew will end ca. 1955)

1952   Tucson Rod and Gun Club shooting range opens

1953   Armistice effectively ends Korean War

1955   Operation Alert 1955, a Cold War defense exercise, sends military dependents from Davis-Monthan Air Force Base to Sabino Canyon for a day

1957   Operation Outdoors begins five-year upgrade of national forest recreation facilities, including those at Sabino Canyon

1959   Sabino Lake cleaned out for the last time (subsequently allowed to silt in)

1960   Lower Bear Canyon Picnic Area opens, extending recreational developments beyond Sabino Canyon into nearby Bear Canyon

1962   First trout planting for put-and-take fishing in Upper Sabino Canyon (last will be 1965)

1964   Murder of young man and abduction of young woman in Upper Sabino Canyon; temporary automobile curfew follows, lasting several months

       Sabino Canyon Visitor Center dedicated

1965   First American combat troops enter Vietnam

       First recreation fees charged, authorized by Land and Water Conservation Fund Act

       Cactus Picnic Area opens

1966   Permanent automobile curfew begins, covering entire recreation area, to curb drunken partying and vandalism at night

1970   Public shuttle raised as potential solution to problems of daytime traffic and overcrowding; community debate begins concerning possible complete ban of private cars

1972   Recreation fees lifted due to changes in congressional authorization

1973   Temporary closure to private cars begins (day as well as night) for upgrade of sanitary facilities; public debate over possible permanent automobile ban intensifies

1974   Partial daytime reopening to private cars follows completion of sanitary facilities upgrade; closure continues above first crossing in Upper Sabino Canyon

1975   Saigon falls to North Vietnamese forces, ending Vietnam War

1978   Pusch Ridge Wilderness created by congressional legislation; Upper and Lower Sabino Canyon, Lower Bear Canyon excluded

        Commercial shuttle service begins to Upper Sabino Canyon only; Lower Sabino Canyon and Lower Bear Canyon remain open to private cars during day

1981   Shuttle service extended to Lower Sabino Canyon and Lower Bear Canyon; complete and permanent closure to private cars begins

1984   Updated and consolidated regulations prohibit private cars, firearms, glass containers, pets, camping, and nudity, as well as harming, removing, or introducing plants and animals

1985   Unrecognized centennial of the "discovery" of Sabino Canyon as a recreational retreat for Tucsonans

Abbreviations for Federal Agencies

CCC   Civilian Conservation Corps

CWA   Civil Works Administration

ECW   Emergency Conservation Works

ERA   Emergency Relief Administration

FPC   Federal Power Commission

USDA   United States Department of Agriculture

USDI   United States Department of the Interior

USGS   United States Geological Survey

WPA   Works Progress Administration

Arizona Historical Society

Notes

Preface

1. Kieran McCarty, *A Frontier Documentary: Sonora and Tucson, 1821–1848* (Tucson: University of Arizona Press, 1997), 39–40. The author is grateful to the late Father McCarty for lending him a typescript copy of the original Spanish text. McCarty's published translation identifies the place with the saguaro forest as Sabino Canyon.
2. Land claim on the arroya of the Cajon Sabino, P. R. Brady, claimant, recorded March 5, 1867, Land Claims vol. I, pp. 75–77, Pima County Recorder, Tucson.
3. David Wentworth Lazaroff, *Sabino Canyon: The Life of a Southwestern Oasis* (Tucson: University of Arizona Press, 1993), 84. The lower limit of the distribution of the Arizona cypress (*Cupressus arizonica*) along Sabino Creek appears to have retreated upstream due to climate change. The tree pictured in the cited publication has since died, several others have disappeared, and there may no longer be a mature cypress in the Sabino Canyon Recreation Area.
4. "A Day at the Dam," *Arizona Weekly Citizen* (Tucson), December 15, 1883.
5. "Tucson District Not a Desert," *Daily Arizona Miner* (Prescott), September 10, 1867. This article is a republication of an item earlier printed in *Southern Arizonian* (Tucson), exact date unknown.

Prologue

1. Peter E. Palmquist, "It *Is* as Hot as H——: Carleton E. Watkins's Photographic Excursion Through Southern Arizona, 1880," *Journal of Arizona History* 28, no. 4 (Winter 1987): 353–72.

Part I. "Rough and Uncivilized"

1. For a detailed history of the city of Tucson through 1980, see C. L. Sonnichsen's book in the list of further reading.

Chapter 1. Discovery

1. E. A. Carr, Colonel 6th Cavalry, Commanding, Fort Lowell, A. T., to Assistant Adjutant General, Hd Qrs Dept of Arizona, Whipple Barracks, A. T., December 11, 1883; vol. 8, July 1883 to June 1885, pp. 88–89; Letters and Telegrams Sent Ft. Lowell, AZ, 1865–91; Records of Posts 1820–1940; Records of United States Army Continental Commands, 1817–1940, Record Group 393; National Archives Building, Washington, D.C. The newspaper articles to which Colonel Carr referred have been lost, but an earlier announcement, which attracted less attention, has survived: "A New Water Company," *Arizona Weekly Citizen* (Tucson), October 6, 1883.

2. "Arizona," *Arizona Weekly Citizen*, March 15, 1884.

3. Notice of water right, Calvin A. Elliott, claimant, recorded May 17, 1883, Land Claims vol. I, p. 648, Pima County Recorder, Tucson. Sabino Canyon isn't mentioned by name in this first claim, which Elliott called the "Santa Catarina Water Right." Amended notice of water right, C. A. Elliott, claimant, recorded July 17, 1884, Land Claims vol. I, p. 676, Pima County Recorder, Tucson. This second document clarifies that Elliott's earlier claim appropriated "all the water of a certain canyon, now commonly known as Sabina Cañon."

4. For a detailed account of Fort Lowell's struggles with its water supply, see David T. Faust and Kenneth A. Randall, "Life at Post: Fort Lowell, Arizona Territory 1873–1891," *Smoke Signal* 74 (Spring 2002): 85–88.

5. General Orders, No. 30, Headquarters of the Army, Adjutant General's Office, Washington, D.C., May 25, 1886; General Orders 1886, box 39; Index of General Orders and Circulars Adjutant General's Office, 1886; Non-Record Publications; Records of the Adjutant General's Office, 1780s-1917, Record Group 94; National Archives Building, Washington, D.C.

6. "Sabino Canyon Water Co," *Arizona Weekly Citizen*, July 12, 1884.

7. In 1889 the Pima Land and Water Company, an Arizona corporation, received congressional authorization to construct a system of canals, dams, and reservoirs across the Fort Lowell Military Reservation, provided that a portion of the water be delivered to the post for irrigation. (See: *Statutes at Large*, 50th Congress, Session II, Chapter 237, 693–94.) One of the proposed dams was at the mouth of Sabino Canyon, but it was never built. The company seems to have had little or no practical effect on the canyon, though its legal rights became an issue in twentieth-century schemes to dam Sabino Creek. Additional information on the company is given in notes to chapters 5 and 8. Further research is needed to clarify its history.

8. "A Day at the Dam," *Arizona Weekly Citizen*, December 15, 1883.

9. "Aqua Pura," *Arizona Weekly Star* (Tucson), February 7, 1884.

10. "City Summary," *Arizona Daily Star* (Tucson), February 12, 1884.

11. "Local News," *Arizona Daily Citizen* (Tucson), March 4, 1885.

12. "A Day at the Dam," *Arizona Weekly Citizen*, December 15, 1883.

Chapter 2. Pioneer Picknickers

1. "Local News," *Arizona Daily Citizen* (Tucson), May 13, 1885.
2. Harrie Grossman Handler, "Willis P. Haynes: Frontier Photographer" (unpublished manuscript, 1977), Early Arizona Photography Seminar, Department of Art, University of Arizona, MS 1086, Eugenie Potter Research Materials, Arizona Historical Society, Tucson. Bruce Hooper, "Willis Pearson Haynes: Arizona Photographer," *Journal of Arizona History* 33, no. 1 (Spring 1992): 85–98.
3. Miss Hughes appears in another photograph taken on the same outing: AHS 15,647, Subjects—Picnics, PC 1000 Tucson General Photo Collection, Arizona Historical Society, Tucson. By 1898, the labeled date on the photo seen here, she had married a professor at the university but left the faculty herself. We'll meet her husband in chapter 6.
4. Robert H. Forbes, *The Penningtons, Pioneers of Early Arizona: A Historical Sketch* (Tucson: Arizona Archeological and Historical Society, 1919), 12–21. Mercedes Sais Quiroz was the ward of William Hudson Kirkland, founder of the ranch mentioned in the preface. Kirkland had business interests in and near the Santa Rita mountains in addition to his "upper rancho" on Sabino Creek.

Chapter 3. Bonanza

1. For a detailed account of Colonel Sykes's enterprises in the Santa Cruz Valley, see: Thomas E. Sheridan, *Landscapes of Fraud: Mission Tumacácori, the Baca Float, and the Betrayal of the O'odham* (Tucson: University of Arizona Press, 2006), 122–37.
2. Homestead grant to Sabino Otero, December 13, 1892, courtesy of Janet Miller, Elkhorn Ranch, Altar Valley, Arizona (photocopy in author's files). See also: "Some of Pima's Stock Ranches," *Arizona Enterprise* (Florence), June 27, 1891. Remains of a dam and a building mentioned in this article can still be found. The Otero ranch is shown on George Roskruge's 1893 Pima County map (chapter 5), where the canyon is labeled "Otero Cañon."
3. "Territorial News," *Arizona Weekly Citizen* (Tucson), May 14, 1892.
4. "Rich Discoveries," *Arizona Daily Star* (Tucson), June 1, 1892.
5. "Rich Discoveries," *Arizona Daily Star*. Despite this gushing account, doubtless encouraged by Sykes himself, he wasn't the first to say he had found mineral wealth in Sabino Canyon. Calvin Elliott filed a mining claim in the mouth of the canyon the same year he announced his plan to dam the creek: Sabina Mine, C. A. Elliott, claimant, recorded December 4, 1883, Mining Claims bk. T, pp. 490–91, Pima County Recorder, Tucson. Interestingly, another mine was staked in the canyon while Sykes and his associates were claiming theirs: Lucky Kick Mine, Geo. Darms and W. K. Large [?], claimants, recorded June 1, 1892, Mining Claims bk. CC, p. 580, Pima County Recorder. (The claimants' names are poorly legible.)
6. Articles of Incorporation of the Sabino Gold Mining Co., Charles P. Sykes, Edward Wastell, and Joseph Hayes, incorporators, recorded November 23, 1895, New York,

filed December 2, 1895, Articles of Incorporation bk. 1, pp. 395–97, Pima County Recorder. The mines claimed were Bonanza, Broadwell, Colorado, Elizia, Heaton, Patterson, Promontory, Rough and Ready, Stem Winder, and Sykes. The author has located six of these.

7. The author has found no clear evidence of fraud in connection with the Sabino Gold Mining Company, despite certain suggestive circumstances, including the presence of a photographer when Sykes claimed to have found gold in Sabino Canyon. The mines were located in a geologically plausible area, near the major Sabino Canyon Fault and a tributary fault just to its north. A reported endorsement by Theodore B. Comstock, director of the University of Arizona's School of Mines, lends credibility to the venture.

8. Elizia Mining Claim, Sabino Gold Mining Co., claimant, C. P. Sykes, representative, recorded April 21, 1897, Mining Claims Book FF, p. 493, Pima County Recorder, Tucson.

Chapter 4. The Man from Cornwall

1. Mrs. George F. Kitt, ed., "Reminiscences of Geo. J. Roskruge," MS 697, George James Roskruge Papers, Arizona Historical Society, Tucson.

2. George J. Roskruge, "Map showing proposed water supply for the [City of Tucson?]," Arizona Historical Society, Tucson. This blueprint copy of a map drawn in Roskruge's hand bears the inked annotation "1899" and shows a dam and reservoir at Calvin Elliott's site. The date is consistent with Roskruge's apparent age in the photograph with his assistants, as well as with the annotation "about 1900" on the reverse of several of the prints reproduced in this chapter. (The map could not be relocated in the archive in 2021. A partial photocopy is in the author's files.)

3. Jim Turner, "A Nice Place to Visit: A Brief History of Sabino Canyon," *Smoke Signal* 81 (2006).

4. "Educational System of the Old Pueblo," *Arizona Republican* (Phoenix), March 26, 1906. See also: "Tucson School Marms," *Bisbee Daily Review*, March 31, 1906.

5. "Roskruge Funeral Services to Be in Charge of Masons," *Arizona Daily Star* (Tucson), July 28, 1928.

6. Raymond M. Turner, Robert R. Webb, Janice E. Bowers, and James Rodney Hastings, *The Changing Mile Revisited: An Ecological Study of Vegetation Change with Time in the Lower Mile of an Arid and Semiarid Region* (Tucson: University of Arizona Press, 2003), 188–91. It's unclear whether artifacts at the photo station were left by Roskruge or by the ecologists.

Chapter 5. Getting There, Late Nineteenth Century

1. "Sabino Canyon," *Arizona Weekly Citizen* (Tucson), April 25, 1885.

2. George E. P. Smith, "Groundwater Supply and Irrigation in the Rillito Valley," *University of Arizona Agricultural Experiment Station Bulletin* 64 (1910): 110–11. The small ciénega just east of the fort was the head of its *acequias* and key to the choice

of its location. This area, called "The Narrows" by Smith, dried up during the twentieth century as the basin's water table declined.

3. A fast-moving party of men on bicycles and women in carriages proudly reported the return trip took two hours, twenty-five minutes, including a twenty-five-minute rest at Fort Lowell. See: "Local News," *Arizona Daily Star* (Tucson), July 27, 1892.

4. The label "Sabino" or "Sabina" appears on a map created four years earlier, though this one was not generally available to the public: "A Map of the Fort Lowell A. T. Military Reservation showing proposed system of dams, waterways, canals, and storage reservoirs of Pima Land and Water Compy to be constructed under authority of an act of Congress approved February 25th 1889." Copies of this map are bound into the three reports cited in chapter 8, note 3. See also chapter 1, note 7.

5. David Wentworth Lazaroff, *Sabino Canyon: The Life of a Southwestern Oasis* (Tucson: University of Arizona Press, 1993), 85–88.

6. Margaret Mitchell, "Oral History Interview with Virginia Roberts Flaccus Daughter of Clara Fish Roberts" (1984), AV 0395, Arizona Historical Society, Tucson.

Part II. Engineers at the Oasis

1. For more detailed descriptions of the turn-of-the-century environmental crisis, see Michael F. Logan's book in the list of further reading, chapters 8–9. See also: Robert H. Webb, Julio L. Betancourt, R. Roy Johnson, and Raymond M. Turner, *Requiem for the Santa Cruz: An Environmental History of an Arizona River* (Tucson: University of Arizona Press, 2014), chapters 5–6.

2. The effects of the fuel shortage may have reached Sabino Canyon thanks to access provided to woodcutters by the same roads early picnickers traveled. Most of the larger mesquites near the Sabino Canyon Visitor Center have sawed-off stumps at their centers—an indication of historical clear-cutting, though the time period is uncertain. The plant community may still be recovering. Both the resprouted mesquites and the saguaros that eventually took root beneath their canopies are increasing in stature, though some mesquites are now suffering from renewed drought, likely related to global climate change.

Chapter 6. The Professor's Idea

1. Water appropriation in Sabino Canyon, S. M. Woodward and Rochester Ford, claimants, recorded March 26, 1901, Land Claims vol. 2, pp. 62–63, Pima County Recorder, Tucson.

2. G. E. P. Smith, "My Trips into the Cordon of Mountains Surrounding Tucson," (Tucson: self-published brochure, 1967), 12; box 10, folder 12, MS 280, Papers of George E. P. Smith, Special Collections, University of Arizona Libraries, Tucson. Chapter V is the chief basis for this account of the 1901 survey.

3. Smith, "My Trips," 12.

4. Smith, "My Trips," 13.

5. "Prof. Woodward Honored by Friends," *Arizona Daily Star* (Tucson), October 16, 1904.

6. Smith's brochure includes a brief description of the streamgage; Smith, "My Trips," 16.

7. Phyllis Ball, *A Photographic History of the University of Arizona* (Tucson: privately printed, 1986), 43; distributed by University of Arizona Press. The year after this photograph was taken, Professor Forbes married Georgie Scott, whom we encountered with her friends in Sabino Canyon at the end of chapter 2. But perhaps the best-remembered faculty member pictured here is Miss Foucar, who would later found the charitable Marshall Foundation with her husband, and be acquitted after shooting him the following year.

Chapter 7. Men in Green

1. Royal S. Kellogg, *Report of a Trip into the Santa Catalina Mountains*, 1902; typescript copy in author's files. Kellogg Mountain, in the Santa Catalinas, is named in Royal Kellogg's honor. The phrase "lower Sabiño Canyon" in the title of the photograph may be confusing to a modern reader. Prior to the 1930s, areas of the canyon in and near its higher-elevation headwaters were often called "upper Sabino Canyon," while lower-elevation areas, including the entire section in today's Sabino Canyon Recreation Area, were called "lower Sabino Canyon." Today we would say the photograph was taken in "Upper Sabino," and apply "Lower Sabino" to the area roughly from Sabino Lake southward to the canyon mouth.

2. "Good! Good!" *Arizona Daily Star* (Tucson), July 17, 1902. "Catalina Forest Reserve," *Tucson Citizen*, July 17, 1902.

3. Historians of the Santa Catalina Mountains, and especially of the role of the Forest Service in the early years, are indebted to a naturalist at the Sabino Canyon Visitor Center for her unpublished work: Anne E. Harrison, *The Santa Catalinas: A Description and History* (Tucson: Sabino Canyon Visitor Center, 1969). The author has donated a copy to the University of Arizona Libraries, Special Collections.

4. La-Vere Shoenfelt Anderson, "Tulsan Traces Tribes," *Tulsa Daily World*, May 5, 1935. This article provides a summary of Thomas Meagher's life to 1933.

5. Forest Supervisor, Santa Rita and Santa Catalina Forest Reserves, Tucson, Arizona to Forester, Washington, D.C., July 11, 1905; T. F. Meagher, "Copy book No. 2, Santa Rita and Santa Catalina Forest Reserves, Arizona, from February 14th to December 1905" (unpublished record book), Supervisor's Office, Coronado National Forest, Tucson.

6. Special thanks to William B. Gillespie, forest archaeologist for Coronado National Forest, since retired, for his collaboration in identifying the location of Thomas Meagher's long-vanished Sabino Canyon shack. It appears on maps in chapters 12 and 14.

7. "Tucson's Summer Resort a Fact," *Arizona Daily Star*, May 18, 1906. A stop in the mountain forests was named Meagher's Paradise. See also: "Ho, for Mount Lemon!!" *Arizona Daily Star*, June 1, 1906.

8. "Grazing and Forest Reserve," *Arizona Daily Star*, January 17, 1906.

Chapter 8. Power and Water

1. "Water Power for Tucson," *Arizona Daily Star* (Tucson), December, 25, 1902.

2. "Originator of Sabino Idea Made Survey 35 Years Ago," *Arizona Daily Star*, February 21, 1936. Mr. Hughes's interest in Sabino Creek preceded Professor Woodward's arrival in Tucson. Hughes was president of the Pima Land and Water Company in 1889, when Congress authorized it to develop water sources on the Fort Lowell Military Reservation. See chapter 1, note 7.

3. Articles of Incorporation of Great Western Power Company, filed and recorded April 28, 1906, Articles of Incorporation bk. 5, pp. 216–18, Pima County Recorder, Tucson. The narrative that follows is based in part on three reports filed simultaneously by the District Engineer in the Forest Service's Albuquerque office: (a) Lyle A. Whitsit, "Report on the Hydro-Electric Project in Sabino Canyon on the Coronado Forest: Federal Power and Water Co. Applicant for Preliminary Permit" (1915), Supervisor's Office, Coronado National Forest, Tucson, (b) as above, "New State Development Company," (c) as above, "John W. Daily."

4. In its early years, the Great Western Power Company considered two different designs for the dam at Woodward's site: a 300-foot concrete dam and a 180-foot rock-fill dam. For this and other details of the company's plans, see: AZ 171, Papers of William Burnham Alexander, Special Collections, University of Arizona Libraries, Tucson.

5. The eastern consortium, which Alexander called the Chicago Syndicate, included Charles B., Edward A., and Edward J. Shedd of Chicago; William F. Cox of New York City; and James R. Severance of Oberlin, Ohio. E. J. Shedd, Cox, and Severance took over as president, vice president, and secretary of the Great Western Power Company, respectively.

6. "Sabino Project Means Much to This City," *Arizona Daily Star*, February 15, 1910. "Water Matters Discussed by Councilmen," *Arizona Daily Star*, April 17, 1910. "Great Resort Proposed for Sabino Canyon," *Arizona Daily Star*, May 22, 1910.

7. Untitled editorial, *Arizona Daily Star*, December 22, 1910. See also: "Sabino Canyon Project Meets with a Delay," *Arizona Daily Star*, December 15, 1910. Note the continued support of the project by L. C. Hughes.

8. "Sabino Canyon Water Rights to Be Contested," *Arizona Daily Star*, February 3, 1911.

9. "Water Wealth Tucson Needs Others Want," *Arizona Daily Star*, November 24, 1911. "Gets Warrant for Officer Power Co.," *Arizona Daily Star*, November 25, 1911.

10. Eagle Milling Co. advertisement, *Arizona Daily Star* (Tucson), November 11, 1911.

11. William B. Alexander, Scituate, Mass., to W. J. Brian [Bryan] Washington, D.C., April 8, 1913, documents related to Great Western Power Company, Supervisor's Office, Coronado National Forest, Tucson. It can't have helped that Alexander misspelled the secretary's name.

12. "Take Up Water for City in Sabino Canyon," *Arizona Daily Star*, May 2, 1913. That same night, Ruthrauff and Cochran also claimed water rights to Sycamore Creek,

which drained into the site of the Great Western Power Company's proposed reservoir in Bear Canyon.

13. "Engineer Cobb Makes Complete Report on Tucson Water Plans," *Arizona Daily Star*, October 23, 1913.

14. This was not the end of John Daily's interest in Sabino Canyon. Much later he partnered in an obscure and unsuccessful effort to revive interest in a dam and reservoir at Professor Woodward's site: the Sabino Canyon Water and Power Company. See: "Sabino Company Is Incorporated," *Arizona Daily Star*, June 13, 1930.

15. James Dix Schuyler, *Reservoirs for Irrigation, Water-Power, and Domestic Water-Supply* (New York: John Wiley & Sons, 1901), 350–51. In the plans of the Catalina Reservoir and Electric Company, water from the east fork of Sabino Creek was to be diverted through a tunnel to supplement runoff from the Bear Creek watershed.

16. William B. Alexander, New York, N.Y., to Duncan Stuart, Tacoma Park, D.C., May 15, 1929, Great Western Power Company documents, Coronado National Forest.

17. Alexander, William Burnham, "History of Reservoirs No. 1 and No. 2" (unpublished, ca. 1911), AZ 171, Papers of William Burnham Alexander. This graph demonstrates the unreliability of Sabino Creek and Bear Creek as water sources. Had the two dams begun service at the start of 1905, an exceptionally wet year, both reservoirs would have filled to capacity, only to decline to empty or nearly so during 1910. "Extreme drought" and forest fires indicated during that year may have helped set the stage for flooding that destroyed the streamgage in 1912.

18. The Shoshone Dam originated in the ambitions of private companies connected with the famous showman William F. Cody. Cody eventually turned over his rights to the U.S. Reclamation Service, which designed and built the dam. In 1946 the structure was renamed the Buffalo Bill Dam in Cody's honor, and later its height was increased to 350 feet. It's still in service today. Closer to home, the Theodore Roosevelt Dam, east of Phoenix, was dedicated by T. R. himself in 1911. It was another U.S. Reclamation Service project. At 280 feet, it was then the world's tallest dam of masonry construction. In 1996 it was raised to 357 feet, nearly but not quite the height of the Great Western Power Company's proposed dam in Sabino Canyon. It, too, is still in service.

Chapter 9. Military Occupation

1. The Sabino Canyon encampment tradition was broken only in the memorably wet spring of 1905, when flooding of Sabino Creek seems to have made conditions inhospitable there. The cadets instead spent several miserably rainy days in nearby Ventana Canyon. When food ran low and resupply wagons from the university were unable to cross the swollen Rillito, two resourceful cadets managed to send provisions across on a cable ordinarily used to transfer milk during high water. See: "Arizona Cadets Are Expecting Big Trip," *Bisbee Daily Review*, February 1, 1907.

2. "On the War Path," *Arizona Daily Star* (Tucson), November 26, 1903.

3. "Cadets Home from the Canyon," *Tucson Citizen*, April 20, 1907.

4. The encampments were initiated by K. C. Babcock, successor to F. Y. Adams as president of the University of Arizona, and they correspond closely to his tenure (1903–10). In late 1916, at the request of University President R. B. von KleinSmid, five hundred acres were set aside from Coronado National Forest lands west of Sabino Canyon for cadet training, apparently at Ventana Canyon, location of the 1905 encampment (note 1, above). The extent of that site's subsequent use is unknown to the author. See: "Military Camp for U. of A.," *Graham Guardian* (Safford, Ariz.), January 12, 1917.

5. Corp. Y. S. Bonillas, "Map Showing Route of the March and Camp of University of Arizona Batallion [*sic*] of Cadets" (1903?), G4331 R3 1903, Tucson Map Collection, Arizona Historical Society, Tucson. Drawn by a cadet who served as acting engineering officer during the 1903 encampment, this map indicates "Targets on the Rocks" in the position of the painted figures seen today. The artifacts show up in much better condition in photographs taken during the late 1930s, when nearby trees were removed in preparation for an artificial lake (chapter 18).

Chapter 10. One Visit

1. The Uphams and their friends took a slightly unusual route, crossing the Rillito directly north of Fort Lowell and following primitive roads northeastward across hilly terrain to Sabino Canyon. The route can be reconstructed from photographs reproduced in this chapter and others taken the same day. All are preserved in the Muriel Upham Collection (PC 142), Arizona Historical Society, Tucson, scattered among folders in boxes 1 and 4.

2. "Aqua Pura," *Arizona Weekly Star* (Tucson), February 7, 1884.

Chapter 11. Gunplay

1. *Acts, Resolutions and Memorials of the Regular Session Fourth Legislature of the State of Arizona* (Phoenix, 1919). "State Statute Bans Guns on Game Preserve," *Arizona Daily Star* (Tucson), September 16, 1920. "Motorists Find Trip to Sabino Canyon Treat as Beauty of Scenery Becomes Known," *Arizona Daily Star*, December 2, 1923. Limited shooting would return with the opening of a permitted rifle range in 1953 (chapter 22).

Chapter 12. On the Trail

1. "Better Trail to Catalinas Is New Plan," *Arizona Daily Star* (Tucson), May 10, 1911. "Road Building Is Started by Power Company," *Arizona Daily Star*, May 11, 1911. "Better Roads to Catalinas Their Objects," *Arizona Daily Star*, May 13, 1911. "Still Seek Best Route to Catalinas," *Arizona Daily Star*, May 18, 1911.

2. "Trail Making Is to Start Immediately," *Arizona Daily Star*, June 3, 1911. "Sabino Trail Work Is to Be Hurried," *Arizona Daily Star*, June 8, 1911.

3. "Forestry Will Have Its Own Telephones," *Arizona Daily Star* (Tucson), August 24, 1911.

4. "The Catalina Mountains," *Arizona Daily Star*, May 26, 1912. A nearly identical notice was published in the *Tucson Citizen*, same date.

5. Oswald Weigelt, "Trip to the Santa Catalina Mountains" (ca. 1913), Mrs. Otto Weigelt biofile, Arizona Historical Society, Tucson. The lively story summarized in this chapter is based on Weigelt's unpublished account. Original punctuation has been preserved in direct quotations.

6. "Mt. Lemon Trail Map Distributed," *Arizona Daily Star*, May 30, 1912.

7. Pete Cowgill, "Pack Trains Were Lone Suppliers to Homes in Catalina Mountains," *Arizona Daily Star*, August 7, 1987.

8. Ed Knagge died tragically in his late eighties after being beaten and robbed at his home in Tucson. See: "Roadbuilder Edwin Knagge, 89, Dies of Injuries," *Arizona Daily Star*, April 19, 1986.

9. For a full description of the construction of the Catalina Highway (officially called the Hitchcock Highway), as well as a more detailed account of the Knagge pack train, see Suzanne Hensel's book in the list of further reading.

Chapter 13. Postcard Perfect

1. "Guess Who?" *Arizona Daily Star* (Tucson), March 3, 1912.

2. "79. Sabino Canon," B 91476, Buehman Photo Collection, Places—Sabino Canyon, Arizona Historical Society, Tucson.

3. For beer aficionados: the brand can be identified by the labels in other photographs taken on the same occasion.

4. Walter Donaldson and Joe Young, "My Mammy" (New York: Irving Berlin, Inc., 1921). The song was famously performed in blackface by Al Jolson in the final scene of *The Jazz Singer* (Warner Brothers, 1927). It's uncomfortable viewing today.

5. Henry Ford and Samuel Crowther, *My Life and Work* (Garden City, NY: Garden City Publishing Co., 1922), 72.

Chapter 14. Getting There, Early Twentieth Century

1. G. E. P. Smith, "My Trips into the Cordon of Mountains Surrounding Tucson," (Tucson: self-published brochure, 1967), 16–17; box 10, folder 12, MS 280, Papers of George E. P. Smith, Special Collections, University of Arizona Libraries, Tucson.

2. Smith, "My Trips," 18–19. The day's adventures weren't quite over. During the return trip, Cochran and Smith drove westward along the Rillito, looking for a better crossing, and, failing to find one, camped north of town. Smith, unwilling to wait for the flow to lessen, stripped naked and waded across in the dark, carrying his clothing in a bundle over his head. He then dressed and walked through the desert to his home at the university.

3. "The City in Brief," *Arizona Daily Star* (Tucson), March 10, 1908.

4. "No Chance to Get Off the Road Now," *Arizona Daily Star*, May 24, 1910. According to the *Star*, the "philanthropists" had also marked the route to Mission San Xavier del Bac, though at only about a tenth the density of bottles.

5. The crossing north of the fort may sometimes have been drier than the other—an advantage in certain seasons. In 1903 the cadets chose the eastern crossing for their return march.

6. The terminus of the upper road, as it existed in Roskruge's time, seems to be indicated by a wooden post near the present one-mile marker. On the steep slope below the post is the eroded trace of the Sabino Canyon fault. This feature, likely attractive to mining prospectors, may have been the road's original destination. (It was not among the claims of the Sabino Gold Mining Company.) It's possible that the road was later extended to facilitate construction of Professor Woodward's streamgage.

7. Glenton G. Sykes was the son of Godfrey Sykes, engineer, scientist, and explorer, who immigrated to the United States from England in 1879. Glenton and his brother, Gilbert, were sent to school in England in 1911 and served in the British military during the Great War. After returning to the United States, both worked briefly as firefighters in the Santa Catalinas. Glenton soon followed his father into the engineering profession, and Gilbert served many years with the Forest Service. The author is unaware of any familial relationship between Godfrey Sykes and Colonel C. P. Sykes of the Sabino Gold Mining Company.

Part III. The Great Expansion

1. Irving Berlin, "Blue Skies" (New York: Irving Berlin, Inc., 1926). Like the song "My Mammy" (chapter 13, note 4), this song was performed by Al Jolson in *The Jazz Singer*, a film on the cusp of the talkie era.

2. O. C. Merrill to Joseph Wittman, April 15, 1929, documents related to Joseph Wittman project No. 741, Supervisor's Office, Coronado National Forest, Tucson. Ben C. Hill, City Attorney, "Protest of City of Tucson in the Matter of the Application of Joseph Wittman," June 3, 1929, Wittman project documents. A. H. Condron, Secretary, Tucson Chamber of Commerce, to O. C. Merrill, June 27, 1929, Wittman project documents.

3. William B. Alexander to D. Stuart, May 15, 1929, documents related to Great Western Power Company, Supervisor's Office, Coronado National Forest.

4. "U.S. Engineer to Survey Canyon Dam," *Arizona Daily Star* (Tucson), October 27, 1929.

Chapter 15. Alphabet Soup

1. For a detailed account of federal relief programs in Arizona during the Great Depression, see: William S. Collins, *The New Deal in Arizona* (Phoenix: Arizona State Parks Board, 1999).

2. *Coronado Bulletin*, July 7, 1933, Supervisor's Office, Coronado National Forest, Tucson.

3. A twenty-year-old man fell and broke his leg while trying the same stunt in 1953. Six years later the USGS moved the cable and its car a few hundred feet downstream. Whatever the reason for the change, it had a positive effect on safety. By that date a

small dam had been built in Lower Sabino Canyon (chapter 18), and anyone losing grip on the cable would drop into a lake. The USGS streamgage was decommissioned in 1974 and later replaced with one in the lakebed.

4. *Coronado Bulletin*, November 17, 1933, Supervisor's Office, Coronado National Forest.

5. There are hints that another ranger station, in what we today call Lower Sabino, may have bridged the gap in time between the structures completed by Supervisor Meagher in 1905 and by the CCC in 1934. See: "Motorists Find Trip to Sabino Canyon Treat as Beauty of Scenery Becomes Known," *Arizona Daily Star* (Tucson), December 2, 1923. Concerning Gilbert Sykes, see chapter 14, note 7.

6. L. J. Arnold and Z. G. Smith, "Sabino Canyon Camp Ground Coronado National Forest Arizona" (unpublished map, February 1934), Supervisor's Office, Coronado National Forest.

7. MS 1193, Mary Estill Caldwell Personal Papers, Arizona Historical Society, Tucson. Albums 3 and 10 include photographs showing a wooden building in the Picnic Grounds, about 1912. See also the article cited in note 5.

8. Trails created by the CWA are among the most poorly documented of all Depression-era improvements in Sabino Canyon. In addition to the nearly forgotten Sabino Canyon Trail restoration, the CWA constructed a link, still in use today, between the Picnic Grounds and the Phoneline Trail. Two other likely CWA-created trails are mentioned in the notes to chapter 17.

9. Because of incomplete records, as well as the turnover and simultaneous activities of government relief agencies, it is impossible to ascertain the agency responsible for every Depression-era improvement in Sabino Canyon. The caretaker's cabin, for example, while attributed to the CWA, appears to have been unfinished when that agency terminated, and may have been completed later by CCC boys. A debris flow down Rattlesnake Canyon destroyed the CCC's footbridge in 2006.

Chapter 16. Reservoir Renaissance

1. "Improvements for Sabino Canyon Proposed to Make It an Attractive Resort," *Arizona Daily Star* (Tucson), February 25, 1923. "Sabino Repair Costs Surprise," *Arizona Daily Star*, December 21, 1929.

2. "Jobless Will Have Work on Road Project," *Arizona Daily Star*, December 31, 1930. Coronado National Forest initially planned to extend the road up Sabino Canyon beyond the Picnic Grounds, but this wouldn't happen until the start of New Deal funding.

3. "Road Workers Show Thanks," *Tucson Daily Citizen*, March 10, 1931.

4. A. H. Condron, "What Sabino Canyon Means to Tucson," *Tucson* 9, no. 4 (April 1936): 5, 12; Arizona Historical Society, Tucson. This article by the secretary of the Tucson Chamber of Commerce provides a useful summary of events related to the chamber's Sabino Canyon projects through the date of its publication, though it's not accurate in every detail.

5. William Misbaugh to Isabella Greenway, June 27, 1934, MS 311, John Campbell Greenway and Isabella Greenway papers, folder 690, Arizona Historical Society, Tucson.

6. Frank C. W. Pooler, Regional Forester, to Greenway, October 16, 1934, Greenway papers, folder 690.

7. Long, C. A., "Project No. 741 Report on Application of Joseph Wittman Project State of Arizona" (1930), Supervisor's Office, Coronado National Forest, Tucson. Despite Long's doubts about the project's feasibility, he approved it with several provisos, including that the applicant grant the City of Tucson the right to buy out the project after ten years.

8. "Sabino Project to Be Approved," *Tucson Daily Citizen*, October 26, 1934. "Sabino Project Work Is Begun," *Arizona Daily Star*, October 27, 1934.

9. "Progress Made on Road Work," *Arizona Daily Star* (Tucson), November 2, 1934. The article describes an inspection the previous day. Condron is not mentioned, but he frequently joined inspections in Sabino Canyon as a representative of the Tucson Chamber of Commerce.

10. William Holzhauser, "Lake in Catalinas Assured," *Tucson* 7, no. 11 (November 1934): 5, 17; Arizona Historical Society, Tucson.

11. Letter to the editor by Mrs. Howard Burkett, *Arizona Daily Star*, February 20, 1935.

12. Howard Caffrey to Greenway, November 14, 1934, Greenway papers, folder 690.

13. Misbaugh to Greenway, March 21, 1935, Greenway papers, folder 691.

14. Mernice Murphy, ed., *Outstanding Projects—Work Division Emergency Relief Administration of Arizona Volume II* (Phoenix: Arizona Board of Public Welfare, 1935), 17–19, Arizona Historical Society, Tucson. Occasional present-day use of the technical term "vented low-water crossings" for these small dams is questionable at best and historically unprecedented.

15. The WPA was created under the authority of the Emergency Relief Appropriation Act of 1935. The reader may recall Thomas Meagher's work on the Indian-Pioneer History Project, one of many valuable cultural programs supported by the WPA (chapter 7).

16. Greenway to Col. Lawrence Westbrook, October 20, 1935, Greenway papers, folder 691.

17. Gladys Lytle to Caffrey, November 1, 1935, Greenway papers, folder 691.

18. Caffrey to Lytle, November 1, 1935, Greenway papers, folder 691.

19. Lytle to Greenway, November 7, 1935, Greenway papers, folder 691.

20. Lytle to Caffrey, November 7, 1935, Greenway papers, folder 691.

21. "$750,000 for Sabino Dam Is Granted by Comptroller from Federal Treasury," *Arizona Daily Star*, November 8, 1935.

22. For a full account of Greenway's life, see Kristie Miller's book in the list of further reading.

Chapter 17. The End of the Road

1. Isabella Greenway to Albert Condron, December 23, 1935, MS 311, John Campbell Greenway and Isabella Greenway papers, folder 691, Arizona Historical Society, Tucson.

2. Howard O. Hunter to W. J. Jamieson, December 18, 1935, Greenway papers, folder 692.

3. Howard Caffrey to William Misbaugh and Condron, January 13, 1936, Greenway papers, folder 692.

4. Condron to Greenway, January 23, 1936, Greenway papers, folder 692.

5. Condron to Greenway, February 27, 1936, Greenway papers, folder 692.

6. "WPA Projects Make Progress Review of Program Reveals," *Arizona Daily Star* (Tucson), February 1, 1936.

7. The Sabino Canyon Trail segment visible in the photograph leads to a small saddle on the peak of a ridge. Beyond there the trail descends the opposite side of the ridge, as shown on the map in chapter 14. A separate trail runs uphill from the saddle to join the Phoneline Trail. This link between the Sabino Canyon and Phoneline Trails postdates them both. (It may have been a CWA creation.) Both the older trail segment seen in the photograph and the later linking trail were restored in 2005, at which time the linking trail was misidentified as part of the original Sabino Canyon Trail.

8. Folk history has often connected Anderson Dam with Deputy Sheriff John D. Anderson, who is said to have met his death while rescuing a boy from a nearby cliff. The connection is spurious. Deputy Anderson did die as described, but at Woodward's dam site, more than a mile farther upstream, and in 1948, years after the name "Anderson Dam" had come into use (chapter 21). For an earlier use of the name, see: "Sabino Canyon Is Tucson's Most Popular Playground," *Arizona Daily Star*, February 23, 1940.

9. Condron to Greenway, April 9, 1936, Greenway papers, folder 693.

10. "Sabino Project Gets into Hair," *Arizona Daily Star* (Tucson), June 2, 1936.

11. Misbaugh to Greenway, March 25, 1936, Greenway papers, folder 693. Misbaugh wrote not as a member of the Tucson Chamber of Commerce but rather in his capacity as chairman of the Pima County Planning Board.

12. "Back to Woods Habit Gaining," *Arizona Daily Star*, September 16, 1936.

13. "County and City Unanimous in Support of Sabino Dam," *Arizona Daily Star*, September 11, 1936.

14. "Sabino Canyon Dam—Tucson: Report of the District Engineer," *Arizona Sheriff and Police Journal*, June 1937, 39–53. In addition to the project's recreational values, Wyman cited its potential benefits for water conservation, either by regulating streamflow for efficient groundwater recharge in the Tucson Basin or by diverting a portion for municipal use. Formally, this report had been requested by the state WPA administrator in March 1936, when the agency had released limited funding to the army for surveys and plans. To satisfy the requirements of the Flood Control Act of 1936, Wyman filed a second, less extensive report concluding that the dam could not be justified for flood control benefits alone.

15. Some figures in this account have been rounded for clarity.

16. "C. C. Committee Dropping Plan," *Arizona Daily Star*, May 16, 1937.

17. "Hopkins Blasts Hopes for Sabino Dam Plans in Letter About Cost," *Arizona Daily Star*, May 21, 1937.

18. F. C. Harrington to Condron, July 27, 1937, Greenway papers, folder 693. The revised WPA application was formally denied by a state WPA official a month later, on August 25. Even the minimal $600 sponsor's contribution offered in the original application, years earlier, may have been an error. It wasn't clear that Pima County could legally contribute funds for improvements on federal lands. See: Greenway to Harry Hopkins, September 31, 1935, Greenway papers, folder 691.

19. "Profane Duet Buries Sabino Dam Proposal," *Arizona Daily Star*, August 5, 1937.

20. The August 4 meeting of the chamber's board of directors effectively ended efforts to secure an application for the dam under Pima County's sponsorship. Misbaugh and Condron later made a brief, failed attempt to persuade the Forest Service to take over the project, and the junior chamber of commerce and the Tucson Trades Council unsuccessfully circulated a petition to revive the dam by holding a bond election.

21. "Sabino Plans Set by Board," *Arizona Daily Star*, June 17, 1937. The fresh-appearing trail at bottom left in the photo may be another example of work done by CWA laborers during the winter of 1933–34. It originally extended roughly three-quarters of a mile up the canyon floor from Anderson Dam, but its upper end has since been buried by flood deposits.

22. Climate change would eventually have affected the lake in ways that couldn't have been foreseen during the 1930s. Not only would the variability in its depth have been increased by greater extremes of precipitation and drought, but also the lake's longevity might have been reduced as forest fires and more intense flooding increased the sediment loads of flood waters. See: David W. Lazaroff, Philip C. Rosen, and Charles H. Lowe Jr., *Amphibians, Reptiles, and Their Habitats at Sabino Canyon* (Tucson: University of Arizona Press, 2006), 39–48.

23. "The Sabino Dam Issue," editorial, *Arizona Daily Star*, June 9, 1937.

24. "Condron Quits C. C. Position," *Arizona Daily Star*, August 6, 1937.

Chapter 18. A Lake at Last

1. "Lake in Sabino Canyon Sought," *Arizona Daily Star* (Tucson), March 18, 1937.

2. The height of the spillway may have been limited to avoid flooding the weir at the USGS streamgage, installed at Calvin Elliott's dam site five years earlier (chapter 15).

3. "Small Dam Goes Up in Sabino Canyon," *Tucson Daily Citizen*, June 15, 1937.

4. "Diary of Edgar B Raudebaugh Camp & Project Supt. Sabino Coronado National Forest," October 27, 1937–February 25, 1938 notebook, January 20 and 22 entries, NAU.MS.19, E. B. Raudebaugh Collection, series 2, folder 13, Special Collections and Archives Dept., Cline Library, Northern Arizona University, Flagstaff.

5. Robert White, "Fred Winn's Lake Inspiration Leaves Forest Service Agog," *Arizona Daily Star*, February 11, 1938.

6. White, "Fred Winn's Lake Inspiration." Two years after this article appeared, Tucson's Sunshine Climate Club arranged for a pair of young women to be photographed in cactus clothing: a brassiere fashioned from the tops of two saguaros and a skirt of prickly pear pads. The photos were published in hundreds of newspapers and, on April 7, 1941, in *Life* magazine.

7. Z. G. Smith and A. R. Curtis, "Lower Sabino Recreational Area Coronado National Forest Arizona" (unpublished map, November–December 1935), Supervisor's Office, Coronado National Forest, Tucson.

8. "2000 See Sabino Dam Ceremonies," *Arizona Daily Star* (Tucson), April 11, 1938.

9. "Youth Drowns in Sabino Lake," *Arizona Daily Star*, June 3, 1938.

10. "Coroner's Jury Studies Death," *Arizona Daily Star*, June 4, 1938. Despite the official disclaimer, Coronado National Forest continued to make improvements for the benefit of swimmers. Note the handrail attached to the dam in the next photograph in this chapter. It was installed the month after the quoted statement.

11. "Hook, Line and Sinker . . . Hall Swears It's the Truth," George Hall, *Arizona Daily Star*, May 28, 1939.

12. "Soft Life Is Anathema to Fred Winn," *Arizona Daily Star*, April 25, 1943.

Chapter 19. Camping Out

1. "Forest Service Has Transients," *Arizona Daily Star* (Tucson), August 12, 1936. Fragmentary and contradictory records concerning the Sabino Canyon Camp make it difficult to construct a precise chronology. Many contemporaneous accounts failed to track the camp's evolving status. Residents were often called "transients" after they'd been recognized as settled local citizens, and their community was sometimes labeled an "ERA camp" after that agency had terminated in 1938.

2. "Rain Takes the Camp by Storm," *Oasis* vol. 2, no. 19 (October 1, 1935), MS 1478, Civilian Conservation Corps newsletters, Arizona Historical Society, Tucson. The account quotes the chorus of a popular song: Billy Hill and Peter de Rose, "Rain" (New York: Shapiro, Bernstein & Co., 1934).

3. "Duckings Are Now the Rage," *Oasis* vol. 2, no. 19 (October 1, 1935), MS 1478, Civilian Conservation Corps newsletters. Note the early use of the inaccurate word "bridge" for one of the stream crossings in Upper Sabino Canyon.

4. "Transient Camp Is Threatened by Forest Fire," *Arizona Daily Star*, June 12, 1936. "Sunburn Worse Than Forest Fire for Men Fighting Blaze," *Arizona Daily Star*, June 13, 1936.

5. "Quiz Fails to Solve Armory Park Murder," *Arizona Daily Star*, June 27, 1936.

6. Baker may have taken many of the pictures documenting ERA and WPA accomplishments in Upper Sabino, though these photographs are usually uncredited in government publications and archives. The photos of the fourth crossing, in this chapter, and of the third, in chapter 16, have been attributed to him. See: "New Lakes Add to Charm of Beautiful Sabino Canyon," *Arizona Daily Star* (Tucson), February 20, 1937.

7. "Diary of Edgar B Raudebaugh Camp & Project Supt. Sabino Canyon Coronado National Forest," July 16–October 27, 1937 notebook, first entry, NAU.MS.19, E. B. Raudebaugh Collection, series 2, folder 12, Special Collections and Archives Dept., Cline Library, Northern Arizona University, Flagstaff. In this and other excerpts from the Raudebaugh work diaries, punctuation and spelling are quoted as written.

8. "Diary of Edgar B Raudebaugh," July 16–October 27, 1937 notebook, July 26 entry, Raudebaugh Collection, series 2, folder 12.

9. "Forest Service Camp Men Ask a Beerless Canyon," *Arizona Daily Star*, November 8, 1938. Certain entries in Raudebaugh's diaries from late 1938 and early 1939 appear to refer to a camp resident's addiction to a narcotic drug.

10. "Diary of Edgar B Raudebaugh," July 16–October 27, 1937 notebook, August 4 entry, Raudebaugh Collection, series 2, folder 12.

11. "Diary of Edgar B Raudebaugh," February 26–June 17, 1938 notebook, March 8 entry, Raudebaugh Collection, series 2, folder 14.

12. "Falls from Car, Prisoner Is Hurt," *Arizona Daily Star*, September 15, 1937.

13. "Pooch Finds Woman, Is Now Declared Hero," *Arizona Daily Star*, May 19, 1936.

14. "Diary of Edgar B Raudebaugh," February 26–June 17, 1938 notebook, June 2 entry, Raudebaugh Collection, series 2, folder 14.

15. Ducks: "Authentic Report of Spring Season Found on Forest," *Arizona Daily Star*, February 16, 1938. Deer: "Diary of Edgar B Raudebaugh," July 16–October 27, 1937 notebook, October 16 entry, Raudebaugh Collection, series 2, folder 12. Gila monster: "Diary of Edgar B Raudebaugh," February 26–June 17, 1938 notebook, April 18 entry, Raudebaugh Collection, series 2, folder 14.

16. "Diary of Edgar B Raudebaugh," October 17, 1937–February 25, 1938 notebook, November 26 entry, Raudebaugh Collection, series 2, folder 13.

17. "Thousands View Colorful Entries in Annual Tucson Rodeo Parade," *Tucson Daily Citizen*, February 19, 1938. The captions for two photographs in the article are reversed.

18. "Diary of Edgar B Raudebaugh," March 1–June 30, 1939 notebook, June 3 and June 10 entries, Raudebaugh Collection, series 2, folder 17.

19. "Diary of Edgar B Raudebaugh," March 1–June 30, 1939 notebook, June 23 entry, Raudebaugh Collection, series 2, folder 17.

20. "Diary of Edgar B Raudebaugh," March 1–June 30, 1939 notebook, last entry, Raudebaugh Collection, series 2, folder 17.

Chapter 20. Getting There, Great Depression

1. The bridge, which had spanned the Rillito on the road to Sabino Canyon since 1917, burned in 1938. Motorists returned to a ground-level crossing for nearly a year while a new concrete-and-steel structure was built. See: "Fire Destroys Sabino Bridge," *Arizona Daily Star* (Tucson), May 5, 1938.

2. *Coronado Bulletin*, June 15, 1937, Supervisor's Office, Coronado National Forest, Tucson. Samuel P. Snow, 1939, "Coronado National Forest Arizona-New Mexico Catalina-Rincon Division Recreation Plan," Supervisors Office, Tucson.

3. Ethel Stiffler Carpenter, *Letters from Tucson, 1933–1942*, ed. Roger E. Carpenter (Tucson: published privately by editor, 2009), 163.

4. In 1962 the trailer campground was converted into a group picnic area. Camping was at times allowed in certain facilities constructed after the Second World War (Cactus and Lower Bear, both outside Sabino Canyon proper), but today there is no permitted camping anywhere in the Sabino Canyon Recreation Area.

Part IV. Growing Pains and Pleasures

1. "Canyon's Lure Still Evident," *Arizona Daily Star* (Tucson), May 18, 1943.

2. The speed limit on Sabino Canyon Road was lifted after the war, but in May 1947, the Pima County Board of Supervisors passed an ordinance returning it to 35 mph. The action was in response to multiple automobile accidents. See: "Speed Reduced on Sabino Road," *Arizona Daily Star*, May 6, 1947.

Chapter 21. Incident at the Old Dam Site

1. W. R. Harrod, "Deputy Sheriff John Anderson Falls to Death in Sabino Rescue Attempt," *Arizona Daily Star* (Tucson), August 10, 1948. For more on the incident, see also: "Deputy Killed Rescuing Boy," *Tucson Daily Citizen*, August 9, 1948. Jim Hart, "Rescued Youth Tells of Fall," *Arizona Daily Star*, August 10, 1948.

2. "Body Is Found in Canyon Pool," *Arizona Daily Star*, July 16, 1938. "Fall Is Fatal for Boy Here," *Arizona Daily Star*, August 29, 1940.

3. For many years after the introduction of a shuttlebus service in the 1970s, drivers perpetuated a false narrative placing this incident at Anderson Dam in Upper Sabino Canyon. See chapter 17, note 8.

4. "The Death of a Rescuer," *Life* 25(8): 36–37 (August 23, 1948).

Chapter 22. Keeping Up

1. The reader may recall that Major Theodore Wyman's 1936 report cited flood protection for existing and future recreational developments as a justification for approving the dam at the Woodward site (chapter 17).

2. "Sabino Fishing Season Opens for First Time at 4 a.m. Today," *Arizona Daily Star* (Tucson), May 5, 1951. Newspaper photographs like these are especially valuable in illuminating Sabino Canyon's postwar history. Many interesting personal photos of Sabino Canyon from this period sit in shoeboxes and albums in private homes—not yet considered by their owners to be "historical" enough for public archives. As time passes this will change, and researchers will be grateful for it.

3. Dean Prichard, "Flood Water Ruins Sabino Picnic Area," *Arizona Daily Star* (Tucson), March 24, 1954.

4. "Rifle Range Opening Will Be Held Sunday," *Arizona Daily Star*, February 12, 1953.

5. Best remembered among the federal prison's inmates is Gordon Hirabayashi, who served time there for resisting the forced relocation of Japanese-American citizens to internment camps during the Second World War. Four decades later his convic-

tion was reversed, and in 1999 he returned for a ceremony naming a campground on the site in his honor.

6. "D-M's 'Operation Alert' Goes Smoothly," *Arizona Daily Star*, June 16, 1955.

7. Robert Moore, "Old Picnicking Spot to Become Pima County's Newest Park," *Arizona Daily Star*, April 6, 1952. Five years later the Arizona Parks Board briefly considered acquiring Sabino Canyon for a state park. See: "State to Ask U.S. Aid in Park Survey," *Arizona Daily Star*, October 22, 1957.

8. "New Park Opening in Canyon," *Arizona Daily Star*, February 28, 1960. The new development was named the *Lower* Bear Canyon Picnic Ground presumably to distinguish it from picnic areas farther up the same canyon, reached via the Catalina Highway. The picnic ground has since been dismantled.

9. "Sabino Gets Another Picnic Area," *Tucson Daily Citizen*, November 4, 1963.

10. Kingsley Wood, "Sabino Visitors Center Dedicated by Officials," *Arizona Daily Star*, June 14, 1964.

11. Lou Pavlovich, "Fishermen Fight for Rose Canyon Dam," *Tucson Daily Citizen*, August 1, 1957. See also: Pavlovich, "Dam Holds Key to Resort Future," *Tucson Daily Citizen*, August 3, 1957.

12. "Water Resources and Recreational Lakes," editorial, *Arizona Daily Star*, September 5, 1959.

13. Tom Foust, "No Trout in Sabino This Spring," *Arizona Daily Star*, April 14, 1966.

14. Siltation of the lake and of the ponds behind the historical stone crossings has continued into the twenty-first century, exacerbated by an increase in the intensity of flooding. The deepening sand has buried attractive reaches of Sabino Creek and reduced habitat for native aquatic life.

15. The reader may have noticed the similarity to the better-publicized role of wildfire in western pine forests. Both flooding and fire, while potentially dangerous to human life and property, are essential elements in their respective ecosystems. Artificial flooding and prescribed fire are partial remedies when these natural disturbances are suppressed.

16. The Pusch Ridge Wilderness was one of multiple such areas created in western national forests by the Endangered American Wilderness Act, signed by President Jimmy Carter on February 24, 1978. Arizona Congressman Morris Udall was its sponsor, and Pusch Ridge was the first wilderness listed in its text.

Chapter 23. Caretakers

1. Special thanks to Karen Hans and to Donald and Betty Early for the privilege of interviewing them for this chapter, and to Tom Early for kindly offering additional information.

2. Helen Pasternak, "Few Dull Days for Caretaker," *Tucson Daily Citizen*, June 14, 1965.

3. "2 Sisters Escape Death in Sabino Flash Flood," *Arizona Daily Star* (Tucson), August 18, 1955.

4. "Old Fort Rifle Range Found," *Arizona Daily Star*, July 6, 1962. There is also the possibility, not investigated by the author, that University of Arizona cadets used surplus army equipment for target practice during Sabino Canyon encampments (chapter 9).

5. "Sabino Canyon Caretaker Retiring after 16 Years," *Tucson Daily Citizen*, December 13, 1966.

6. The visiting friend has been tentatively identified as Coronado National Forest employee Norman B. Cobb, possibly retired by the time of the photograph.

7. Pasternak, "Few Dull Days."

8. Pasternak, "Few Dull Days."

Chapter 24. Troubled Times

1. "Picnickers Pollute Stream at Sabino," *Arizona Daily Star* (Tucson), May 25, 1912. The article suggests that rather than dumping the remains of their lunches into the creek, picnickers should leave them on the ground to "furnish welcome food for the birds and animals"—by modern standards, hardly an improvement.

2. Katie Lee, "Life on the Rocks," *Journal of Arizona History* 49, no. 4 (Winter 2008): 318. The italics are Ms. Lee's.

3. "On Defacing Nature," editorial, *Arizona Daily Star*, March 27, 1948.

4. "Litterbugs Strew Refuse in Sabino," *Arizona Daily Star* (Tucson), April 26, 1954.

5. "Bay Area Travel Editor Amazed at Low Food Prices in Tucson," *Arizona Daily Star*, January 30, 1959.

6. "Sabino Caretaker Fails to Get Point of Prank," *Arizona Daily Star*, February 18, 1959. The stunt seems to have been part of a student fundraising effort. In a photograph for the article, a note set on the sacks of cans appears to read "CAMPUS CHEST DRIVE."

7. "Sabino Canyon Suffers from Beer Can Blight," *Arizona Daily Star*, May 3, 1962.

8. "Slobbovia in Sabino," editorial, *Tucson Daily Citizen*, July 3, 1964. The reference is to Lower Slobbovia, a miserable and backward kingdom dreamed up by Al Capp for his satirical comic strip, *L'il Abner*.

9. "Litterbug Turns Up as Brother," *Tucson Daily Citizen*, May 26, 1962.

10. "Car Flips in Canyon; Tires Stolen," *Tucson Daily Citizen*, May 6, 1963. It seems likely that wheels were stolen with tires attached, despite the wording in the article.

11. "Four Dyed-in-the-Hand Car Looters Arrested," *Arizona Daily Star*, May 28, 1957.

12. Charles Bowden, "Sabino Canyon: Is It Too Good to Waste on People?" *Weekender* magazine, *Tucson Citizen*, September 19, 1981.

13. "New Public Picnic Area in Sabino Canyon Open," *Arizona Daily Star*, November 4, 1963.

14. "Just in Passing," *Arizona Daily Star*, May 18, 1963.

15. "Boy Makes 'Thing' Go 100 m.p.h.," *Tucson Daily Citizen*, June 20, 1957.

16. "Sports Car Plunges into Canyon; Girl Badly Injured," *Tucson Daily Citizen*, April 29, 1963.

17. "Car Flips off Canyon Road; UA Student Killed; 2 Hurt," *Tucson Daily Citizen*, May 4, 1963.
18. "No Clues in Sight on Sabino Slayer," *Tucson Daily Citizen*, January 13, 1964.
19. "Globe Man Accused of Sabino Canyon Slaying, Abduction," *Arizona Daily Star*, January 27, 1964.
20. "No Clues in Sight." By coincidence, in April another man confessed to the sexual assaults in 1961 and 1962. His accomplice wasn't apprehended.

Chapter 25. On the Mend

1. "Action, Please!," query by Bob DeVore, *Tucson Daily Citizen*, July 16, 1963.
2. "Action, Please!," by DeVore.
3. Today the Land and Water Conservation Fund is financed by royalties paid to the federal government for offshore oil and gas mining.
4. K. W. Misner, "Beautiful Sabino Canyon Defiled," letter to editor, *Tucson Daily Citizen*, March 11, 1970.
5. William Whitlaw, "Have They Nothing Better to Do?," letter to editor, *Tucson Daily Citizen*, May 13, 1969.
6. Ernie Heltsley, "Nude Scene Enjoyable, Actor Namath Decides," *Arizona Daily Star* (Tucson), April 25, 1970.
7. Betty Meuser, "The Hollywood Dollar," letter to editor, *Arizona Daily Star*, May 7, 1970.
8. Helen Pasternak, "Litterbugs in Canyon Are Costly," *Tucson Daily Citizen*, April 2, 1969.
9. H. Donald Harris, "Beer Cans in Sabino," letter to editor, *Arizona Daily Star*, February 18, 1969.
10. Pete Cowgill, "On the Trail," *Arizona Daily Star*, December 30, 1971.
11. Cowgill, "On the Trail." Part of Tucson's Randolph Park has since been renamed John C. Reid Park.
12. Cowgill, "Sabino Facing Problems," *Arizona Daily Star*, April 23, 1970.
13. Particulars for the following five letters to editors: Margaret MacIver Hoops, "Not So Great for Some," *Arizona Daily Star*, February 16, 1974; Tom Pittenger, "To Preserve Sabino," *Tucson Daily Citizen*, February 19, 1974; Anthony Caporaso, "Border on Ludicrous," *Arizona Daily Star*, February 22, 1974; Merle J. Westerfeld, "Don't Limit Sabino," *Tucson Daily Citizen*, March 1, 1974; Peter Johnson, "Sabino Sans Cars," *Arizona Daily Star*, March 4, 1974.
14. P. K. Weis (photo), "Sabino Hikers Leave Cars Behind," *Tucson Daily Citizen*, March 18, 1974. Readers who owned Volkswagens during these years may sigh with nostalgia, wince at the memory, or both. Edward Stiles (text), and P. K. Weis (photos), "People Boom Afoot in Sabino," *Tucson Daily Citizen*, March 11, 1974.
15. Cowgill, "Shuttle for Sabino," *Arizona Daily Star*, May 2, 1974.
16. "Cars in the Canyon," editorial, *Tucson Daily Citizen*, August 7, 1974.

17. A significant if somewhat peripheral issue attracting attention during this period was pollution of Sabino Creek's headwaters by the town of Summerhaven, with possible effects on water quality as far downstream as Sabino Canyon. The situation was resolved in 1985, when a new sewage treatment plant began discharging effluent into a different watershed.

18. "Sabino's Shuttle," *Tucson Citizen*, June 6, 1978.

19. Charles Bowden, "Sabino Canyon: Is It Too Good to Waste on People?," *Weekender* magazine, *Tucson Citizen*, September 19, 1981.

20. Bowden, "Sabino Canyon," *Weekender* magazine cover. The photograph was originally published mirror reversed.

21. Edward Stiles, "Sabino Car Closure Sparks Acrid Exchange," *Tucson Citizen*, October 2, 1981.

Chapter 26. Being There, Late Twentieth Century

1. Thanks for this insight to Robert C. Barnacastle, cofounder (with the author) of the Sabino Canyon Volunteer Naturalists.

2. Santa Catalina Ranger District, Coronado N. F., "Visitor's Guide to Sabino Canyon: A Desert Oasis" (Albuquerque: Southwest Natural and Cultural Heritage Association, 1985). The publisher has since been renamed the Public Lands Interpretive Association.

3. Jane Poston, "Preserve for Wealthy," letter to editor, *Arizona Daily Star* (Tucson), October 9, 1982.

4. By mid-2022 the adult shuttle fare to Upper Sabino had nearly quadrupled again, to $15.00.

5. Robert B. Tippeconnic, Forest Supervisor, *Special Closure Coronado National Forest USDA - Forest Service*, November 5, 1984.

6. "Diary of Edgar B Raudebaugh Camp & Project Supt. Sabino Coronado," February 26–June 26, 1938 notebook, April 2 entry; E. B. Raudebaugh Collection (NAU. MS.19), Series 2, Folder 14, Special Collections and Archives Dept., Cline Library, Northern Arizona University. Raudebaugh also evicted two boys from the women's restroom—another facility inadvertently creating opportunities for mischief.

7. In this context the reader may recall the "DANGER KEEP OFF" sign posted at the spillway around the time the dam was completed (chapter 18).

Further Reading

Barnes, Mary Ellen. *The Road to Mount Lemmon*. Tucson: University of Arizona Press, 2009.

Eppinga, Jane. *Tucson Arizona*. Charleston, S.C.: Arcadia Publishing, 2000. (Images of America series.)

Greenough, Sara, Diane Waggoner, Sarah Kennel, and Matthew S. Wittkovsky. *The Art of the American Snapshot: From the Collection of Robert E. Jackson*. Washington, D.C.: National Gallery of Art, 2007.

Hensel, Suzanne. *Look to the Mountains*. Mount Lemmon, Ariz.: Mt. Lemmon Woman's Club, 2003.

Lazaroff, David Wentworth. *Sabino Canyon: The Life of a Southwestern Oasis*. Tucson: University of Arizona Press, 1993.

Logan, Michael F. *The Lessening Stream: An Environmental History of the Santa Cruz River*. Tucson: University of Arizona Press, 2002.

Miller, Kristie. *Isabella Greenway: An Enterprising Woman*. Tucson: University of Arizona Press, 2004.

Sonnichsen, C. L. *Tucson: The Life and Times of an American City*. Norman: University of Oklahoma Press, 1982.

Southwestern Mission Research Center. *Tucson: A Short History*. Tucson: Southwestern Mission Research Center, 1986.

Speelman, Mike. *Historic Photos of Tucson*. Nashville, Tenn.: Turner Publishing Company, 2007.

Woosley, Anne I., and the Arizona Historical Society. *Early Tucson*. Images of America. Charleston, S.C.: Arcadia Publishing, 2008.

USDA Forest Service, Southwestern Region

Filmography

This is a chronological list, through 1985, of theater-released films with scenes shot at Sabino Canyon. The author has been unable to review the first three films to confirm Sabino Canyon footage.

Episodes in television series, including *Gunsmoke*, *Bonanza*, and *High Chaparral*, also include scenes filmed at the canyon.

The Halfbreed's Treachery (silent). 1912. Lubin Manufacturing Co., director unknown (Harry Solter?). Romaine Fielding, Edna Payne, Burton L. King.

The Poor Nut (silent). 1927. Jess Smith Productions, Richard Wallace, director. Jack Mulhall, Charlie Murray.

Under a Texas Moon. 1930. Warner Brothers, Michael Curtiz, director. Frank Fay, Raquel Torres.

The Return of the Cisco Kid. 1939. Twentieth Century Fox, Herbert I. Leeds, director. Warner Baxter, Lynn Bari, Cesar Romero.

Relentless. 1948. Cavalier Productions, George Sherman, director. Robert Young, Marguerite Chapman.

Ten Wanted Men. 1955. Ranown Pictures Corporation and Scott-Brown Productions, Bruce Humberstone, director. Randolph Scott, Jocelyn Brando, Richard Boone.

Buchanan Rides Alone. 1958. Columbia Pictures, Bud Boetticher, director. Randolph Scott.

Heller in Pink Tights. 1960. Paramount Pictures, George Cukor, director. Sophia Loren, Anthony Quinn.

The Deadly Companions. 1961. Carousel Productions, Sam Peckinpah, director. Maureen O'Hara, Brian Keith.

A Thunder of Drums. 1961. Robert J. Enders Productions and Metro-Goldwyn-Mayer, Joseph M. Newman, director. Richard Boone, George Hamilton, Luana Patten, Arthur O'Connell.

Return of the Gunfighter. 1967. King Brothers Productions, James Neilson, director. Robert Taylor, Chad Everett, Ana Martin. (Direct to television in United States, 1967; released to theaters elsewhere, beginning 1966.)

The Last Challenge. 1967. Metro-Goldwyn-Mayer, Richard Thorpe, director. Glenn Ford, Angie Dickenson, Chad Everett.

C. C. and Company. 1970. Namanco and Rogallan Productions, Seymour Robbie, director. Joe Namath, Ann-Margret.

The Soul of Nigger Charley. 1973. Paramount Pictures, Larry Spangler, director. Fred Williamson, D'Urville Martin, Denise Nicholas, Pedro Armendáriz Jr.

Posse. 1975. Bryna Productions, Kirk Douglas, director. Kirk Douglas, Bruce Dern.

Illustration Credits

Photographs and maps are as valuable as textual sources in reconstructing Sabino Canyon's past. Abbreviated credits accompany this book's illustrations where they appear, and more detailed information is given here, keyed to page numbers.

Camera positions, expressed as latitude and longitude in decimal degrees, follow the credits for many of the photographs. Precision varies, with an estimated position error from seven feet to more than thirty feet, depending on the number of satellites accessible to a Global Positioning System (GPS) device in the topographically rugged Sabino Canyon environment.

Many historical views in the canyon are extremely challenging to recognize today due to recreational developments, changes in vegetation, and effects of severe flooding. Camera positions now buried by heavily vegetated sediments at Sabino Lake are particularly difficult to locate, and those listed here are necessarily approximate. No camera positions are given for photographs taken outside national forest boundaries or seen only in newspapers and magazines, and certain locations have been withheld to protect historical features.

Cover, top   *Women seated on boulders, Sabino Creek*. Item L, album 2, box 14, PC 240, Sykes Family Collection, Arizona Historical Society, Tucson. (32.32237, −110.80998)

Cover, bottom   *Shuttlebus crossing stream*. Photograph by the author, May 11, 1991.

ii   *Young people climbing boulder*. Item R, folder 42, MS 1193, Mary Estill Caldwell Personal Papers, Arizona Historical Society, Tucson. (32.32368, −110.80652)

27   *Group on ledge, detail.* AHS 93064, Portraits—Maria Alexander, PC 1000 Tucson
        General Photo Collection, Arizona Historical Society, Tucson. (32.31491,
        −110.81149)

28   *Children and adults on sloping rocks.* AHS 18720, PC 60, Willis Pearson Haynes
        Photograph Collection, Arizona Historical Society, Tucson. (32.31505,
        −110.81108)

29   *Large group posed against cliff.* AHS 52598, Subjects—Picnics, PC 1000, Tucson
        General Photo Collection, Arizona Historical Society, Tucson. (32.31718,
        −110.81102)

31   *Two men carrying woman.* AHS 95733, PC 111, Clara Fish Roberts Photograph
        Collection, Arizona Historical Society, Tucson. (32.31635, −110.81052)

32   *Picnic, 1897.* AHS 95736, PC 111, Clara Fish Roberts Photograph Collection,
        Arizona Historical Society, Tucson. (32.31637, −110.81042)

33   *Drinking from creek.* AHS 95738, PC 111, Clara Fish Roberts Photograph Collec-
        tion, Arizona Historical Society, Tucson. (32.31698, −110.81067)

34   *Men posed among large boulders.* AHS 24377, Places—Sabino Canyon, PC
        1000, Tucson General Photo Collection, Arizona Historical Society, Tucson.
        (32.32618, −110.80303)

35   *University students posed among rocks.* N-10243, Students 1891–1900—Events—
        Picnics and Hikes, University of Arizona Photograph Collection, Special Col-
        lections, University of Arizona Libraries, Tucson. (32.31708, −110.81107)

36   *Woman and child at stream.* Item F, folder 15, MS 1085, Beppie Leslie Culin
        Papers, Arizona Historical Society, Tucson. (32.31708, −110.81082)

38   *Group holding hands.* AHS 46778, Subjects—Picnics, PC 1000, Tucson General
        Photo Collection, Arizona Historical Society, Tucson. (32.31882, −110.80960)

42   *Hotel notecard.* Hotel Santa Rita notecard, MS 879, Joseph Enos Wise Papers,
        Arizona Historical Society, Tucson.

45   *Gold mining prospect.* Photograph by the author, July 29, 2010.

46   *Charles Patterson Sykes.* AHS 41045, Portraits—Colonel Charles P. and Mrs. Sykes,
        PC 1000, Tucson General Photo Collection, Arizona Historical Society, Tucson.

46   *Mary Elizabeth Knight Sykes.* AHS 41046, Portraits—Colonel Charles P. and Mrs.
        Sykes, PC 1000, Tucson General Photo Collection, Arizona Historical Society,
        Tucson.

47   *Panoramic view up canyon.* Photograph by the author, January 18, 2018. (32.32209,
        −110.81115)

50   *Surveyors at stream.* AHS 46233, PC 114, George James Roskruge Photograph
        Collection, Arizona Historical Society, Tucson. (32.31695, −110.81059)

52–53   *Modern/historical panorama.* Background: photograph by the author, June 9,
        2011. Superimposed, left to right: AHS 45839, 45837, 45847, 45832, 45835,
        45833, PC 114, George James Roskruge Photograph Collection, Arizona His-
        torical Society, Tucson. (32.31803, −110.81047)

53   *Cairn and chiseled X.* Photograph by the author, May 30, 2011. (32.31803,
        −110.81047)

57   *Travelers at Fort Lowell.* AHS 48647, PC 60, Willis Pearson Haynes Photograph
        Collection, Arizona Historical Society, Tucson.

58–60   *Tucson area map, 1893 (shown twice).* "Official Map of Pima County Arizona,"
        George J. Roskruge, 1893; 4333, P4 1893, Map Collection, History and Ar-
        chives Division, Arizona State Library, Archives and Public Records, Phoenix.

62   *Mud wagon stagecoach.* N-2476, Students 1891–1900—Events—Picnics and
        Hikes, Arizona, Southwestern, and Miscellaneous Photographs, University
        of Arizona Photograph Collection, Special Collections, University of Arizona
        Libraries, Tucson. (32.31470, −110.81180)

64   *Woman at streamgage.* AHS 29645, Places—Sabino Canyon, PC 1000 Tucson
        General Photo Collection, Arizona Historical Society, Tucson. (32.32345,
        −110.80770)

67   *Santa Cruz River flood, 1889.* AHS 2922, Places—Santa Cruz River, PC 1000,
        Tucson General Photo Collection, Arizona Historical Society, Tucson.

70   *Professor Woodward's dam site.* Photograph by the author, December 20, 2017.
        (32.35702, −110.77751)

73   *Visitors at streamgage.* AHS 62886, PC 142, Upham Family Photographs, Arizona
        Historical Society, Tucson. (32.32344, −110.80771)

74   *University of Arizona faculty.* University faculty, 1901, folder 2, Faculty—
        1891–1910, University of Arizona Photograph Collection, Special Collections,
        University of Arizona Libraries, Tucson.

78   *View down canyon, 1902.* "Giant Cactus in Lower Sabiño Canyon," R. S. Kellogg,
        1912; category Coronado—Scenery, Historical Photograph Collection, Forest
        Service Southwestern Regional Office, Albuquerque. (32.33275, −110.79020)

82   *Thomas F. Meagher.* Whi 30433, "Tom Meagher," Robertson & Co., Muskogee,
        Indian Territory, undated; William A. Jones Photographs, Wisconsin Histori-
        cal Images, Wisconsin Historical Society, Madison.

85   *Survey mark.* Photograph by the author, January 24, 2018.

88   *Diversion tunnel.* "The portal of the Tunnel near the Proposed Sabino Dam,"
      T. W. Norcross, 1911; documents related to the Great Western Power Com-
      pany, Supervisor's Office, Coronado National Forest, Tucson. (32.35522,
      −110.77955)

92–93 *Map of reservoirs.* "General Plan of Sabino Canyon Project Showing Proposed
      Diversion Made for the Great Western Power Co.," William B. Alexander,
      1908; AZ 171, Papers of William Burnham Alexander, Special Collections,
      University of Arizona Libraries, Tucson.

94   *William B. Alexander and friends.* AHS 25924, Portraits—Frank Kelton, PC 1000,
      Tucson General Photo Collection, Arizona Historical Society, Tucson.

99   *Tents at roadside.* AHS 28589, Places—Sabino Canyon, PC 1000, Tucson General
      Photo Collection, Arizona Historical Society, Tucson. (32.31551, −110.81005)

100   *Cadets with rifles and game.* AHS 28592, Places—Sabino Canyon, PC 1000, Tuc-
      son General Photo Collection, Arizona Historical Society, Tucson. (32.31600,
      −110.81070)

101   *Uniformed cadets in formation.* Item w, folder 1, Military Camps—Arizona,
      Arizona, Southwestern, and Miscellaneous Photographs collection, Special
      Collections, University of Arizona Libraries, Tucson. (32.31275, −110.81227)

102   *Cadets lined up, early morning.* Item q, folder 2, Military Camps—Arizona,
      Arizona, Southwestern, and Miscellaneous Photographs Collection, Special
      Collections, University of Arizona Libraries, Tucson. (32.31311, −110.81223)

103   *Painted figures, bullet holes.* Photograph by the author, October 19, 2020.

106   *Surrey at adobe ruin.* AHS 62347, PC 142, Upham Family Photographs, Arizona
      Historical Society, Tucson.

107   *Women, saguaro, and canteen.* AHS 62889, PC 142, Upham Family Photographs,
      Arizona Historical Society, Tucson.

108   *Surrey approaching canyon.* AHS 62879, PC 142, Upham Family Photographs,
      Arizona Historical Society, Tucson. (32.31526, −110.81724)

109   *Woman waving stick.* AHS 92919, PC 142, Upham Family Photographs, Arizona
      Historical Society, Tucson. (32.32345, −110.80790)

110   *Group on boulder, man with raised pistol.* AHS 92917, PC 142, Upham Family
      Photographs, Arizona Historical Society, Tucson. (32.32390, −110.80730)

110   *Couple seated on rock, man pointing.* AHS 92920, PC 142, Upham Family Photo-
      graphs, Arizona Historical Society, Tucson. (32.32444, −110.80606)

112   *Two seated on boulders, passing cup.* AHS 92921, PC 142, Upham Family Photo-
      graphs, Arizona Historical Society, Tucson. (32.32500, −110.80573)

112   *Surrey crossing sandy wash.* AHS 62887, PC 142, Upham Family Photographs, Arizona Historical Society, Tucson.

117   *Group with multiple firearms.* B 68670, Places—Sabino Canyon, Buehman Photo Collection, Arizona Historical Society, Tucson. (32.31743, −110.81127)

118   *Group posed at fallen cottonwood.* AHS 95639, PC 111, Clara Fish Roberts Photograph Collection, Arizona Historical Society, Tucson. (32.32150, −110.80938)

119   *Woman with pistol and holster (two photos).* AHS 95828 (left), AHS 95829 (right), PC 111, Clara Fish Roberts Photograph Collection, Arizona Historical Society, Tucson. (32.32286, −110.80936)

120   *Woman with raised pistol, horses.* AHS 62883, PC 142, Upham Family Photographs, Arizona Historical Society, Tucson. (32.32247, −110.81012)

121   *University students with owl.* "Great hunters from the University, 1902," folder 84, MS 1095, Mansfield Family Records, Arizona Historical Society, Tucson. (32.31732, −110.81117)

122   *Man with rifle (two photos).* Items A^{2}C (left), A^{2}D (right), smaller album, PC 257, Margaret Eldred Collection, Arizona Historical Society, Tucson. (32.32345, −110.80683)

125   *Men, mounts, and pack animals on trail.* "A portion of the completed road," T. W. Norcross, 1911; documents related to the Great Western Power Company, Supervisor's Office, Coronado National Forest, Tucson. (32.31600, −110.80818)

126   *Wooden telephone pole.* Photograph by the author, April 3, 2012. (32.32453, −110.80080)

128–129   *Trail map, 1912.* Tucson Chamber of Commerce, "The Catalina Mountains Arizona's Finest Summer Resort," *Arizona Daily Star*, May 26, 1912; courtesy Arizona Historical Society, Tucson.

131   *Visitors at small waterfall.* AHS 41351, Subjects—Mountains—Santa Catalina, PC 1000, Tucson General Photo Collection, Arizona Historical Society, Tucson. (32.32485, −110.80577)

134   *Group at large tree.* AHS 42081, Subjects—Mountains—Mt. Lemmon, PC 1000, Tucson General Photo Collection, Arizona Historical Society, Tucson.

136   *Burros carrying lumber.* Untitled negative, personal collection of Terry DeWald.

138   *Two horseback riders on trail.* Item P, folder 53, MS 1193, Mary Estill Caldwell Personal Papers, Arizona Historical Society, Tucson. (32.34320, −110.77869)

140   *Stereoview, large family.* AHS 11473, PC 260, Stereoview Collection, Arizona Historical Society, Tucson. (32.316420, −110.80997)

141   *Women in formal dress, wading.* AHS 24449, Portraits—Myrtle Drachman, PC 1000, Tucson General Photo Collection, Arizona Historical Society, Arizona Historical Society, Tucson. (32.31748, −110.81112)

142   *Postcard, two men on bank of stream.* "Sabino Canyon, Tucson, Ariz.," postcard no. 24, H. D. Corbett Stationery Co., Tucson; author's collection. (32.31804, −110.81133)

143   *Postcard, carriages in the Picnic Grounds.* "Sabino Canyon, Catalina Mountains. Tucson, Arizona," postcard no. 238, Rudolph Rasmessen, Tucson; author's collection. (32.32108, −110.81043)

144   *Women and children picnicking.* AHS 92902, PC 142, Upham Family Photographs, Arizona Historical Society, Tucson. (32.32340; −110.80845)

145   *Family among boulders in stream.* AHS 51357, Portraits—Mr. and Mrs. H. Virgil Failor, PC 1000, Tucson General Photo Collection, Arizona Historical Society, Tucson. (32.32587, −110.80473)

146   *Postcard: power company streamgage.* "Sabino Canyon, Catalina Mountains. Tucson, Arizona," postcard no. 227, Rudolph Rasmessen, Tucson; author's collection. (32.32337, −110.80813)

146   *Postcard, Sabino Canyon Trail and seated man.* "Sabino Canyon. Catalina Mountains. Tucson, Arizona," postcard no. 215, Rudolph Rasmessen, Tucson; author's collection. (32.33693, −110.78633)

148   *Men and women on angular boulders.* Item AW, PC 86, Mary Jones Montgomery Photograph Album, Arizona Historical Society, Tucson. (32.32358, −110.80773)

148   *Men with beer bottles.* Item AL, PC 86, Mary Jones Montgomery Photograph Album, Arizona Historical Society, Tucson. (32.32345, −110.80784)

150   *Young couples.* Left: Item W, PC 86, Mary Jones Montgomery Photograph Album, Arizona Historical Society, Tucson. Right: Item L, larger album, PC 257, Margaret Eldred Collection, Arizona Historical Society, Tucson. (left: 32.32318, −110.80890; right: 32.32555, −110.80548)

152   *Uniformed man with companions.* Item A6B, PC 248, Geraldine Fenollosa Album, Arizona Historical Society, Tucson. (32.32372, −110.81110)

153   *Women with cigarettes.* Item A, folder 2006, MS 1276, Ivancovich Family Collection, Arizona Historical Society, Tucson. (32.32232, −110.81012)

154   *Women in bathing suits.* "Miss Common [?] and J 1922," folder 2, Sabino Canyon (Ariz.) photographs, Arizona, Southwestern, and Miscellaneous Photographs, Special Collections, University of Arizona Libraries, Tucson.

155   *Visitors and parked cars.* Item H, folder 52, PC 240, Sykes Family Collection, Arizona Historical Society, Tucson. (32.32207, −110.81080)

160–162   *Tucson area map, 1905 (shown twice).* "Tucson Quadrangle" (1:125,000), June, 1905 edition, United States Geological Survey; scan courtesy Arizona Historical Society, Tucson.

164   *Early automobile crossing Rillito.* Item N, Photograph Album of John H. Gardiner, MS 1115, Gardiner Family Papers, Arizona Historical Society, Tucson.

165   *Family in two carriages.* AHS 51379, Portraits—Mr. and Mrs. H. Virgil Failor, PC 1000, Tucson General Photo Collection, Arizona Historical Society, Arizona Historical Society, Tucson. (32.32343, −110.80905)

166   *Unpaved road through desert.* Item 7AC, album 7, MS 1193, Mary Estill Caldwell Personal Papers, Arizona Historical Society, Tucson. (32.30033, −110.82360)

167   *Three women and large car.* Item E, folder 52, PC 240, Sykes Family Collection, Arizona Historical Society, Tucson. (32.31717, −110.81448)

168   *Laborers on road.* #02-1119, RG 52 Highway Department, History and Archives Division, Arizona State Library, Archives and Public Records, Phoenix. (32.32454, −110.80608)

170   *Downtown Tucson, 1926.* B 27898, Places—Tucson—Streets—Congress—Post 1925, Buehman Photo Collection, Arizona Historical Society, Tucson.

175   *Man at USGS streamgage.* Negative 3257 (stake 3228), Desert Laboratory Repeat Photography Collection, United States Geological Survey, Tucson. (32.31682, −110.81043)

176   *Boy suspended from cable (two photos).* Items BC (left), CW (right), album 4, MS 1198, Fenster School Collection, Arizona Historical Society, Tucson. (32.31697, −110.81078)

178   *CCC boys making adobe bricks.* AHS 17329, MS 875, Frederic Winn Papers, Arizona Historical Society, Tucson. (32.31108, −110.81824)

179   *House, Lowell Ranger Station, being built.* "Front Porch Lowell Ranger Station," CCC Photos and Photo Log file, Supervisor's Office, Coronado National Forest, Tucson. (32.31099, −110.81796)

180   *House, Lowell Ranger Station, completed.* "Lowell Ranger Station dwelling," 1930s—CNF Photos file, Supervisor's Office, Coronado National Forest, Tucson. (32.31052, −110.81799)

182   *CWA picnic set.* 95-GP-955-292479; Recreation Improvements—Arizona; 95-GP
       Photographs Relating to National Forests, Resource Management Practices,
       Personnel, and Cultural and Economic History, ca. 1897–ca. 1980; RG 95 Re-
       cords of the Forest Service, 1870–2008; Still Pictures Unit, National Archives,
       College Park, Md. (32.32280, –110.80990)

183   *CWA restroom.* 95-GP-955-292477; Recreation Improvements—Arizona; 95-GP
       Photographs Relating to National Forests, Resource Management Practices,
       Personnel, and Cultural and Economic History, ca. 1897–ca. 1980; RG 95 Re-
       cords of the Forest Service, 1870–2008; Still Pictures Unit, National Archives
       at College Park, Md. (32.32412, –110.80612)

184   *Caretaker's cabin.* "Sabino Caretaker's Cabin 1929 [*sic*]," CNF Photographic
       Record Book 1, Photographs of Forest Activities 1927 to ———, Supervisor's
       Office, Coronado National Forest, Tucson. (32.32205, –110.81087)

184   *Stepping stones, Sabino Canyon Trail.* 288717, category Coronado National
       Forest—Recreation, Historical Photograph Collection, Forest Service South-
       western Regional Office, Albuquerque. (32.32603, –110.80317)

191   *ERA men beginning road work.* #96-1614, RG 89 Arizona Board of Public
       Welfare, History and Archives Division, Arizona State Library, Archives and
       Public Records, Phoenix. (32.32433, –110.80601)

192   *Inspectors, site of first crossing.* #05-8000, Emergency Relief Administration, RG 89
       Arizona Board of Public Welfare, History and Archives Division, Arizona State
       Library, Archives and Public Records, Phoenix. (32.32487, –110.80593)

193   *Construction crane, first crossing.* #05-8001, Emergency Relief Administration,
       RG 89 Arizona Board of Public Welfare, History and Archives Division, Arizona
       State Library, Archives and Public Records, Phoenix. (32.32487, –110.80593)

194   *Wooden forms, first crossing.* #96-1615, RG 89 Arizona Board of Public Welfare,
       History and Archives Division, Arizona State Library, Archives and Public
       Records, Phoenix. (32.32505, –110.80560)

194   *First crossing, completed.* #05-8003, Emergency Relief Administration, RG 89 Ar-
       izona Board of Public Welfare, History and Archives Division, Arizona State
       Library, Archives and Public Records, Phoenix. (32.32488, –110.80595)

197   *Pond at third crossing.* #98-3869, RG 89 Arizona Board of Public Welfare,
       History and Archives Division, Arizona State Library, Archives and Public
       Records, Phoenix. (32.32634, –110.80300)

199   *Fourth crossing under construction.* #98-3867, RG 89 Arizona Board of Public
       Welfare, History and Archives Division, Arizona State Library, Archives and
       Public Records, Phoenix. (32.32813, –110.80140)

202   *Isabella Greenway.* B 205809, Portraits—Isabella Greenway, Buehman Photo
       Collection, Arizona Historical Society, Tucson.

205   *Postcard, fifth crossing.* "The River Crossing Bridge No. 5, Sabino Canyon near
       Tucson, Arizona," postcard no. B7612, Frasher's Inc., Pomona, Calif.; author's
       collection. (32.32923, −110.79876)

205   *WPA plaque, fifth crossing.* Author photograph, March 3, 2012.

206   *WPA road construction, unstable slope.* "Sabino Rec. Rd. Along Grade at Sta.
       #70," Arizona folder, 69-PR Pictorial Report, 1935–1943; RG 69 Records of
       the Work Projects Administration, 1922–1944; Still Pictures Unit, National
       Archives, College Park, Md. (32.33432, −110.78961)

207   *Anderson Dam and cypress.* "Sabino Canyon," CNF Photographic Record Book 1,
       Photographs of Forest Activities 1927 to ———, Supervisor's Office, Coro-
       nado National Forest, Tucson. (32.33930, −110.78544)

209   *Seventh crossing.* 69-NS-30160, Arizona Construction; 69-NS WPA Informa-
       tion Division State Files; RG 69 Records of the Work Projects Administra-
       tion, 1922–1944; Still Pictures Unit, National Archives, College Park, Md.
       (32.32993, −110.79455)

210   *Swimmers at seventh crossing.* "Swimming Pool Sabino Canyon," Arizona Con-
       struction; 69-NS WPA Information Division State Files; RG 69 Records of
       the Work Projects Administration, 1922–1944; Still Pictures Unit, National
       Archives, College Park, Md. (32.33007, −110.79447)

212   *Theodore Wyman Jr.* uclamss_1429_7793, LSC.1429, Los Angeles Times Pho-
       tographic Archive, Special Collections, Charles E. Young Research Library,
       University of California, Los Angeles.

216   *End-of-road switchbacks.* 344980, category Coronado National Forest—
       Recreation, Historical Photograph Collection, Forest Service Southwestern
       Regional Office, Albuquerque. (32.34062, −110.78410)

218   *Albert H. Condron.* B 37358, Portraits—Albert Harlan Condron, Buehman Photo
       Collection, Arizona Historical Society, Tucson.

221   *Group posed on ledge, Lower Sabino.* Item AO, folder 37, MS 1193, Mary Estill
       Caldwell Personal Papers, Arizona Historical Society, Tucson. (32.31477,
       −110.81152)

222   *Scaffolding for dam construction.* NAU.PH.99.4.3.21, E. B. Raudebaugh Collec-
       tion, Special Collections and Archives Department, Cline Library, Northern
       Arizona University, Flagstaff. (32.31457, −110.81102)

222 *Dam under construction.* NAU.PH.99.4.3.20, E. B. Raudebaugh Collection, Special Collections and Archives Department, Cline Library, Northern Arizona University, Flagstaff. (32.31525, –110.81165)

226 *Boys on completed dam.* "Sabino Canyon Lake and Dam, Sabino Canyon Recreational Area 1938," CCC Photos and Photo Log file, Supervisor's Office, Coronado National Forest, Tucson. (32.31450, –110.81109)

227 *Swing set below dam.* "Use of Recreational Equipment, Sabino Canyon Recreational Area March 1938," CNF Photographic Record Book 1, Photographs of Forest Activities 1927 to ———, Supervisor's Office, Coronado National Forest, Tucson. (32.31435, –110.81196)

228 *View of dam and lake.* 360319, category Coronado National Forest—Engineering, Historical Photograph Collection, Forest Service Southwestern Regional Office, Albuquerque. (32.31368, –110.81309)

229 *Dedication ceremony, Sabino Dam.* NAU.PH.99.4.1.18, E. B. Raudebaugh Collection, Special Collections and Archives Department, Cline Library, Northern Arizona University, Flagstaff. (32.31475, –110.81205)

230 *Swimmers in Sabino Lake.* 371917, CNF Photographic Record Book 1, Photographs of Forest Activities 1927 to ———, Supervisor's Office, Coronado National Forest, Tucson. (32.31587, –110.81058)

231 *Girl photographing picnickers.* 370919, CNF Photographic Record Book 1, Photographs of Forest Activities 1927 to ———, Supervisor's Office, Coronado National Forest, Tucson. (32.31592, –110.81075)

233 *Fishing from dam, 1939.* AHS 7239, Subjects—Mountains, PC 1000, Tucson General Photo Collection, Arizona Historical Society, Tucson. (32.31530, –110.81152)

234 *Fred Winn.* AHS 14374, Portraits—Mr. and Mrs. Frederic Winn (Ada Pierce), PC 1000, Tucson General Photo Collection, Arizona Historical Society, Tucson.

237 *Fourth crossing, tents in background.* #98-3868, RG 89 Arizona Board of Public Welfare, History and Archives Division, Arizona State Library, Archives and Public Records, Phoenix. (32.32779, –110.80145)

238 *Drawing of laborers.* Bill Griffin, "Sabino Canyon," *Oasis* vol. 2, no. 19 (October 1, 1935), Tucson Transient Camp, Pima County, Arizona; MS 1478, Civilian Conservation Corps Newsletters, Arizona Historical Society, Tucson.

241 *Workers' camp overview.* "Sabino Transient Camp. July 1936," CCC Photos and Photo Log file, Supervisor's Office, Coronado National Forest, Tucson. (32.32818, –110.79918)

242 *Inspectors at dam-construction scaffold.* 347096, category Coronado National Forest—Personnel, Historical Photograph Collection, Forest Service Southwestern Regional Office, Albuquerque. (32.31496, −110.81166)

246 *Family wading, Lower Sabino.* 349287, category Coronado National Forest—Recreation, Historical Photograph Collection, Forest Service Southwestern Regional Office, Albuquerque. (32.31435, −110.81142)

247 *Fourth crossing, camp buildings beyond.* NAU.PH.99.4.3.16, E. B. Raudebaugh Collection, Special Collections and Archives Department, Cline Library, Northern Arizona University, Flagstaff. (32.32779, −110.80147)

248 *Forest Service float, Rodeo Parade.* NAU.PH.99.4.4.3, E. B. Raudebaugh Collection, Special Collections and Archives Department, Cline Library, Northern Arizona University, Flagstaff.

250 *Edgar Raudebaugh.* Personal collection of Mary Lou Raudebaugh Morrow.

251 *Rusted engine in stream.* Photograph by the author, December 20, 2019.

255 *Postcard, cars on road into Upper Sabino.* "Sabino Canyon Drive Tucson, Arizona," postcard no. E-31, L. L. Cook Co., Milwaukee, Wis.; author's collection. (32.31750, −110.81365)

256 *Family in trailer camp, Lower Sabino.* 406581, category Coronado National Forest—Recreation, Historical Photograph Collection, Forest Service Southwestern Regional Office, Albuquerque. (32.30942, −110.81002)

258–259 *Tucson area map, 1936.* "Points of Interest of Tucson and Vicinity," Tucson Chamber of Commerce and Sunshine Climate Club, 1936; G4334 T8 1936 M3, Tucson Map Collection, Arizona Historical Society, Tucson.

260 *Crowded fishermen, Sabino Lake.* Photograph by S. C. Warman, *Tucson Daily Citizen*, published May 5, 1951, p.1; courtesy *Arizona Daily Star*, Tucson; © Tucson Citizen; published by permission of Lee Enterprises, Omaha, Nebr.

263 *Red Cross float, Rodeo Parade, 1941.* AHS 9041, Places—Tucson—Celebrations—Rodeo 1940s, PC 1000, Tucson General Photo Collection, Arizona Historical Society, Tucson.

268 *Newspaper coverage, death during rescue attempt. Arizona Daily Star*, August 10, 1948, p. 1; © Arizona Daily Star; published by permission of Lee Enterprises, Omaha, Nebr.

273 *Dredging equipment, Sabino Lake.* Photograph by Thomas R. Ellinwood, *Arizona Daily Star*, March 1951 (unpublished at that time); © Arizona Daily Star; published by permission of Lee Enterprises, Omaha, Nebr. (32.31530, −110.81106)

274   *Fishing from Sabino Dam, 1951.* Photograph by Bernie Roth, *Arizona Daily Star*, published May 6, 1951, p. 11A; © Arizona Daily Star; published by permission of Lee Enterprises, Omaha, Nebr. (32.31527, −110.81148)

276   *Prisoners' inscription.* Photograph by the author, January 31, 2011.

278   *Postcard, visitors at waterfall.* "Waterfalls in Sabino Canyon," postcard L-120, Lollesgard Specialty Company, Tucson and Phoenix; author's collection.

279   *Newspaper coverage, "Operation Alert."* "D-M's 'Operation Alert' Goes Smoothly," *Arizona Daily Star*, June 16, 1955, p. 1B; © Arizona Daily Star; published by permission of Lee Enterprises, Omaha, Nebr. (Photographs credited to "Wong-Sheaffer," a studio run by photographers Tunney Wong and Jack Sheaffer.)

281   *Mimicking target practice, Bear Canyon.* AHS 93001, PC 142, Upham Family Photographs, Arizona Historical Society, Tucson. (32.31080, −110.79903)

282   *Lower Bear Canyon sign.* Untitled negatives, Historic Photographs Santa Catalina Ranger District, Supervisor's Office, Coronado National Forest, Tucson. (32.31227, −110.80118)

283   *Young picnickers, Lower Bear Canyon.* Untitled negative, Historic Photographs Santa Catalina Ranger District, Supervisor's Office, Coronado National Forest, Tucson. (32.31198, −110.79880)

284   *Caretaker at new picnic table.* Untitled negative, Historic Photographs Santa Catalina Ranger District, Supervisor's Office, Coronado National Forest, Tucson. (32.31342, −110.81363)

285   *Sabino Canyon Visitor Center.* Untitled negative, Historic Photographs Santa Catalina Ranger District, Supervisor's Office, Coronado National Forest, Tucson. (32.30983, −110.82233)

286   *Girls at exhibit, visitor center.* Untitled print, category Interp/Photos, Regional Black and White Photos, Forest Service Southwestern Regional Office, Albuquerque.

288   *Ranger-led nature walk.* Untitled print, Historic Photographs Santa Catalina Ranger District, Supervisor's Office, Coronado National Forest, Tucson. (32.31937, −110.81690)

290   *Man on horseback, woman at stream.* Item C, folder 30, MS 1120, Robert M. Riddell Papers, Arizona Historical Society, Tucson. (32.32247, −110.80993)

291   Heller in Pink Tights *lobby card. Heller in Pink Tights* mini lobby card, Paramount Pictures Corporation, 1960; author's collection; © Paramount Pictures Corp. All Rights Reserved. (32.33940, −110.78572)

293   *Flood damage at second crossing.* "Below 2," courtesy Donald and Betty Early. (32.32572, −110.80475)

294   *Streamside vegetation.* Photograph by the author, August 21, 1988.

299   *Caretaker's cabin.* Untitled print, courtesy Donald and Betty Early. (32.32204, −110.81103)

300   *Pierre and Hazel Early, seated with friend.* Untitled print, courtesy Donald and Betty Early.

301   *Pierre Early, standing.* "Pierre October 1952," courtesy Donald and Betty Early.

302   *Karen Early with pets.* Untitled print by Edwin M. Hunt, courtesy Donald and Betty Early. (32.32187, −110.81131)

303   *Karen Early's horse, Sabino.* Untitled print by Edwin M. Hunt, courtesy Donald and Betty Early. (32.32202, −110.81179)

304   *Karen Early with Sabino.* Untitled print by Edwin M. Hunt, courtesy Donald and Betty Early. (32.32220, −110.81183)

305   *View up canyon to Thimble Peak.* Untitled print, courtesy Donald and Betty Early. (32.32202, −110.81107)

309   *Staged litter scene at table.* 468416, Historic Photographs Santa Catalina Ranger District, Supervisor's Office, Coronado National Forest, Tucson. (32.31637, −110.81045)

310   *Newspaper coverage, beer can litter.* "Saturday Night Party Clutters up Picnic Area," *Arizona Daily Star*, April 26, 1954, p. 1A; © Arizona Daily Star; published by permission of Lee Enterprises, Omaha, Nebr.

312   *Litterbug statue.* Untitled negative, Historic Photographs Santa Catalina Ranger District, Supervisor's Office, Coronado National Forest, Tucson. (32.32202, −110.81103)

314   *Car on fifth crossing.* AHS 83155, Places—Sabino Canyon, PC 1000, Tucson General Photo Collection, Arizona Historical Society, Tucson. (32.32915, −110.79875)

314   *Swimmers in Sabino Creek.* Untitled print, CNF Photographic Record Book 1, Photographs of Forest Activities 1927 to ———, Supervisor's Office, Coronado National Forest, Tucson. (32.32337, −110.80787)

316   *Family picnic, Upper Sabino.* 95-G-491970, Box 226 Camping AZ-CA, Camping and Picnicking—Arizona; 95-G General photographic files of the Forest Service, 1897–1965; RG 95 Records of the Forest Service, 1870–2008; Still Pictures Unit, National Archives, College Park, Md. (32.33005, −110.79477)

318   *Vandalized picnic table.* Untitled negative, Historic Photographs Santa Catalina Ranger District, Supervisor's Office, Coronado National Forest, Tucson. (32.31395, −110.81245)

319   *Painted graffiti.* "Vandalism Sabino Canyon End of Road," negative, Historic
       Photographs Santa Catalina Ranger District, Supervisor's Office, Coronado
       National Forest, Tucson. (32.34393, −110.78055)

322   *Newspaper coverage, crime victims.* "No Clues in Sight on Sabino Slayer," *Tucson
       Daily Citizen*, January 13, 1964, p. 1; © Tucson Citizen; published by permis-
       sion of Lee Enterprises, Omaha, Nebr.

325   *Ranger closing gate.* Untitled negative, Historic Photographs Santa Catalina
       Ranger District, Supervisor's Office, Coronado National Forest, Tucson.
       (32.30905, −110.82380)

329   *Newspaper coverage, ticket-vending machine.* "No One-Armed Bandit," *Tucson
       Daily Citizen*, December 10, 1965, p.41; © Tucson Citizen; published by per-
       mission of Lee Enterprises, Omaha, Nebr.

332   *Joe Namath on motorcycle.* Photograph by Art Grasberger, *Tucson Daily Citi-
       zen*, published April 24, 1970; print distributed by Associated Press, author's
       collection; © Tucson Citizen; published by permission of Lee Enterprises,
       Omaha, Nebr.

334   *Litter cleanup by fraternity members.* Untitled negative, Historic Photographs
       Santa Catalina Ranger District, Supervisor's Office, Coronado National Forest,
       Tucson. (32.33693, −110.78678)

338   *Automobiles crowding roadsides.* Photograph by P. K. Weis, *Tucson Daily Cit-
       izen*, published March 18, 1974, p.4; courtesy *Arizona Daily Star*, Tucson;
       © Tucson Citizen; published by permission of Lee Enterprises, Omaha, Nebr.

339   *Newspaper coverage, "People Boom Afoot."* Edward Stiles (text) and P. K. Weis
       (photographs), "People Boom Afoot in Sabino," *Tucson Daily Citizen*,
       March 11, 1974, p. 19; © Tucson Citizen; published by permission of Lee
       Enterprises, Omaha, Nebr.

341   *Shuttle approaching fifth crossing.* Photograph by H. Darr Beiser, *Tucson Daily
       Citizen*, published June 6, 1978, p. 1A; courtesy *Arizona Daily Star*, Tucson;
       © Tucson Citizen; published by permission of Lee Enterprises, Omaha, Nebr.
       (32.32898, −110.79848)

343   *Many visitors at Sabino Lake.* Photograph by Peter Weinberger, *Tucson Daily
       Citizen*, published September 19, 1981 in *Weekender* magazine, p.12; courtesy
       Arizona Daily Star, Tucson; © Tucson Citizen; published by permission of Lee
       Enterprises, Omaha, Nebr. (32.31331, −110.81323)

344   *Boy diving into creek.* Photograph by Peter Weinberger, *Tucson Daily Citizen*,
       published September 19, 1981 (mirror reversed) in *Weekender* magazine, p.1;
       courtesy *Arizona Daily Star*, Tucson; © Tucson Citizen; published by permis-
       sion of Lee Enterprises, Omaha, Nebr. (32.31702, −110.81083)

349   *Shuttle at the second crossing, Upper Sabino.* Photograph by the author, December 15, 1991.

350–351 *Sabino Canyon map, 1985.* "Sabino Canyon Recreation Area and Vicinity," map drawn by Patricia Eisenberg, in "Visitors Guide to Sabino Canyon: A Desert Oasis," Southwest Natural and Cultural Heritage Association, Albuquerque, 1985; author's collection. The publisher has since been renamed the Public Lands Interpretive Association.

353   *Walkers on road, Upper Sabino.* Photograph by the author, May 29, 1991.

354   *Family with stroller, second crossing.* Photograph by the author, March 14, 1992.

354   *Runners splashing, fifth crossing.* Photograph by the author, March 14, 1992.

355   *Birders at Sabino Lake.* Photograph by the author, December 19, 1998.

355   *Children at Sabino Dam spillway.* Photograph by the author, July 21, 1984.

356   *Families on rocks, Anderson Dam.* Photograph by the author, March 14, 1992.

359   *Woman reading on boulder, Upper Sabino.* Photograph by the author, September 10, 1988. (32.32498, −110.80581)

360   *Women and girl snacking at stream, 1992.* Photograph by the author, March 14, 1992.

362   *Men picnicking at stream, 1890.* AHS 24378, Places—Sabino Canyon, PC 1000, Tucson General Photo Collection, Arizona Historical Society, Tucson. (32.31678, −110.81035)

363   *Survey crew picnicking, ca. 1899.* AHS 19460, PC 114, George James Roskruge Photograph Collection, Arizona Historical Society, Tucson. (32.31647, −110.81055)

364   *Men and women picnicking in shade, ca. 1907.* AHS 62882, PC 142, Upham Family Photographs, Arizona Historical Society, Tucson. (32.32253, −110.81017)

364   *Adults and children picnicking on sand, ca. 1907.* Item 4DD, Album 4, MS 1193, Mary Estill Caldwell Personal Papers, Arizona Historical Society, Tucson. (32.32350, −110.80805)

366   *Women picnicking on ledge, 1920s.* AHS 54851, Subjects—Picnics, PC 1000, Tucson General Photo Collection, Arizona Historical Society, Tucson. (32.32350, −110.80807)

367   *Small family at picnic table, 1938.* 37192, category Coronado National Forest—Recreation, Historical Photograph Collection, Forest Service Southwestern Regional Office, Albuquerque. (32.31401, −110.81269)

368   *Family picnicking on rocks, 1941.* 406584, category Coronado National Forest—Recreation, Historical Photograph Collection, Forest Service Southwestern Regional Office, Albuquerque. (32.33940, −110.78563)

369   *Elaborate picnic at table, 1951.* 95-G-489538, Box 226 Camping AZ-CA, Camping and Picnicking—Arizona; 95-G General photographic files of the Forest Service, 1897–1965; RG 95 Records of the Forest Service, 1870–2008; Still Pictures Unit, National Archives, College Park, Md. (32.32195, −110.81032)

373   *Sunlight on canyon floor.* Photograph by the author, December 9, 2020. (32.31885, −110.81138)

384   *Man and two women on blanket.* "Mr. Tussing, his fiancee Miss Vail, & Bertha Carpenter," AHS 69368, Places—Sabino Canyon, PC 1000, Tucson General Photo Collection, Arizona Historical Society, Tucson.

408   *Group on seesaws.* 360317, category Coronado National Forest—Recreation, Historical Photograph Collection, Forest Service Southwestern Regional Office, Albuquerque. (32.31435, −110.81200)

428   *Two men standing in creek.* "Haskell and Al Bernard in Sabino Canyon, 1902," folder 84, MS 1095, Mansfield Family Records, Arizona Historical Society, Tucson. (32.31732, −110.81118)

437   *Author and wife.* Photograph by the author, August 10, 2013. (32.32485, −110.80577)

Arizona Historical Society

Index

A page number in **bold** indicates a photograph. The letter *m* indicates a map. The letter *n* indicates an endnote. Extended captions have been indexed as text.

Professor Woodward's streamgage, **64**, 72–73, **73**, 84, 109, **109**, 157, 162m, 163

public transportation. *See* shuttle

Pusch Ridge Wilderness, 3m, 295, 350–351m, 351, 403n16

Quinn, Anthony, 291

Quiroz, Mercedes Sais (Mrs. Charles A. Shibell), 39, 387n4 (chap. 2)

railroad. *See* Southern Pacific Railroad

ranger cabin, 2m, 80, 128, 128–29m, 132, 135, 162m, 163. *See also* Lowell Ranger Station (later, Lowell Administrative Site)

Rasmessen, Rudolph, **vi**, 143, 147, 278

Rattlesnake Canyon, 2m, 3m, 143–44, 181, 299, 350–51m, 351, 369. *See also* Rattlesnake Creek

Rattlesnake Creek, 2m, 3m, 43, 80, 105, 185–86. *See also* Rattlesnake Canyon

Raudebaugh, Edgar B., 243–50, **250**, 357

recreational activities. *See* bicycles; birding; camping; drinking: alcohol; driving (recreational); fishing; hunting; picnics; shooting (recreational); swimming; walking and hiking

recreation fees, 153, **153**, 280, 328–30, 335

regulations, 357–58

Reilly, Phil, 71

reservoirs, 19, 52, 60m, 61, 70–71, 83, 86, 92, 92–93m, 124, 208, 388n2 (chap. 4). *See also* Calvin Elliott's dam site; Professor Woodward's dam site

restrooms, 181, 183, **183**, 186, 336, 396n7

Riddell, Robert, 290, **290**

rifle range (shooting range), 3m, 275, 350–351m, 351, 357, 371m

Rillito, 15, 16, 16m, 23, 59, 86, 128–29m, 160–61m, 258–59m, 388n2 (chap. 5), 392n1, 394n2; road crossing, 55–56, 112, **112**, 158, 161, 164, **164**, 167, 253, 392n1, 394n2 (chap. 14), 395n5, 401n1

roads in Sabino Canyon: to Bear Canyon, 283; in Lower Sabino Canyon, 99, **99**, 101, **101**; in Upper Sabino Canyon, 52, **52–53**, **168**, 185, 187, 189–91, **191**, 200, 205–8, **206**, 216–17, **216**, 220, 235, 255, **255**, 320, 353, **353**; maps, 2m, 3m, 60m, 61, 162m, 163, 257, 258–59m, 350–51m, 351

roads into Santa Catalina Mountains, 80, 123–25, **125**, 135, 137, 257. *See also* Catalina Highway (Mount Lemmon Road)

roads to Sabino Canyon from Tucson, 25, 55–56, 108, **108**, 157–59, 166–67, **166**, **167**, 211, 253, 338, **338**, 347, 393n1; maps, 58–59m, 59, 60m, 61, 160–61m, 161, 162m, 163, 257, 258–59m. *See also* Rillito: road crossing; Sabino Canyon Road

Rockefeller, Guy, Jr., 265–69

Rockefeller, Guy, Sr., 265–66

Rock Peak, 2m, 109, **109**, **146**, 147, 160–61m, 162m, 163

Rodeo Parade, 248, **248**, 304

Roosevelt, Eleanor, 188, 202

Roosevelt, Franklin Delano (FDR), 173, 202

Roosevelt, Theodore, 77, 79, 202

Roser, Raymond E., 333

Roskruge, George J., 37, 49–53, **50**, 58–59m, 59, 60m, 61, 363, **363**, 388n2 (chap. 4)

Rough and Ready Mine, 45, **45**

Rough Riders, 79, 202

Rowton, Sue, 290, **290**

Ruthrauff, J. Mos, 90–91, 391n12

Sabino (horse), 303, **303**, 304, **304**

Sabino Canyon (name): early uses of, ix–x, 15, 21, 58–59m, 59, 60m, 389n4 (chap. 5); origin of, x, 42, 207, 303

Sabino Canyon, early descriptions, 20–22, 25

Sabino Canyon Camp (transient camp), 3m, 219–20, 224, 231–232, 235–251, **237**, **241**, **247**, 400n1

Sabino Canyon Road, 257, 258–59m, 347. *See also* roads to Sabino Canyon from Tucson

Sabino Canyon Trail, 2m, 3m, 69, 77, 80, 84, 123–24, 128, 128–29m, **146**, 147, 162m, 163, **184**, 185–86, 206–7, **206**, 398n7

Sabino Canyon Visitor Center, 3m, 285–289, **285**, **286**, 317, 350–51m, 351

Sabino Canyon Volunteer Naturalists, 372, 406n1

Sabino Creek: color and taste, 113; and climate change 372, 399n22; early descriptions, xi, 20, 25; flow variability, 73, 392n17; pollution, 307, 404n1, 406n17. *See also* floods (Sabino Creek)

Sabino Dam (Lower Sabino Canyon), 3m, 220–24, **222**, 226, **226**, 228–29, **228**, **229**, 233, **233**, 242, **242**, 343, **343**. *See also* Sabino Lake (Lower Sabino Canyon)

About the Author

David Wentworth Lazaroff developed a deep and continuing interest in Sabino Canyon while working as an environmental education specialist for Coronado National Forest from 1977 to 1986. He is now an independent writer and photographer living in Tucson. This is Lazaroff's third book about Sabino Canyon to be published by the University of Arizona Press.

The photograph is of the author and his wife, Cherie, at the first stream crossing in Upper Sabino Canyon, August 10, 2013.

Author photograph

THE SOUTHWEST CENTER SERIES

Jeffrey M. Banister, Editor

Ignaz Pfefferkorn, *Sonora: A Description of the Province*

Carl Lumholtz, *New Trails in Mexico*

Buford Pickens, *The Missions of Northern Sonora: A 1935 Field Documentation*

Gary Paul Nabhan, editor, *Counting Sheep: Twenty Ways of Seeing Desert Bighorn*

Eileen Oktavec, *Answered Prayers: Miracles and Milagros Along the Border*

Curtis M. Hinsley and David R. Wilcox, editors, *Frank Hamilton Cushing and the Hemenway Southwestern Archaeological Expedition, 1886–1889,* volume 1: *The Southwest in the American Imagination: The Writings of Sylvester Baxter, 1881–1899*

Lawrence J. Taylor and Maeve Hickey, *The Road to Mexico*

Donna J. Guy and Thomas E. Sheridan, editors, *Contested Ground: Comparative Frontiers on the Northern and Southern Edges of the Spanish Empire*

Julian D. Hayden, *The Sierra Pinacate*

Paul S. Martin, David Yetman, Mark Fishbein, Phil Jenkins, Thomas R. Van Devender, and Rebecca K. Wilson, editors, *Gentry's Rio Mayo Plants: The Tropical Deciduous Forest and Environs of Northwest Mexico*

W. J. McGee, *Trails to Tiburón: The 1894 and 1895 Field Diaries of W J McGee,* transcribed by Hazel McFeely Fontana, annotated and with an introduction by Bernard L. Fontana

Richard Stephen Felger, *Flora of the Gran Desierto and Río Colorado of Northwestern Mexico*

Donald Bahr, editor, *O'odham Creation and Related Events: As Told to Ruth Benedict in 1927 in Prose, Oratory, and Song by the Pimas William Blackwater, Thomas Vanyiko, Clara Ahiel, William Stevens, Oliver Wellington, and Kisto*

Dan L. Fischer, *Early Southwest Ornithologists, 1528–1900*

Thomas Bowen, editor, *Backcountry Pilot: Flying Adventures with Ike Russell*

Federico José María Ronstadt, *Borderman: Memoirs of Federico José María Ronstadt,* edited by Edward F. Ronstadt

Curtis M. Hinsley and David R. Wilcox, editors, *Frank Hamilton Cushing and the Hemenway Southwestern Archaeological Expedition, 1886–1889,* volume 2: *The Lost Itinerary of Frank Hamilton Cushing*

Neil Goodwin, *Like a Brother: Grenville Goodwin's Apache Years, 1928–1939*

Katherine G. Morrissey and Kirsten Jensen, editors, *Picturing Arizona: The Photographic Record of the 1930s*

Bill Broyles and Michael Berman, *Sunshot: Peril and Wonder in the Gran Desierto*

David W. Lazaroff, Philip C. Rosen, and Charles H. Lowe Jr., *Amphibians, Reptiles, and Their Habitats at Sabino Canyon*

David Yetman, *The Organ Pipe Cactus*

Gloria Fraser Giffords, *Sanctuaries of Earth, Stone, and Light: The Churches of Northern New Spain, 1530–1821*

David Yetman, *The Great Cacti: Ethnobotany and Biogeography*

John Messina, *Álamos, Sonora: Architecture and Urbanism in the Dry Tropics*

Laura L. Cummings, *Pachucas and Pachucos in Tucson: Situated Border Lives*

Bernard L. Fontana and Edward McCain, *A Gift of Angels: The Art of Mission San Xavier del Bac*

David A. Yetman, *The Ópatas: In Search of a Sonoran People*

Julian D. Hayden, *Field Man: The Life of a Desert Archaeologist*, edited by Bill Broyles and Diane Boyer

Bill Broyles, Gayle Harrison Hartmann, Thomas E. Sheridan, Gary Paul Nabhan, and Mary Charlotte Thurtle, *Last Water on the Devil's Highway: A Cultural and Natural History of Tinajas Altas*

Thomas E. Sheridan, *Arizona: A History, Revised Edition*

Richard S. Felger and Benjamin Theodore Wilder, *Plant Life of a Desert Archipelago: Flora of the Sonoran Islands in the Gulf of California*

David Burkhalter, *Baja California Missions: In the Footsteps of the Padres*

Guillermo Núñez Noriega, *Just Between Us: An Ethnography of Male Identity and Intimacy in Rural Communities of Northern Mexico*

Cathy Moser Marlett, *Shells on a Desert Shore: Mollusks in the Seri World*

Rebecca A. Carte, *Capturing the Landscapes of New Spain: Baltasar Obregón and the 1564 Ibarra Expedition*

Gary Paul Nabhan, editor, *Ethnobiology for the Future: Linking Cultural and Ecological Diversity*

James S. Griffith, *Saints, Statues, and Stories: A Folklorist Looks at the Religious Art of Sonora*

David Yetman, Alberto Búrquez, Kevin Hultine, and Michael Sanderson, with Frank S. Crosswhite, *The Saguaro Cactus: A Natural History*

Carolyn Niethammer, *A Desert Feast: Celebrating Tucson's Culinary Heritage*

Gary Paul Nabhan, editor, *The Nature of Desert Nature*

David Yetman, *Natural Landmarks of Arizona*

Michael Chiago Sr. and Amadeo M. Rea, *Michael Chiago: O'odham Lifeways Through Art*

David Wentworth Lazaroff, *Picturing Sabino: A Photographic History of a Southwestern Canyon*